STUDIES IN OPEN EDUCATION

STUDIES IN OPEN EDUCATION

Edited by

Bernard Spodek
University of Illinois at Urbana-Champaign
and
Herbert J. Walberg
University of Illinois at Chicago Circle

AGATHON PRESS, NEW YORK

Distributed to the trade by
SCHOCKEN BOOKS, NEW YORK

Address all inquiries to the publisher:
AGATHON PRESS, INC.
150 Fifth Avenue
New York, N. Y. 10011

Distributed to the trade by
Schocken Books Inc.
200 Madison Avenue
New York, N. Y. 10016

Printed in the United States

ACKNOWLEDGMENTS: Portions of Chapter 6
previously appeared in Richard M. Brandt's "Three
Weeks in British Infant Schools" in *Current Research
and Perspectives in Open Education,* D. Dwain
Hern, Joel Burdin, and Lilian Katz, eds.
(Washington: American Association of Elementary-
Kindergarten-Nursery Educators, 1973). We are
grateful to The Macmillan Company for permission
to reprint in Chapter 14 substantial excerpts from
Vincent R. Rogers' *Teaching in the British Primary
School,* Copyright © 1970 by Vincent R. Rogers.

Library of Congress Cataloging in Publication Data

Spodek, Bernard
    Studies in open education.
      Includes bibliographies.
      1.   Open plan schools—Addresses, essays, lectures.
I.   Walberg, Herbert J., 1937—   joint editor.
II.   Title.
LB1029.06S66   372.1'3   73—19109
ISBN 0-87586-045-1

Contributors

J. Myron Atkin is Dean of the College of Education, University of Illinois at Urbana-Champaign. He earned his Ph.D. in science education at New York University in 1956. He taught for five years in elementary schools and two years in secondary schools before joining the University of Illinois faculty as an assistant professor in 1955. Atkin has been President of the Council for Elementary Science International, a member of the Board of Directors of the National Association for Research in Science Teaching, Chairman of the Section on Education of the American Association for the Advancement of Science, and a member of the Executive Board of the American Educational Research Association. His current research interests are centered on comparative studies of strategies for educational change in industrialized nations.

Richard M. Brandt is Dean of the School of Education, University of Virginia. He was formerly Chairman of the Department of Foundations of Education at the University, and in prior years on the staff of the Institute for Child Study, University of Maryland. He has also taught in public schools in Michigan and at the University of Delaware. He received his Ed.D. in human development education at the University of Maryland in 1954. He is author of a recent book, *Studying Behavior in Natural Settings* (New York: Holt, Rinehart and Winston, Inc., 1972) and several dozen articles and monographs in educational and child development journals.

Jerome E. DeBruin is currently in assistant professor of elementary science education at the University of Toledo. He received his Ph.D. in elementary science education from the University of Illinois in 1972. He has worked with consultants from England on the implementation of open education in the United States and was a research assistant in the Open Education Fellowship Program at the University of Illinois.

Nancy L. Dill is assistant professor of education, Queens College of The City University of New York. She received her Ed.D. in curriculum and teaching from Teachers College, Columbia University, in 1969. She was formerly Director of Junior-Intermediate Work, Church Training Department, Tennessee Baptist Convention. In the past she has conducted USOE-funded research utilizing systems theory and network analysis in the study of change processes in education. Currently she is engaged in research on the use of media (videotape recording and photography) in studying educational phenomena.

John Dopyera, Dean of Faculty at Pacific Oaks College and Children's School in Pasadena, California, was formerly associate professor of early childhood education at Pennsylvania State University. Prior to this he was involved in teaching and evaluation projects at Syracuse University in early education, teacher preparation, adult literacy, and adolescent development within the framework of compensatory education projects. He earned his Ph.D. in school psychology from Syracuse University in 1971. His interests range from alternative approaches in early childhood teacher preparation, naturalistic documentation of early childhood education programs, and the assessment of development in children as well as the environments which influence this process.

Judith T. Evans, a Senior Research Associate at Educational Research Corporation, received her doctorate in human development from the Harvard Graduate School of Education. Her study of open education was the result of work done as Director of Research and Evaluation at Education Development Center (EDC) in Newton, Mass. Research teams from EDC tried to adapt open education concepts and techniques to schools in four cities. This study was conducted to clarify the different definitions of open education that arose in the field. She is interested in cognitive development, social action programs, evaluation, test construction, and statistics.

Ronald W. Henderson is associate professor of educational psychology at the University of Arizona. He was formerly at the University of Oregon, and Director of the Arizona Center for Early Childhood Education, a component of the National Program on Early Childhood Education. He received his doctorate in educational psychology in 1966 from the University of Arizona, where he became interested in environmental influences on learning and performance while studying as a Woodrow Wilson Fellow in anthropology. His investigations of the role of social influence in learning is reflected in more than 25 research papers and reports on educational applications.

Margaret Z. Lay is associate professor of education and human development at Syracuse University, New York. She received her doctorate in psychological foundations of education at the University of Florida in 1967. She has developed and is currently field-replicating an open environment model called "responsive care" in several day-care settings. Her previous research and writings have focused on effects of programming on young children's behavior and on alternative approaches to teacher education.

James B. Macdonald is Distinguished Professor of Education, University of North Carolina—Greensboro. He received his Ph.D. from the University of Wisconsin in 1956. Macdonald was formerly at the University of Wisconsin—Milwaukee and Madison, New York University, and the University of Texas—Austin, where he served as Director of Research and the Laboratory School, Director of Doctoral Studies, Chairman of Elementary Education and Curriculum and Instruction at various times. He is the author of more than 60 articles, research monographs, yearbook chapters, etc., in curriculum theory and social foundations of education. During the academic year 1967-68, Macdonald served as visiting professor at the Curriculum Laboratory, Goldsmiths' College, University of London.

Theodore Manolakes is presently Professor of Elementary Education at the University of Illinois and Co-Director of the Illinois Open Education Fellowship Program. He is also Director of the Illinois-Bristol Exchange Program which coordinates student exchanges between the University of Bristol, England, and the University of Illinois. Manolakes received his Ed.D. from Teachers College, Columbia University in 1960. He has taught in the elementary schools of New York State, lectured at Hunter College and is former Chairman of the Department of Elementary Education, University of Illinois.

David T. Miles is Associate Professor of Guidance and Educational Psychology at the School of Medicine of Southern Illinois University, Carbondale. He received his Ph.D. in educational psychology from Southern Illinois University in 1967. He has co-authored a book and published articles on instructional objectives. His research has been in the areas of creative problem-solving, teacher training, curriculum design, and affective education. He is presently investigating procedures for behavioral self-clarification of self-esteem and instructional values clarification.

Vincent R. Rogers is Professor of Education and Director of the Center for Open Education at the University of Connecticut at Storrs. He is a former Fulbright Scholar, author of *The Social Studies in English Education*, (Heinemann, 1968), *Teaching in the British Primary School* (Macmillan, 1970), co-author of the *Social Science Seminar Series* (Charles E. Merrill, 1965), editor of *A Source Book For Social Studies* (Macmillan, 1969), and the author of numerous articles on education in England and the United States of America. He has been active in the curriculum-reform movement of the 1960's in the United States and has recently become involved in educational projects in Africa and Italy.

Bernard Spodek is Professor of Early Childhood Education in the Department of Elementary Education, University of Illinois-Urbana-Champaign campus, and is presently co-director of the Program for Teacher Trainers in Open Education. He received his Ed.D. in early childhood education from Teachers College, Columbia University in 1962. He taught for nine years at the nursery, kindergarten and elementary levels in public, private and laboratory schools. Upon completion of his doctoral work, Spodek joined the faculty of the University of Wisconsin—Milwaukee where he remained for four years before coming to the University of Illinois.

Spodek has been a member of a number of organizations related to early childhood education and has been on the governing board of the National Association for the Education of Young Children. He has written a number of books and articles relating to early childhood education and open education. His present interests are in the area of open education and teacher preparation.

Susan Christie Thomas is a Teacher-Developer at Education Development Center, Newton, Massachusetts, preparing curriculum for *Exploring Childhood,* a course being designed for adolescent students who learn about child development as they work with children. A graduate of Northwestern University, she holds an M.Ed. from the Harvard Graduate School of Education. Her work in education has combined public school teaching, curriculum development, evaluation, teacher education, and community involvement in school reform.

Herbert J. Walberg, Professor of Human Development and Learning and Research Professor of Urban Education at the University of Illinois at Chicago Circle, was formerly at the Educational Testing Service in Princeton, Harvard University and the University of Wisconsin. He received his Ph.D. in Educational Psychology from the University of Chicago in 1964. He is author of more than 80 research papers on creativity, developmental and social psychology, social environments of learning, evaluation, and statistics, and has contributed as author, chapter author, or editor to 15 books.

Contents

PART ONE: INTRODUCTION

PART TWO: CURRICULUM AND OBJECTIVES

PART THREE: STUDYING CLASSROOMS

Preface

WHAT is "open education"? This is the central question of this book, and the chapter authors have approached it from a variety of presuppositions and points of view. Such variation was deliberately planned, for neither open education nor the study of the concept and its practice should become an orthodoxy. At the same time, if the concept has features that set it apart from other forms of education, methods of educational inquiry, though they vary from one investigation to the next, ought to converge upon its distinctive features.

To make the intent of this book more explicit, it is useful to mention Max Weber's* specification of the three forms of corporate organization—charismatic, bureaucratic, and collegial. The first form of organization centers on an exalted leader or clique, perhaps with elite protégés or disciples endowed with derived charisma. The appeal is to the emotions, to doctrinal fervor, to bandwagons and fads. Generally the organization grows by making "converts" who have suppressed their critical faculties to undergo "peak experiences." Bureaucratic organization is a system of hierarchical control, legalistic norms, and abstract rules. The appeal is to consistency, standardization, efficiency, and the precedence of means over ends. Growth stems from the increased impersonal application of general rules to particular cases by subordinate operatives. Collegial organization is democratic and egalitarian. Its appeal is to thoroughness and deliberation rather than emotion and efficiency. Its growth stems from technical expertise, adversarial positions, and openness of inquiry.

In the view of the editors, charismatic or bureaucratic expansion of open education could harm both the theory and practice of teaching. It seems to us that what are most needed at this time are comprehensible descriptions of open education by colleagues with different standpoints.

* Max Weber, *The Theory of Social and Economic Organization*. New York: Oxford University Press, 1947.

Such a collection allows the reader to exercise his critical judgment and to formulate his own understanding and evaluation. It is in this open-minded spirit of inquiry that we have asked the chapter authors to contribute to this book.

One important aspect of open education may appear to have been inadvertently omitted—its effectiveness in producing higher academic achievement, in supporting intellectual development, and in promoting such elusive traits as autonomy, creativity, self-esteem, and integrity. The decision not to solicit a treatment of this aspect was made for several reasons. First, it seemed more important to understand and characterize the processes of open education before relating them to outcomes. Second, even now we know of no systematic experiment that would permit a valid evaluation of outcomes. Third, while recognizing that most school people as well as parents will want to examine a thorough evaluation of outcomes before adopting open education, it seemed premature to carry out such evaluation at the time we conceived the idea of this book since many open classrooms were just being tried out. It would have been like pulling out sprouting plants to examine the roots. Now that open education has taken hold in a number of communities, it does seem appropriate to begin long-term evaluations of outcomes, using a variety of devices to collect the necessary information. We hope that the work in this book on process will help to lay the groundwork for such outcomes research.

Finally, we acknowledge several debts. We are grateful to the University of Illinois for the colleagues, facilities, and environment that supported the editing of this book. We are particularly grateful to the Program for Teacher Training in Open Education at the Champaign-Urbana Campus, supported by the U.S. Office of Education under the Education Professions Development Act, and to the Urban Education Research Program at the Chicago Circle Campus. We need to thank Jean Patterson, who typed portions of the manuscript and who kept communications going between the editors and the authors. We thank our wives Prudence and Mahka for their support and understanding.

BERNARD SPODEK
HERBERT J. WALBERG

Urbana
Chicago
September, 1973

PART ONE

Introduction

CHAPTER 1

Open Education: Romance or Liberation?

Bernard Spodek, *University of Illinois*

IT HAS been called "open education" in the United States, "informal education" in England. It is an educational movement that has few of the characteristics of typical educational movements. It is derived from no explicit theory; there are no heavily funded educational projects developing it, nor are there specific educational products associated with it. It is a form of education that some consider formless, that goes under a variety of names and sometimes exists without any label at all. What is it then? What does it look like? How do you do it and how do you know if you are *really* doing it? How do you justify it? How do you study it?

Because of its characteristics, open education has remained elusive. Although leaders can be identified, it remains a grass-roots movement. There is no single Mecca to which one can come to find "truth" (unless, as Vincent Rogers says in Chapter 14, one views the English primary school scene as the American educational pilgrim's Mecca). But individuals in schools, school systems, and teacher preparation institutes in all parts of the United States have been attracted to the ideas and are "doing it" in their own way.

Another reason for open education's elusiveness is its justification and characterization by the use of slogans often phrased in the form of assumptions. Scheffler (1960) has defined slogans as "rallying symbols of the key ideas and attitudes of (educational) movements, ideas and attitudes that may be more fully and literally expressed elsewhere" (p. 36). Slogans represent ideological points of view. Although such statements are often fuzzy, Bernier and Williams (1973) suggest that their ambiguity serves an important purpose by "sustaining social cohesion, binding individuals together who would disagree if precision were achieved" (p. 48). Keeping statements ill-defined allows many people

3

to rally to their support while holding different points of view. Fuzziness, therefore, can be useful in increasing the popularity of any point of view.

Although ambiguity has advantages, it also has disadvantages. In order to understand a phenomenon, one must be clear about what it is. We need to analyze, clarify, and justify open education and determine its requisite attributes even though the necessary act of clarification might lead to increased disagreement.

Another reason for the elusiveness of open education is the fear on the part of many of its practitioners that to clarify is to codify. The very openness of this educational form means that it is constantly being changed and redefined. Many of the movement's strongest advocates have observed other approaches to education that had promising beginnings die as the forms became ritualized. Fuzziness allows for flexibility and the acceptance of a wide range of practice. It allows for the continuous shift in acceptable procedures without the need to justify each shift. This ability to accept change is an important attribute of open education. It represents a response to specific situations and conditions as well as a response to deepening understandings and the development of new insights on the part of practitioners. It also represents an acceptance of a wide range of teaching styles.

Because of its elusiveness, open education has been difficult to study and analyze. It is sometimes felt that the mere recounting of experience is the way in which individuals can be helped to understand what took place. Sharing descriptions as well as reactions to occurrences allows the listener to become aware of aspects of classroom practice that would be left out of analysis and would be distorted by generalizations. In addition, the wide variance in the implementation of open education raises questions about generalizing from any studies; yet without study, analysis, and theory it will be difficult to advance the field.

Too often in hearing a description of what open education is, one is tempted to respond, "Yes, that's part of it." Every definition seems to overlap with other definitions, but no one definition presents a full-enough characterization. This results from the fact that open education represents an open system of thought, one that is constantly being modified. As Nancy Dill points out in Chapter 10, open systems in a changing environment either change or perish. Although open education does represent an educational ideology, it is a nondoctrinaire approach, and therefore it is in a continual state of flux.

The absence of definitive statements of what open education is and the absence of formal doctrine may ultimately be one of the strengths of open education. But this strength also creates one of its major problems. Individuals, practitioners as well as theorists, develop their own interpretations of open education which differ from, or even contradict, others. Without some clear consensus it will continue to be difficult to define open education.

Defining Open Education

Since open education is such an elusive phenomenon, it has often been suggested that the best way to define it is to state what it is not. This eliminates the confusion between open education and other approaches to education, but without defining the range of approaches that can legitimately bear that label.

Possibly the most important disclaimer to make is that open education is neither an organizational arrangement for schools nor an architectural form. Too often open schools are confused with "open area" or "open architecture" schools. The construction of new buildings without typical classroom separations, often arranged into large units or "pods," has led to the term *open area*. Development of these buildings is often advocated by those who feel that the elimination of internal physical barriers in school buildings will lead to greater flexibility in school programs. Children can be organized into various-sized groups for different purposes, and children can be moved to different instructional areas with ease. In addition, organizing into larger instructional groups may allow for varying staffing patterns in schools, including team teaching and differentiated staffing patterns. A better match between children and learning resources may occur.

New organizational patterns, however, often lead to less rather than more flexibility—with team teaching leading to departmentalization, and differentiated staffing increasing teacher specialization. In addition, open areas can create problems of acoustical separation, so that noise in one area will disrupt quiet activities in another area. The carpeted floors in open areas are often less soil-resistant and more difficult to clean than hard-surfaced floors, thus leading teachers to avoid messy activities that could create confrontations with maintenance personnel.

Many of the problems of open-area schools can be overcome if they have leadership and a teaching staff willing to move away from traditional goals and methods, as well as open communication and a sense of cohesiveness among the staff. Otherwise a "least common denominator" approach to education may be created. If teachers in such a school are not in agreement on educational policy or on issues regarding how much noise or movement can be tolerated, the teachers may seek to teach in the least-offensive manner possible, so as not to antagonize a colleague. Conformity and repression, rather than experimentation and sharing, can result, even with an open plan.

Similarly, team teaching and individualized instruction programs, which are often confused with open education, can result in rigidity rather than flexibility. Individualized instruction tends to rely heavily on prescribed materials. While a child may be working alone, the main component of the educational enterprise that is varied for him is pace. In team teaching, the deployment of staff may be more "efficient," but it is seldom more responsive to the needs of children. Children may be organized by achievement levels or by subject interests, but the slotting of children and teachers into prescribed niches is anything but open. In addition, the tyranny of scheduling required to mesh the work of many may lead to compartmentalization, departmentalization, and regimentation.

Open education can occur in open-area schools just as it can occur in traditional buildings when teachers collaborate. Open education can occur in nongraded as well as graded schools. Some patterns of school organization do have greater potential for flexibility than others, and particular institutional arrangements often have specific consequences. Large institutions, for example, tend to be organized bureaucratically, but this does not always hold true. Some small schools can be more bureaucratic than larger schools, and schools using varied organizational arrangements have become open.

Just as open education cannot be characterized by institutional organization, it also cannot be characterized by classroom organization. Arrangement of the room into activity centers, scheduling of a long activity period in the day, availability of large amounts of manipulative materials, or an emphasis on arts and crafts does not necessarily make for an open classroom.

Nor does an open classroom mean a classroom that is characterized by a "hands-off" policy, where either teacher or children can simply "do their own thing." While freedom, autonomy, and pupil involvement in decisionmaking are essential to the open classroom, the teacher is not disengaged as a person of authority, nor is he less responsible for his actions. Both teachers and children may have great authority in determining what happens in an open classroom, but the decision is always made within a context of mutuality.

Studying Open Education

Although differentiating between open education and other approaches to education is a useful exercise in limiting the confusion among different programs, it does not clarify what open education is. Indeed, one of the important threads in the study of open education has been its definition. Given the fact that it is a new movement that stems from many sources, this is a necessary first step. The process has included theoretical study, primarily the identification and analysis of goals, assumptions, and ideological bases of open education and a tracing of their roots. It has also included empirical study, observing open education in practice and abstracting the essence of open education from these observations. Many studies combine these two approaches.

Since the movement evolved from practice rather than from theory, the study of open education is valuable. Conceptualization has been the second step. The evolution of open education is linked to a number of historical threads as well as to existing contemporary conditions. James Macdonald, in Chapter 3, points out some of the historical antecedents of open education. The philosophies of Jean Jacques Rousseau, Friedrich Froebel, and John Dewey as well as the practice of Robert Owen, Maria Montessori, and Rachel and Margaret MacMillan provide some of the roots of open education. Open education, however, also has its roots in human interests and forms of knowledge.

In their analytic review of the literature in Chapter 2, Susan C. Thomas and Herbert J. Walberg document some of these historic roots. Not only are the writings of contemporary critics and practitioners consistent with the characteristics of open education, but so are the writings of progressive educators and child-centered advocates of earlier eras, such as Tolstoy. Despite this consistency, the contemporary conception of open education is different from earlier approaches to child-centered education. It is not simply "progressive education warmed over," although there are roots in progressivism.

The analysis of historical antecedents of open education is only part of the theoretical study. In a practice-based approach to education, much of the study must consist of observing practice, abstracting assumptions upon which practice seems to be based, and verifying these assumptions by submitting them to the judgments of practitioners. Those assumptions about which there is sufficient consensus are accepted as valid, and others which do not meet this criterion are discarded. Such analysis has been the basis of works such as those by Barth (1972) and Bussis and Chittenden (1970).

From these statements of assumptions and from descriptions of practice, it is possible to begin to abstract some of the characteristics of open education. Validation of these characteristics would depend upon agreement of practitioners in the field. Statements about these characteristics could be translated into items in an observational schedule to be used to describe the degree of openness in a classroom. Such studies as those by Walberg and Thomas (Chapter 8) and by Judith T. Evans (Chapter 9) use these strategies.

Other studies of open classrooms have used previously existing observational instruments, as did Richard M. Brandt (Chapter 6), or have developed specific instruments for the purpose of studying open education. John Dopyera and Margaret Lay (Chapter 7) developed an instrument to study openness as a single characteristic of any classroom. Nancy L. Dill (Chapter 10) used systems analysis to study open classrooms—a somewhat different approach to observational study. Conceiving of the classroom as an open system allowed this strategy to be used effectively. In each study, open classrooms look significantly different from traditional classrooms, even when instruments not specifically designed to be sensitive to characteristics of open classrooms were used.

Another area of study relates to the implementation of open education. J. Myron Atkin, in Chapter 11, characterizes open education as a grass-roots movement whose development was nurtured by conditions in England which may be absent from the current American educational scene. However, schools and school systems in the United States are developing programs of open education. Teacher training institutions are trying to develop ways of helping teachers move into open education. Little is still known about how best to prepare teachers for open classrooms and about what personal, cultural, and institutional conditions best support a move to open classrooms. Bernard Spodek and Theodore Manolakes, in Chapter 12, describe one approach to teacher training and the hypotheses raised from a study of that approach. Jerome E. De Bruin, in Chapter 13, describes what happened when a group of teachers prepared to develop open classrooms moved into a new school building and attempted to implement what they had learned. Both of these studies raise significant questions for the extension of practice in open education.

Vincent Rogers, in the final chapter, raises more questions about the extension of practice, questions about the use of the British experience and questions about how the open education movement might be extended in the United States. Rogers is hopeful about the continued development of the movement.

Since open education is a relatively new approach to the teaching of children, there are limitations to the studies being made of it. Evaluation of student outcomes becomes difficult because of the absence of appropriate instruments and the questionable propriety of using standardized achievement tests. In addition, few children and teachers have been involved in it long enough to provide stable treatments or to identify long-range effects. Since many of its practitioners consider the worth of open education to be self-evident, there has been little pressure to accumulate evidence of pupil outcomes in order to evaluate open education. Even the identification of goals in open education has been questioned.

David T. Miles and Ronald W. Henderson have addressed themselves to the issue of defining goals for open education. Miles, in Chapter 5, compares high priorities for the traditional and the open classroom and analyzes the relationship between affective, cognitive, and psychomotor goal priorities. He discusses some of the problems in evaluating affective goals in open education. Henderson suggests, in Chapter 4, that the "methods of science can provide a corrective mechanism to determine if our means do in fact lead to the ends which our philosophy dictates." He presents the identification of goals of the Tucson Early Education Model as an example of steps taken to establish behavioral objectives for open education. Although his advocacy of behavioral objectives for open education may be controversial, Henderson's position relating to the use of scientific inquiry in developing verifiable knowledge about open education needs to be considered carefully by all.

A Look to the Future

The present volume represents a scraping of the surface. We are just beginning the practice of open education in the United States in earnest and also just beginning its study. Since this volume was proposed, additional research has been undertaken. New volumes describing practice and providing help for practitioners are being published at an amazing rate. There is still much that we need to know. Thus, it might be helpful to look at where we are and to suggest possible areas for further study.

Research to date has established that there is such a thing as open education, that it is more than just a fuzzy idea in the minds of educational romantics. A body of acceptable theory is being developed. In addition, there is identifiable consistency in classroom treatment among open educators, and there are observable differences between treatments in these classrooms and in traditional classrooms.

We are beginning to identify the structure of open education in theory as well as in practice. Exactly what that structure will be is not yet clear. As a matter of fact, it might be more appropriate to look for *structures* in open education. To borrow an analogy from Noam Chomsky: open education might best be understood in terms of *surface structure* and *deep structure*. Surface structure would include observable classroom practice—the syntax of education. Deep structure would provide the meaning of practice. The former would require increased observation of classroom practice. Learning about the latter would require a study of educational ideologies.

Bernier and Williams (1973) find the ideological roots of open education to be in progressivism. They suggest that it is a form of neoprogressivism, although contemporary practitioners do not manifest the same degree of "moderation, professionalism and grace" as did practitioners of an earlier era. Kohlberg and Mayer (1972) suggest that the roots of open education are in the romantic ideology. The emphases on child freedom allowing the inner "good" to emerge and supporting intellectual and emotional growth as well as physical growth, which can be attributed to open education, are cited as indicators of the romantic ideology.

Perhaps the labeling of the movement as essentially progressive or romantic serves little purpose in understanding the deep structure of open education. Neither of these labels explains the essential ethical or moral position in relation to the nature of childhood or of schooling that is essential to open education.

Macdonald, in Chapter 3, suggests some of the ethical attributes. He views open education as "a contemporary educational expression of the desire for human liberation" through the freeing of intellectual capacity, the desire for justice, equality, and love, and the concern for moral integrity and personal growth. Macdonald's framework of human interests could be useful in studying the ideological base for all educational programs and may be especially productive in studying open education.

The use of studies of deep structure becomes apparent when one realizes that a teacher's actions may be as much a function of his beliefs as of the reward system of schools. The "onion construct" presented in Chapter 12 suggests that an understanding of teacher behavior may very well require an understanding of the deep structure of education: the beliefs that underlie human behavior.

While we need to look at the structures of open education, we also need to give greater attention to the institutional framework in which education takes place. Sarason (1971) has suggested that the success or failure of educational innovation is related to the culture of the school in which innovation is attempted. Studies of school culture—at the classroom level, at the school building level, and at the school system level—will help us to understand the influences that determine the success of efforts to make schools more open.

Finally, we shall need to develop studies to determine outcomes of open education procedures. Beyond the concern for educational accountability, we need to see whether what happens to children in open classrooms is consistent with what we want to happen to them and whether there are consequences of involvement in these programs. Is development enhanced? Do children become more involved in the search for knowledge, freedom, and justice? Knowledge about outcomes of open education may become more and more the focus of study as the movement develops.

References

Barth, R. S., *Open Education and the American School.* New York: Agathon Press, 1972.

Bernier, N. R., and J. E. Williams, *Beyond Beliefs.* Englewood Cliffs, N.J.: Prentice-Hall, 1973.

Bussis, A. M., and E. A. Chittenden, *An Analysis of an Approach to Open Education.* Princeton, N.J.: Educational Testing Service, 1970.

Kohlberg, L., and R. Mayer, "Development As the Aim of Education," *Harvard Educational Review,* 1972, *42,* 449–496.

Sarason, S. B., *The Culture of the School and the Problem of Change.* Boston: Allyn and Bacon, 1971.

Scheffler, I., *The Language of Education.* Springfield, Ill.: Charles C. Thomas, 1960.

CHAPTER 2

An Analytic Review of the Literature

Susan Christie Thomas, *Education Development Center*
Herbert J. Walberg, *University of Illinois*

Introduction

EARLY in 1970, Judith T. Evans and Mary Lela Sherborne, then of the Education Development Center in Newton, Massachusetts, invited one of us to develop and validate observation schedules and rating scales for the "objective identification" of "open education." The other author, with teaching experience in open classrooms in England and United States, agreed to collaborate on the research. We felt that useful published and unpublished writings on open education were available and that it was our obligation, prior to developing instruments, to extract insights from these works and ask people working on open programs around the country to help us check the validity of these insights against their own experience. The project turned out to be far more extensive than originally planned, and we are extremely grateful to people at EDC and elsewhere who supported and helped us in various ways.* This chapter is a summary of the results of the first phase of the project—the content analysis.

*In addition to those colleagues mentioned above, Roland Barth, Dorothy Berman, Maurice Eash, Floralyn Fine, William Genova, Ralph Mosher, and Edward Yeomans consulted or worked with us directly. Marianne Amarel, Charles Ascheim, Sylvia Ashton-Warner, Maurice Belanger, Courtney Cazden, John Cawthorne, Edith H. E. Churchill, Margaret Cline, Ann Cook, Terry Denny, Priscilla Ehrlich, Louise Hauser, David Hawkins, Leo Howard, William Hull, Tony Kallet, Lilian Katz, Herbert Mack, Marjorie Martus, Anita Olds, Henry Olds, Vito Perrone, Charles Rathbone, Elwyn Richardson, Charles Silberman, Bernard Spodek, Christopher Stevenson, Marian Stroud, Patricia Swan, Masako Tanaka, Evelyn Weber, and Lillian Weber responded by mail to our request to help validate the content analysis. Their cooperation does not imply agreement with our purpose and methods nor with one another.

It is important to note at the outset that our work should not be regarded as complete or final; it is a starting point. First, although we made use of collections of educational materials at EDC and universities (Chicago, Harvard, and Illinois), surely some relevant material escaped us. Second, some works we analyzed have been further developed and published in book form (Barth, 1972; Featherstone, 1971), and several excellent works on open education have appeared since 1970 (Hertzberg and Stone, 1971; Murrow and Murrow, 1971; Weber, 1971); some of these are taken up in other chapters in this book. Third, although some writings of some precursors of open education and those with other viewpoints are included to provide contrast, the list could be expanded considerably. Fourth, our methodological biases are psychological and experiential; we employ analytic content analysis and consensual checks. Perhaps those using historical, philosophical, or sociological methods on the same body of literature would produce different findings. Thus we hope that others may expand on our starting point in the several ways that are possible.

AN ANALYTIC FRAMEWORK

Open education, the integrated day, the developmental classroom, informal education: these phrases refer to an educational movement that began in England and that is growing in the United States. As more and more educators—with the desire to put philosophy into practice—are attracted to this movement, it becomes useful to look for consistent and agreed-upon characteristics that distinguish this concept from other approaches to education. The open education approach is founded upon responsiveness to contingency and individuality—of students and of situation. The open education teacher is especially difficult to categorize, precisely because her guiding principle seems to be to respond as sensitively and reflectively as possible to the situational *gestalt* and to the unique child with whom she is interacting.

On the other hand, the mere awareness of the "non-model" quality of open education does not provide any practical help for transmuting idea into action. Some sort of operational definition—albeit one that allows for flexibility and individuality in response to situational variations—is needed. The study upon which this chapter is based was an attempt to provide an analytic basis for such a definition. Basically, our aims were: (1) to define the essential pedagogical features of open education; (2) to develop explicit, concrete indicators of each feature; (3) to check the validity of the indicators with the major writings on the subject and with important theorists and practitioners in the United

States and Great Britain; and (4) to make comparisons with other approaches, such as progressive and affective education.

The open education teacher is distinguished by his awareness of the diversity of children's learning styles. His actions seem guided by the self-posed question: "What use can I be to this particular child at this particular moment?" As a human being and as a teacher, he views himself as a continual learner who will err, but whose job it is to respond, adapt, improvise, and be willing to change. This is not to say, however, that the open education teacher operates in an ideological vacuum. He brings to each decision a set of attitudes and convictions about the nature of children, learning, and schooling. In deciding whether or when to intervene in a child's activity, he tries to use all his experience and resources to perceive the child's needs and interests, both long-range and immediate.

Understanding the teacher's role and assumptions also requires insight into how his behavior permits and encourages children's resourcefulness and individuality. Open educators view the student as a significant decisionmaker in determining the direction, scope, and pace of his education. Both the child and the teacher occupy central positions in the classroom and in the child's instruction—an apparent paradox that perhaps most distinguishes the open education movement. Both parties must jointly assume the decisionmaking function in the classroom and together fashion the child's school experience, tailored both to his choice of immediate goals and to the teacher's long-term goals for him. Open education differs from teacher-centered, child-centered, and materials-centered approaches in that it combines all three, with both the teacher and the child determining goals, materials, and activities collaboratively.

Identifying the Themes

An analysis of open education pedagogical style must then examine the teacher's role—not in isolation, but as it assumes and depends on the presence of children. Since the movement has been more highly developed at the level of primary education, it seemed appropriate to focus this analysis on the complex and interdependent themes recurrent in descriptions of open education for children from five to eight.

To organize the wealth of material relating to the teacher's roles, a conceptual framework was needed. Bussis and Chittenden (1970) proposed conceptualizing the role of the teacher as a network of beliefs and behaviors which could be grouped into ten themes. Their excellent theoretical framework, elaborated and changed based upon our reading of open education writings and upon our own thinking and observations, served as a starting point for content analysis. Our modification centered upon the following eight themes:

INSTRUCTION — Guidance and extension of learning
PROVISIONING — The classroom for learning
DIAGNOSIS — Of learning events
EVALUATION — Of diagnostic information
HUMANENESS — Respect, openness, and warmth
SEEKING — Opportunities to promote growth
SELF-PERCEPTION — Of the teacher
ASSUMPTIONS — Ideas about children and the process of learning

Aspects of these themes overlap, since so many of the characteristics of open education are interrelated. Organizing according to themes facilitates examination of all the elements of classroom operation and provides means for ordering observation and analysis. What may seem arbitrary placement of some characteristics merely illustrates again the complex interdependence of all the characteristics and all the themes.

Defining the Themes

An early step in this study was to select quotations from the literature indicative of each author's attention to each of the themes. Through this process, the definitions of each theme became more specific and concrete. This very large collection of quotations (reproduced in Walberg and Thomas, 1971) then formed the basis for drafting a series of explicit statements, each defining a characteristic of the open education teacher's behavior and attitudes as presented in this literature. We then corresponded with notable practitioners, advisers, advocates, researchers, and theorists of open education and used their responses to arrive at the ninety characteristics which define the eight themes. Brief summaries of each of the eight themes are offered below.

INSTRUCTION refers to the teacher's guidance and extension of learning: how she directs and responds in the classroom. The open education teacher shows a very high degree of individualized instruction and does not operate as the focal point of the classroom. Her instruction is characterized by responsiveness, adaptability, and encouragement of children's choice; much of her instructional time is devoted to listening and observing, with a great deal of less formal questioning and informing than is usually found in classrooms.

PROVISIONING refers to the teacher's responsibility for what is in the classroom and how it affects the children's learning. Under this theme come not only materials, equipment, and furniture which the teacher chooses and arranges but also the procedures and expectations she establishes.

Thus, the organization of time, the grouping of children, provision for their interaction, and the promotion of climate are all part of the teacher's provisioning for learning. As Bussis and Chittenden found, this theme is "central to an educational philosophy that stresses the importance of choice for children" (p. 37). One aspect of provisioning is deciding just when to provide. The teacher supplies a child with a book or a piece of equipment or material at a point when she estimates, as a result of watching and talking with him, that it will further stimulate his inquiry. From provisioning, in a sense, all else follows; but at the same time it is itself a result of the characteristics which make up each of the other themes.

DIAGNOSIS refers to the teacher's involvement as participating observer. She views a child's work not only as a learning experience for the child but also as an opportunity for her to learn about that child. She welcomes not only successful solutions and accurate reporting but also errors and fantasy, as indicators of the child's developmental concerns and thought processes. In open education, seeking diagnostic information in the learning process is important, because it determines instruction. The importance of constant and on-the-spot diagnosing means that the teacher cannot be expected to lay out lesson plans for a month ahead. She must elicit information about the development of her children from day to day and respond to them individually on the basis of what she learns.

EVALUATION in open education is seen as having two purposes: one centers on its usefulness to the student, and the other on its usefulness to the teacher in attempting to help the student. Evaluation is not seen as a way to compare a child's performance with predetermined goals or norms in order to report his strengths and deficiencies to his parents, future teachers, and employers, nor is its function to compare children with their peers. Rather, it is a means of providing a child and those interested in his development with information about his growth and learning. The purpose of this information is to assist him in seeking better ways to contribute to what he chooses to do and whom he chooses to be, and to help him gain the skills necessary to reach his goals.

Reflective evaluation takes place both during class time and after the children have left. The teacher's actions are shaped by a combination of not only her own careful reflection and her discussions with colleagues and advisors but also her on-the-spot evaluation of the diagnostic information she constantly collects in class. Her record-keeping, a characteristic often mentioned in the literature, combines her constant jotting in class and her thoughtful writing about each child outside class time.

HUMANENESS encompasses such characteristics as respect for the individual, honesty, and warmth. The teacher shows her respect for the child by dealing honestly with him, presenting herself openly as a human being who has weaknesses and strengths and who recognizes that the other person is similarly human. Thus, the teacher is freed from the need to appear all-knowing or infallible, and the child is relieved of being in the position of inferiority by virtue of his age or station. The teacher can accept her role of authority—yet not be authoritarian—by earning respect and obedience based on her proven ability and readiness to help and lead. The teacher respects and responds honestly to the work the child does, as well as to the ways he thinks, feels, and acts. In such a situation, where expression of emotions is encouraged as part of growth, an underlying basis of warmth is required in relationships, in order to support healthy growth and to provide the child with the reassuring and stabilizing sense that the people there accept and care for him.

SEEKING, in open education, assumes that the school experience contributes not only to the child's educational development but to the teacher's as well; she too is the beneficiary of the learning milieu she works to provide. Seeking activities to promote continual personal growth is obviously an integral part of the teacher's interaction with the children as well as of her life outside the classroom. It applies, of course, to her participation in workshops, her use of advisors, her education-related conversations during lunchtime and after class, and her pursuit of information about the local community and about new materials and subject matter. But more than this, open education is an approach to teaching which stresses the necessity of the teacher's deep and active personal involvement in classroom change and growth. Seeking personal growth takes place right in the classroom, and the children have much to contribute to it.

In this dimension the open education teacher differs little from the excellent traditional teacher. Yet so many writers on open education and others who are actually involved in the approach lay stress on the necessity of the characteristics which make up this theme that they seem to be saying that the teacher who is not seeking opportunities for personal and professional growth cannot succeed in and should not attempt open education.

SELF-PERCEPTION refers to the way the open education teacher views herself and her role. Prescott (Prescott and Raoul, 1970), in describing the fruition of the integrated day at her school, indicates the importance of this theme when she writes that success with the open education approach is not possible without "a complete understanding on the part of the teacher of her changing role" (p. 16), and she lists among the three "best supports" in her own growth as an open education teacher "the conviction within myself that what we were doing was right" (p. 5). Self-perception (along with the theme of assumptions) intertwines with the six other themes by supporting and sustaining the teacher's actions in the classroom. The teacher's self-perception enables her to formulate and act upon her convictions about children and education—or, conversely, can disable her from ever feeling convinced of her beliefs or from behaving in accord with what she professes to believe. Although traditional teachers may hold many of the same beliefs, it seems to be the willingness to attempt to carry out their implications in the classroom that characterizes open education teachers.

ASSUMPTIONS define the teacher's orientation towards children, knowledge, and the process of learning. These assumptions include faith in children's innate curiosity, in their ability to sustain exploratory behavior, and in their capacity and right to make significant decisions about their learning. The assumptions define desirable conditions for learning: a warm and accepting emotional atmosphere, a dependable and honest source of authority, explicit and reasonable rules, and opportunity for direct interaction with rich and diverse materials. On the other hand, the assumptions put negative value on measurement by norms and conventional tests, the promotion of competition, and the use of threats or bargaining. They reject distinctions between "subjects" or disciplines and between work and play, and they see knowledge as a personal synthesis that cannot be "transmitted."

An interesting thing about the open education movement is that it seems to grow out of many old truths about the nature of effective learning. The difference seems to be that open educators are determined to take seriously what many regard as clichés and to structure their classrooms, their instructional behaviors, and their relationships to children accordingly, instead of trying to rationalize what they were already doing and convince themselves ex post facto that their existing practices are consistent with such beliefs.

CONTENT ANALYSIS

Selection of the Literature

Since publication of the *Plowden Report* (1967), a great deal has been written about open education. After seeking the advice of many educators actively related to open education and collecting bibliographies, we drew up a list of the most frequently cited and important open education writings. We attempted to cover the most informed and influential authors in each of the following categories: *practitioners, advisers and advocates, observers and reporters,* and *researchers and analysts.*

In addition to the literature on open education, we selected a number of other writings which we felt would provide valuable points of comparison; some, in fact, form the background from which open education evolved. Three pre-twentieth-century writers were selected: Plato (1945 translation), because of his enduring influence in education and because he provides a touchstone for comparison; Tolstoy (1967 translation) and Rousseau (1956 translation), because they were early thinkers who drew connections between an optimistic view of human nature and the role of philosophical assumptions in the process of education. Like advocates of open education today, the latter two authors translated their philosophical beliefs into proposals for ways of teaching which are concerned with development of individual potential and based on trust in man's positive nature.

In the twentieth century, we categorized three orientations which warrant comparison to open education. Three representative progressive educators who span the years of this movement were selected for analysis: Dewey and Dewey (1915), Rugg and Shumacker (1928), and Sheehy (1954) represent ideological forerunners of open education, particularly with respect to early childhood education and the first few years of elementary school. The other two categories, *popular critics* and *affective orientation,* are generally contemporary with open education, and the ways in which their viewpoints mirror and differ from those of open education are reflected in this content analysis. *Popular critics* are represented here by Kohl (1967, 1969), whose book *The Open Classroom* is perhaps responsible for the currency of the term "open education," and by Holt (1964, 1967), considered by many to be chief spokesman for more responsive, personal, flexible schools. Teachers themselves, they were included because they fuse their criticism, beliefs, and recommendations to their personal classroom experience and interaction with other practicing teachers. Neill (1960), Leonard (1968), Dennison (1969), and Borton (1970) were included because they present proposals for, or descriptions of, what has been gathered under the term *affective orientation.*

Design of the Analysis

The selected works of the twenty-eight authors or coauthors chosen were examined for their attention to each of the eight themes. Each author was scored on a three-point scale, with a rating of 3 indicating heavy stress on a particular theme, a rating of 2 indicating moderate stress, and a rating of 1 indicating either negative stress or the absence of that theme. Plato's *Republic*, for example, is replete with philosophical assumptions which determine the program of education he describes. These assumptions, however, are for the most part antithetical to those espoused by open educators, and he is therefore rated 1 on the theme of assumptions.

Discussion of the Analysis

In the interest of readability, the authors are grouped here according to the categories described above to facilitate comparison between those of similar orientation and among differing orientations. Discussion of our content analysis of the literature here consists of an interpretation of the ratings rather than the actual numerical ratings, which are summarized in Tables 1 and 2. The complete numerical ratings of each author, along with evidence for their validity and tables comparing both the different categories and the authors within each category, can be found in our original report (Walberg and Thomas, 1971).

Analysts and Researchers
Since the eight themes derive from the ten proposed by Bussis and Chittenden (1970), it is not surprising that analysis of their report resulted in higher rankings. Assumptions and self-perception were the only themes to receive less than full ratings. Although the report cited the importance of these two themes, it offered little description or discussion of their content or influence. The Bussis and Chittenden report represents the conclusions of researchers who have most closely examined the thinking and practices of a specific group of open educators—the participants in the Education Development Center's Follow Through Program, especially its advisers.

The two doctoral dissertations, Barth (1970, and later revised and expanded: Barth, 1972) and Rathbone (1970), represent the most ambitious efforts to examine open education that we found. Both authors studied all available material, visited many British "informal" or "integrated day" classrooms, conducted extensive interviews, and carried on correspondence with proponents of open education. In general, their wider surveys diverge little from the emphasis Bussis and Chittenden found common to the EDC advisers. Where they give less emphasis, it is slight, and as is the case with Bussis and Chittenden's work, middle rating indicates not that the authors devalued that theme but only that it received short shrift relative to the discussion and elaboration given the others.

Both Barth and Rathbone seem able to talk about an ideal, based upon consensus of beliefs, hope, and the best practices. Barth combines discussions of the assumptions he finds underlying the work of open educators with description of their pedagogy and with a narrative in which he contrasts this ideal model with a thorough account of his own difficulties in attempting to implement his ideals. Rathbone compiled a comprehensive set of materials dealing with open education and its related assumptions. He based his analytic description of the movement on examination of these works and on his own observation. He shows how open education works ideally by describing its organizational patterns and its implicit ideology. The second half of his dissertation describes the implications of this educational approach for teacher education.

These two authors, who attempted a comprehensive examination of the movement, treated the eight themes thoroughly. Barth stressed seven themes very strongly; only seeking received less emphasis relative to the others. His narrative suggests that the exigencies of coping with the discouraging year of attempting to initiate and administer an open education program left him and his teachers little time, desire, or energy to seek much more than rest or refuge. Nevertheless, implicit in his recital of his "New Harbor" adventure in implementation is a good deal of seeking behavior as defined by the characteristics we have listed.

Rathbone, too, places strong emphasis upon seven of the eight themes. His less-emphasized theme, evaluation, probably results from some misgivings he holds about the open educators' avoidance of traditional forms of evaluation and mistrust of "hard research." As he states,

> The real challenge posed by Open Education's attitude towards evaluation, of course, is an overall questioning of traditional evaluatory techniques. For when proponents of Open Education do set down the questions they would most like answered, the list does not lend itself to any simple or established system of measurement. . . . Until hard research is available, one can only rely on one's subjective judgment—tempered by thoughtful reflection and a careful reading of the available literature to determine the appropriateness of Open Education for any particular child. (pp. 166–168)

Reporters and Observers

The four sources examined as significant reporters on open education are unanimous in their heavy emphasis on the themes of provisioning, instruction, and assumptions. Self-perception—certainly a rather personal dimension and one to which a classroom visitor is not likely to have access—is least emphasized on the average. Yet, despite this limitation, this theme is still moderately stressed.

Relative to the lengthy *Plowden Report* (1967) and Silberman (1970) or even the Blackie paperback (1967), Featherstone's series of articles on British infant schools is very short. He skims evaluation, humaneness, and seeking. More than the other reporters, however, he is evidently struck by the teachers' confidence in children's ability to learn through open structure, and he emphasizes the need for such conviction. He alone, among the reporters, gives strong stress to the theme of self-perception. He views the teacher's internal frame of reference as a very important ingredient to successful open teaching. His lesser attention to the other three themes could be a function of his not having found them particularly important, or it could be a matter of journalistic necessity of making a choice where space is limited.

Although all these authors except Silberman are reporting their observation of British practices only, Silberman's treatment of these themes does not differ from theirs despite his inclusion of American efforts in North Dakota, Philadelphia, and elsewhere. Indeed, *Crisis in the Classroom* and Blackie's *Inside the Primary School* (by a retired Chief Inspector of Primary Schools of thirty-three years' experience in the Inspectorate) result in identical ratings. Both give strong emphasis to all themes except self-perception and diagnosis. They seem to assume the importance of diagnosis but do not stress it as much as other themes or as do other writers. But they do call attention to the teacher's job of attending to children as individuals whose needs and abilities develop at different times.

Humaneness is the other theme which receives only moderate emphasis in two of these works. One cannot help wondering whether a reason for the lesser emphasis on humaneness in the *Plowden Report* is in part the result of the inevitable impersonality of a government report. Although the *Plowden Report* gives attention to the need to view children as individuals and to attend to their affective experience in school, this theme receives less attention compared with others.

Advisers and Advocates

Ratings of advisers and advocates may be somewhat misleading because each category is represented by short works, written for a specific audience and aimed at dealing with a single aspect of this approach to teaching. For example, Armington's paper (1968) is a proposal to the United States government for the Education Development Center's Follow Through Program. In it he stresses the role of the adviser, which constituted the core of the EDC's efforts in assisting teachers to adopt an open education approach to teaching. He sees advisers as a crucial part of the success of the open education approach and bases his conception of them upon the role of the advisers in Leicestershire. His brief paper includes a clear and concise outline of the key elements of the open classroom; hence the high ratings for seven of the eight themes. He does not, however, include any mention of evaluation. Although this omission may reflect an absence of concern for describing appropriate forms of evaluation, it is also possible that in so short and specific a piece, a less-valued theme falls by the wayside.

Hawkins (1967), too, focuses on a single central idea. His is a philosophic statement about his concept of the core of teaching and learning: "The relationship between the teacher and the child and a third thing . . . knowledge . . . that has to be there and that completes the triangle" (p. 1). Open educators see his paper as a key statement, central to an understanding of instruction. Hawkins does not try to deal with more than one, albeit crucial, aspect of the teacher's performance. Nevertheless, in discussing it, he does include strong emphasis on half of the themes. These, the themes most closely tied to the teaching-learning relationship he is considering, are provisioning, diagnosis, instruction, and assumptions. In addition, he touches on humaneness.

One of Yeomans' pamphlets (1969b) describes a summer workshop for teachers preparing to teach according to the practices and beliefs of the "integrated day." The other aims to interest educators in the integrated day as an approach to primary education. Both works are brief and include practical information such as lists of suggested materials and equipment and descriptions of the day-to-day programming of the workshop. Both stress provisioning and instruction heavily; the former rates high on the themes of seeking, self-perception, and assumptions.

In summary, these ratings probably reflect only in part these authors' estimates of the nature and importance of each of the eight themes. Despite any limitations and possible distortions, however, these authors still unanimously stress the themes of provisioning, instruction, and assumptions. Evaluation receives least attention from the advisers and advocates.

Practitioners

The practitioners strongly agreed on the importance of the theme of instruction. As noted earlier, a distinctive aspect of the open education approach is the concept of an active teacher. The open classroom is conceived of as teacher-centered *and* child-centered; both are crucial to instruction. These practitioners go about helping children to learn by responding to the needs, interests, and readiness of each child as an individual and by respecting his capacity for intelligent decisionmaking. Permissiveness is not to be found in the mode of instruction these teachers practice.

Except in Cazden's accounts, humaneness is another theme on which these practitioners place very high stress. In a paper which is both analysis and catalogue, Cazden (1971) concentrates on methods and approaches to language instruction. In it, the first four themes in our list are strongly present, as are seeking and assumptions. Humaneness and self-perception were perhaps of less interest to her since she concentrated on language acquisition and reading development. An especially low rating for humaneness is based upon the almost total absence of this theme in the interview with the headmistress of Gordonbrock school (Cazden, 1969).

Brown and Precious (1969), heads of associated infant and junior schools, describe the ways in which the "integrated day" has been interpreted in practice in their schools. Their book combines bold assertions with detailed descriptions, even diagrams, which are both evocative and practical. All eight themes are emphasized; hardly any of the 90 specific characteristics goes unexpressed.

Similarly, Prescott and Raoul (1970), American innovators who were trained by educators from Leicestershire, emphasize each of the eight themes as they are defined in this study. Howard (1971) has been engaged over the past several years in the development of open education in his school. While Prescott and Raoul have been working with a limited number of classrooms in a private school, Howard has been an administrator in a city public school system. At the program's inception the children of his school, however, were often poor and accustomed to years of neglect and inadequate education, which had led to community resentment and desperation: "In the formative months of the Boardman School program, . . . it became evident that something had to be done about the deplorable condition of the school's image" (p. 8). Which of these differences or combination of differences account for the relatively lower emphasis he places on the themes of diagnosis, evaluation, seeking, and self-perception can only be speculated upon. His conception of the other four themes—provisioning, instruction, humaneness, and assumptions—agrees with that presented in this report, and he stresses their importance.

The other two authors we selected for analysis as practitioners were less clearly a part of this educational movement at the time they wrote their books. Marshall (1966) and Richardson (1964) are unique and exceptional teachers who, working on their own in the relative isolation of "one-room" country schools, developed their own styles and convictions. Marshall taught for eighteen years in a village which "was really too rural and off the map to attract many suitable candidates" (p. 13); Richardson, for twelve years in a little school at the northern tip of

New Zealand. Their books relate their growth as teachers, the experiences they and their children shared, and reveal the underlying convictions which grew in them as they taught.

Marshall especially stresses the themes of instruction, humaneness, and seeking. She gives less emphasis to provisioning, diagnosis, self-perception, and assumptions. Richardson's book is rated highly on five themes and gives relatively less emphasis to provisioning, diagnosis, and seeking. The somewhat lower rating on provisioning perhaps reflects the isolation of the two teachers' schools from sources of materials other than what their environment provided and what a meager "supplies allowance" could purchase from a limited provincial market or school supplies' list. Similarly, Richardson had little opportunity for courses, colleagues, or advisers from which or whom to seek opportunities for growth. Both teachers made extensive use of the natural resources of their immediate surroundings. These teachers seem to be a special breed, and they differ somewhat from practitioners who are a conscious part of the open education approach.

Summary

Overall, those writing about open education are unanimous in strongly emphasizing the theme of instruction. The teacher has an active role in guiding and extending children's learning, based upon individual attention and involvement with the child and upon encouraging children's independence and also based upon exercise of real choice within a framework of long-term goals. In addition, of the sixteen open education authors or coauthors analyzed, fourteen similarly stressed the theme of provisioning for learning (only Richardson and Marshall differing slightly, as described above). In order for children to share with the teacher the central role in their own instruction, they must be provided with the appropriate range and richness of materials and with conditions (of grouping, timing, emotional atmosphere) which maximize their ability to learn at their own rate and in their own ways. Fourteen of the sixteen rated high on assumptions also. Bussis and Chittenden stressed the importance of this but did not describe it explicitly. Marshall seemed to understand and agree with the open education assumptions described in this report, but she neither spelled them out nor particularly stressed them. Diagnosis, seeking, and humaneness all receive strong emphasis in this literature. In general, the authors agree upon the importance of these three qualities of the teacher, but these themes rate slightly lower than instruction, provisioning, and assumptions in importance. The theme of evaluation receives least attention overall in this literature—a point which is reflected no doubt in the accusations of "irresponsibility" leveled against this movement by its critics.

Writers of Historical Importance

Plato.   Our analysis is based on the relevant sections of Cornford's translation of *The Republic,* Plato's vision of an ideal society. Plato's views on education are developed in the context of a Utopian society and reflect the world view of his own society. On every theme Plato received a negative rating. His assumptions and emphasis are the antithesis of those of open education. He assumes (1) a clearly defined and circumscribed training for a particular function in an apparently static society, and (2) an "ultimate end" for education in the form of a specific belief about the nature of the world. These assumptions contrast with the ideas about knowledge and the process of learning found to be characteristic of open education.

Other Platonic beliefs about education are rooted in these assumptions. For the development of good and wise men and women, Plato believes that education must be strictly regulated; only stories of certain content and moral standards should be allowed; only certain poetry, music, and drama, suitable in form and content for the moral development of children, should be permitted; and learning is sharply divided into subject matter areas.

Plato's scheme is authoritarian, with little scope for the development of individual differences, the encouragement of a child's independence, initiative, or self-expression. Even direct interaction of a child with manipulative and environmental materials and with other children is not considered valuable. With regard to provisioning, instruction, diagnosis, and evaluation, Plato does not advocate considering the individual child's feeling or reasoning processes.

Plato assumes the teacher should be a good and wise person, but particular characteristics, similar to those which define our themes of seeking and self-perception, are not mentioned; the teacher is nondescript. Even "instruction" is usually described in the passive voice.

Rousseau.   In *Emile* (trans. 1956), Rousseau assumes that human nature is essentially good and that each individual's learning proceeds idiosyncratically. His views are in general agreement with those which constitute the themes of assumptions, self-perception, humaneness, and instruction.

Rousseau assumes that children possess a natural curiosity and goodness, which is fettered by society and by the kind of education they receive. He believes that children learn best when they are involved in what they are learning and that their lessons should derive from their own exploratory interests. The teacher should facilitate learning by asking questions and directing attention to new areas, but the starting point should be the child's interests.

The characteristics which make up Rousseau's concept of proper instruction follow from these assumptions and mirror those found in open education. According to Rousseau, instruction should be based upon direct experience. Rousseau especially emphasized the world of nature as providing the appropriate setting and materials for learning. Instruction should be individualized: Rousseau's ideal in *Emile* is portrayed as the tutor who pays attention to what the child understands and wants to learn. Learning should be of a piece, with one question or interest leading to another.

Provisioning was not strongly stressed in *Emile*. Since his theory presupposes a one-to-one situation in a natural environment, rather than a classroom and peer group, the provisioning (for interaction with other children, for activity areas and organization of classroom space, for profusion and diversity of books, equipment, and materials) is usually absent. There is no emphasis in *Emile* on the themes of diagnosis, evaluation, and seeking, at least as conceptualized by open educators.

Tolstoy.   The ratings for Tolstoy are based on his "pedagogical articles" which appeared in the periodical *Yasnaya Polyana* in 1862 and which later were collected under the title *On Education* (1967). Like Plato and Rousseau, Tolstoy wrote on education within a larger philosophical context. Unlike the two earlier writers, however, he directed his attention specifically to the classroom situation, and his ideas were derived from his own experiences while teaching children in this way.

Tolstoy's views generally agree with the characteristics of open education on the themes of assumptions, self-perception, and humaneness, and he gives much importance to these themes in his articles. Where Rousseau and Plato see education as serving specific "ultimate aims" for society, Tolstoy envisions developing individuals for a changing society. He emphasizes that students should not be compelled to study any particular lesson, that the teacher must experiment with many different methods of instruction until those which fit the students' needs are developed, that children must be allowed to find their own ways of learning, and that the children's interests should form the starting point for instruction. The teacher should perceive himself as an attempter, a continual learner. Tolstoy trusts children's ability to operate effectively and feels comfortable about children exercising choice and about modifying plans. He believes they should be free to work out their own conflicts with each other without adult intervention. He gives serious attention to, and shows respect for, children's feelings.

Tolstoy gives moderate attention to the other five open education themes. He shows some agreement with the characteristics which define seeking: teachers talk with one another each Sunday, compare notes, and make tentative plans for the following week. Tolstoy says that his school changed, based in part on conversations between parents and teachers. Although he gives importance to the themes of diagnosis and instruction and generally agrees with the definitions of these themes as found in open education literature, there is not as much actual evidence of child initiative and attention to the pupil's individual needs in these areas as is given by open educators. "Subjects" are defined and separated, and although there is a flexibility about scheduling, it seems to be based more upon group than individual decision.

Regarding evaluation, it is clear that Tolstoy reflected on what was happening in his school and why it happened. Proper evaluation for him comes through observing in the classroom over a long period, not from testing. Provisioning includes no mention of manipulative or environmental materials to which the children have free access; however, children of many ages and abilities learn together. They teach each other, and there appears to be much voluntary grouping and regrouping of children according to interests. Tolstoy also speaks of the necessity of a great variety of books for stimulating and sustaining interest in reading.

Progressive Educators*

Clearly, many of open education's antecedents lie in the progressive movement. The strong showing made by the three representatives selected for our analysis reflect this affinity. These authors, therefore, warrant discussion here.

Within the main themes of what became known as progressive education, there are differences and conflicting interpretations, to be sure; but as set out early in the 1900s, these themes have a ring of consistency which permits us to follow them through not only as theory but in description of practice. The testing of ideas by their consequences meant that theory did not remain in the realm of the abstract but was quickly moved into the world of practice; hence, the activist stance of progressives on many fronts has left a rich catalogue of practice available for analysis.

The three progressives and their work selected for analysis range over the past seventy years. *Schools of Tomorrow* (1915) is undoubtedly one of Dewey's clearest statements on progressive education, with salient illus-

* We thank Professor Maurice J. Eash for conducting the content analysis of progressive educators and drafting most of this section.

trations drawn from public schools visited by his daughter Evelyn. While at Columbia Teachers College, Rugg worked in the Lincoln Laboratory School in developing curriculum and putting progressive theory to test. *The Child-Centered School* (1928) was an early influential statement in disseminating progressive education ideas among the profession. Emma Sheehy's textbook (1954) has been widely used in training teachers for early childhood education. In a manner similar to the Dewey and Rugg documents, she puts theory into practice—though the theory is more implicit—as she addresses her audience of teachers with detailed descriptions of program activities.

The tenets of progressive education run through these three books. For brevity, only six are sketched here:

1. Education, to be effective, must be compatible with the natural growth of the child. This root assumption, which Dewey admitted came from Rousseau, was at the heart of progressive theory and practice.

2. Free movement, physical activity, and the affective component were as much a part of education as cognitive and intellectual processes. Therefore, activity units requiring construction, use of drama, and other physical expression were central to the curriculum.

3. Wholeness was emphasized. The life of the school was not divorced from the life outside; moreover, the quality of living in the present was seen as the best preparation for life in the future—a phrase much repeated in open education materials.

4. Learning by doing was a part of natural education and the primary method by which children learned; therefore, activity units based on children's experiences were developed.

5. Activities in which children engaged in school were not to be pursued capriciously but were to reproduce selectively the conditions of real life within the boundaries of students' understanding.

6. Within the school there must be concern for children's making choices and evaluating consequences.

These tenets, with variations, have a long history in their evolution and reflect a myriad of practices. Though they sometimes proved difficult to carry out in practice, they have been persistent. The role of the teacher is paramount, a significant variable in establishing the conditions where children can operate. Weaknesses of teachers, lack of consistent theory, and limitations of personal and professional resources have contributed to the perversion of these main themes and challenged their usefulness.

Open education obviously has historical roots in progressive education. Ignorance of its antecedent foundations would close it off from a knowledge of the fatal practices which plagued progressive education and placed it in disrepute for a number of decades. Rathbone (1970) warns wisely: "An understanding of both the similarities and the differences between Open Education and the Progressive movement might alert American proponents to potential resistances as well as predict the most receptive groups of parents and schools" (p. 163).

Popular Critics

Holt.   John Holt's first two books, *How Children Fail* (1964) and *How Children Learn* (1967), presented a more difficult rating task. The former, composed of notes and anecdotes written while Holt was teaching and observing in an elementary school, contains reflections on the teaching-learning process, criticism of the organization of contemporary schools, and questions with implications for how the situation should be changed. Although Holt does mention the Leicestershire schools, he does not make explicit recommendations for how a school or classroom should be organized to facilitate the real, as distinct from apparent, learning he thinks schools should foster.

How Children Learn, too, is anecdotal in form and deals with preschool children. The book disappoints expectations suggested by its title, which complements that of Holt's earlier book, because it does not address itself to the issues and questions raised in that book of how schools could and should better facilitate learning; thus, there is little in the second book which is relevant to the open education themes presented in this report.

Holt's first book gives much importance to the themes of diagnosis, evaluation, humaneness, and assumptions. His reports show attentive observation of what particular children are doing, both to diagnose what the child knows and can do and to estimate why the child has made a particular mistake or is stumped at a particular point. He devotes five pages to a description and careful explanation of how a child uses her materials to do her own correcting, without needing or wanting a teacher to point out her errors for her. The form of his books reflects a continuing jotting and evaluation of what was going on in learning activities. Holt expresses strong feelings against testing in the traditional sense for evaluation purposes.

Compared with his especially strong emphasis on diagnosis and evaluation, the other two emphasized themes seem somewhat weaker. On humaneness, Holt underlines the crucial role that he sees the teacher's sincere respect for the children plays in their learning. Holt's assumptions correspond to those defined in this research, for example, that there is no set body of knowledge that should be "transmitted" in schools or that children should learn at their own rate from their own concrete experiences.

Holt does not treat seeking and self-perception as strongly. From references to walks outside the school, conversations with parents, and occasional mention of colleagues, it is apparent that Holt sought opportunities for growth as a teacher in the ways defined in open education literature. For Holt, it seems implicit that the self-perception of the good teacher includes trust that the children can learn independently, an ability to restrain himself from interfering out of his own needs rather than the child's, and a sense of perceiving the child as a continual learner. However, these characteristics are not discussed explicitly.

His treatment of the themes instruction and provisioning is also moderate. Although strong emphasis is given to the diagnostic aspect of instruction, encouragement of real choice and independence and the interdisciplinary nature of learning are less apparent in his descriptions. The classroom problems and tasks which Holt describes appear to be teacher-initiated. With respect to provisioning, Holt mentions the use of some manipulative materials but does not stress their importance or range, nor does he discuss other kinds of materials, the children's grouping and regrouping voluntarily, or many activities going on simultaneously and flexible scheduling.

Kohl. *Thirty-six Children* (1967) describes a teaching experience in a class of American sixth-grade children. *The Open Classroom* (1969) is a "handbook for teachers who want to work in an open environment" (p. 65). In it, Kohl gives substantial attention and emphasis to seven of the themes defined in this report and only slightly less to diagnosis. He is concerned with how change can come about, as well as the direction that the change should take. His attention is directed to how teachers can change their classrooms and themselves. Consistent with his interest in the teacher's change, his work shows much emphasis on self-perception and seeking. He sees a need for teachers to build trust in themselves and in the children, and he encourages and assists them to get in touch with colleagues and parents about what they are doing.

Particular sections of *The Open Classroom* are devoted to the theme of evaluation. Kohl makes explicit his lack of faith in tests and his belief that note-taking and observation of each child and the quality of his particular work are crucial to evaluation. Further, he sees evaluation as necessitating reflection as well as data collection. And from such thoughtful reflection arises the instruction the teacher decides upon for each child.

The necessity for openness, respect, trust, and warmth in relations with the children and in the atmosphere of the classroom as a whole runs through both books. That the teacher should be a real person with feelings and needs is especially stressed. He should minimize those classroom practices which set him up as privileged. Kohl's ideal teacher hangs his coat among those of his students and turns the "teacher's closet" over to the class for storage of materials. Although diagnosis receives less emphasis compared with the other seven themes, Kohl does recognize its importance to instruction and stresses in particular the role of teacher as acute and constant observer.

Affective Orientation

Affective educators, according to Terry Borton (1970), are developing a new field which aims at "balancing the traditional emphasis on skills and cognitive information with an explicit attention to the important areas of feelings, values, and interpersonal behavior" (p. 135). There is no one theoretical foundation on which all affective educators agree. It is the aim which links them together; their methods are eclectic. Affective education includes a whole range of people, and in addition to the four representatives selected for this analysis, many others intending to help children cope with their feelings have entered this field. Most such courses and books, as those by Borton and William Glasser (1969), take for granted a traditional classroom arrangement, with a teacher conducting lessons with the class as a whole unit. They are obviously not conceived with open education in mind, although an open education teacher could decide to call the class together for activities such as those they outline.

Neill.   Dennison (1969) and Neill (1960) are trained therapists who have devoted themselves to educating children. The books of these two men selected for analysis concentrate on the education of children in a school setting and, as such, seemed most likely to provide bases for comparison with open education. Neill, whose major tenet is a belief in the child's right to freedom of choice, presents an approach least like that of open education. His frame of reference (assumptions and self-perception) is, however, very similar; these two themes are strongly stressed. But his treatment of practices, with the exception of humaneness, differs considerably. His is a more permissive, laissez-faire approach; the teacher in his scheme appears to be less active than is expected in open education. Although evaluation and provisioning receive moderate treatment in a manner consistent with the views of open education, attention to seeking, diagnosis, and instruction is almost entirely absent. In fact, lessons appear to be conducted along traditional lines: i.e., whole group instruction in various disciplines.

Leonard.   George Leonard (1968) represents an "affective" orientation rather different from the other three authors considered here. This difference is reflected in his high rating on provisioning and lower ratings on humaneness and self-perception. He sees in technology great promise for the enrichment of man; in Leonard's book, technology is servant to man's ecstasy rather than an agent of depersonalization. Among this group, only he lays heavy stress on provisioning and includes probably more "hardware" than open educators would be comfortable with. None of the other affective writers studied gives strong emphasis to the theme of provisioning. Although all acknowledged its role in learning, they saw it as clearly secondary to the interpersonal relationship between teacher and child.

This relative duality is reflected in the ratings on the theme of humaneness. The other three authors showed great emphasis on this theme, whereas Leonard gave only moderate emphasis; Leonard conceives of the individual as somewhat less needful of the emotional support of teachers. While he takes for granted a humane atmosphere in his ideal school, he does not dwell upon it, and his students of the future appear far more capable of satisfying their emotional needs through their own resources and the skills they learn. Opportunities for practice in techniques of self-awareness and such activities as role-playing are present, but the characteristics which make up open education's theme of humaneness seem somehow slightly irrelevant. Leonard seems to assume that if the child is more self-sufficient the humaneness of the teacher is not so crucial.

In general, the teacher as person fades into the background in his book, and this lack of emphasis is reflected in lower ratings on seeking and self-perception; the teacher as *teacher* remains active, however. Leonard gives strong emphasis not only to the theme of provisioning but also to those of diagnosis, instruction, evaluation and assumptions.

Dennison.   Of all these "affective" authors, George Dennison (1969) most closely reflects the open education approach. On seven of the eight themes, his book showed that strong emphasis on provisioning alone may be related to a difference in ultimate priorities. Although Dennison is greatly concerned with the child's intellectual learning and development of skills, one might legitimately assume from reading his book that for him, when "either-or" choices must be made, emotional growth takes precedence over cognitive growth. To the extent that emotional growth is facilitated by richness of interpersonal relationships and to the extent that intellectual growth is based upon interaction with the material environment uninterpreted by a sensitive adult, some conflict in allocation of resources comes into play. Dennison's First Street School had the "luxurious intimacy" of small size and a very low pupil/teacher ratio. Provisioning—in the form of providing *adults*—had highest priority and greatest importance. This view differs somewhat from the open education theme.

Borton.   In *Reach, Touch and Teach* (1970), Borton surveys suggestions of other educators for what might constitute an education which would help both students and teachers become more in touch with their own and one another's feelings, and he also offers his own suggestions for curricular modifications and innovations. He gives only moderate emphasis to the themes of instruction, provisioning, and diagnosis. Generally the context is one of a whole-class lesson within a scheduled time period, with the "materials" being one's own elicited feelings. Flexibility of time, space, activities, and grouping is limited. Although the child as an individual is recognized as important, diagnosis on an individualized basis with close attention to each child's thought processes, needs, and interests is not specifically mentioned. Evaluation receives a low rating, because it is not discussed. Borton's attention to the themes of humaneness, seeking, self-perception, and assumptions, however, is generally consistent with that of the open education writers.

None of these writers deals exclusively with early elementary school children. This difference, as well as their affective orientation, may have something to do with their emphases.

OVERALL COMPARISON

Table 1 presents a summary of this content analysis arranged according to the individual author's mean score on all eight themes and the overall mean of the authors in each group. Not surprisingly, the two groups of writers who set themselves the task of describing open education have the highest overall ratings (analysts/researchers and reporters/observers). The next-highest groups are popular critics and practitioners. It is interesting to note that the two writers grouped under popular critics have also been practitioners and base their criticisms of, and comments on, contemporary education upon their own experiences and efforts. The progressive educators are only slightly lower than these two groups in their agreement and emphasis on these eight themes. The means of the affective orientation selections and of the advisers/advocates fall almost exactly halfway between a 2 and a 3 rating. The lowest rating of any group analyzed here belongs to the writers of historical importance. Here one should notice, however, the gradually rising ratings of the three authors selected, from Plato's "closed education" through Rousseau to Tolstoy. This historical trend continues in the progressives' relatively high rating.

Table 1. Summary of Content Analysis by Individual and Group

Analysts/Researchers		Writers of Historical Importance	
Bussis-Chittenden (1970)	2.75	Tolstoy (1967)	2.47
Barth (1970)	2.88	Rousseau (1956)	2.12
Rathbone (1970)	2.88	Rolstoy (1967)	2.38
Overall	2.83	Overall	1.83

Reporters/Observers		Progressive Educators	
Plowden (1967)	2.75	Dewey (1915)	2.50
Blackie (1967)	2.75	Rugg & Shumacker (1928)	2.50
Featherstone (1967)	2.62	Sheehy (1954)	2.75
Silberman (1970)	2.75	Overall	2.58
Overall	2.72		

Advisers/Advocates		Popular Critics	
Armington (1968)	2.75	Holt (1964, 1967)	2.50
Hawkins (1967)	2.12	Kohl (1967, 1969)	2.88
Yeomans (1969)	2.50	Overall	2.69
Overall	2.47		

Practitioners.		Affective Orientation	
Cazden (1969, 1973)	2.62	Neill (1960)	2.00
Brown & Precious (1969)	3.00	Leonard (1968)	2.62
Prescott & Raoul (1970)	3.00	Dennison (1969)	2.87
Howard (1968, 1971)	2.50	Borton (1970)	2.38
Richardson (1964)	2.62	Overall	2.47
Marshall (1966)	2.25		
Overall	2.66		

A comparison among the groups of authors based on the mean scores for each of the themes (Table 2) indicates more specific areas of similarity and difference between open education authors and those of other orientations. Here it can be seen that open educators stress provisioning and diagnosis more strongly than any other group except the progressives. Open educators and progressives alone unanimously emphasize the theme of instruction as defined in this report. Only the popular critics pay more attention to the theme of evaluation than the open educators, whereas humaneness is stressed more strongly by three of the other groups: the progressives, the popular critics, and the affective educators. Seeking is the only theme on which the open education authors averaged higher than all other groups. On self-perception, open education falls right in the middle, above the historical writers and the progressives but below the two contemporary groups. Despite the overall high mean of open education on the theme of assumptions, all the other groups (except the historical writers) were even higher.

Looking at the progressive educators alone in comparison with those

Table 2. A Summary of a Content Analysis by Theme and Group (Open Educators)

	Analysts/Re-Searchers	Reporters/Observers	Advisers/Advocates	Practitioners	Open Education Overall Means*	Writers of Historical Importance	Progressive Educators	Popular Critical	Affective Orientation
Provisioning for learning	3.00	3.00	3.00	2.66	2.88	1.66	3.00	2.50	2.25
Diagnosis of learning events	3.00	2.50	2.66	2.50	2.63	1.33	3.00	2.50	2.25
Instruction—guidance and extension of learning	3.00	3.00	3.00	3.00	3.00	2.00	3.00	2.50	2.25
Reflective evaluation of diagnostic information	2.66	2.75	1.33	2.50	2.38	1.33	2.00	3.00	2.25
Humaneness—respect, openness, and warmth	3.00	2.50	2.00	2.66	2.56	2.33	3.00	3.00	2.75
Seeking opportunities to promote growth	2.66	2.75	2.33	2.66	2.63	1.33	1.33	2.50	2.25
Self-perception of the teacher	2.66	2.25	2.33	2.50	2.44	2.33	2.33	2.50	2.75
Assumptions—ideas about children and the process of learning	2.66	3.00	3.00	2.83	2.88	2.33	3.00	3.00	3.00

*These means represent the average of all sixteen authors and coauthors.

writing about open education, one notes that they treat the themes of provisioning, diagnosis, humaneness, and assumptions more thoroughly than the open educators considered as a whole. Both groups give very strong attention to or agreement on the themes of evaluation, seeking, and self-perception.

A similar comparison between the writers grouped under affective orientation and the open education writers reveals that affective educators give relatively more importance and emphasis to the themes of self-perception and humaneness and, as a group, less attention to the themes of provisioning, diagnosis, instruction, evaluation, and seeking. Both groups stress assumptions, although the open education literature taken as a whole shows slightly less emphasis in this area.

CONCLUSION

Why the foregoing? More than anything else, we view it as a starting point. There are many difficulties and much subjectivity in attempting to rank works in this manner, but it does offer a method for identifying systematic trends in a body of literature. We hope some useful purposes have been served: at the very least, we have found some consistent differences between open education authors and others. The thinking is evolutionary (especially from Rousseau and the progressives), rather than revolutionary, but is distinctive and will, if nothing else, give engaged educators a fresh point of view, a touchstone for educational practice. Our definitions of the eight themes in the revised list of characteristics (Walberg and Thomas, 1971; Appendix D) present a means for learning about distinctive characteristics of open education. The comments on the authors and their writings may serve as a guide to further reading and refinement of points of view.

In general, there has been an absence of systematic theorizing among the open educators. Their ideas seem to derive inductively from the practice of teaching. Meanwhile "romantic critics" of education and others have been rendering a devastating picture of contemporary education and offering few constructive alternatives, while some "Establishment educationists" are wondering whether indeed their practices are viable or oppressive and how they may be adapted. Open education, as described in the writings we reviewed, offers a chance for real attention to individual learning, respect for the child, authentic relationships, and opportunities for both teacher and child to participate in significant learning. These factors may help to explain the widespread interest in the movement. But the concept requires more scrutiny by philosophers, psychologists, and others who contribute to educational ideology. There are many valid questions to ask about new educational concepts, and perhaps we have identified some elements of these questions here.

References

Armington, D. E., "A Plan for Continuing Growth," proposal submitted to United States Office of Education, December 1968.

Ashton-Warner, Sylvia, *Teacher*. New York: Simon and Schuster, 1963.

Barth, R. S., *Open Education: Assumptions About Learning and Knowledge*. Doctoral dissertation, Harvard University, 1970.

Barth, R. S., *Open Education and the American School*. New York: Agathon Press, 1972.

Blackie, J., *Inside the Primary School*. London: Her Majesty's Stationery Office, 1967; New York: Schocken Books, 1971.

Borton, T., *Reach, Touch and Teach: Student Concerns and Process Education*. New York: McGraw-Hill, 1970.

Brown, Mary, and N. Precious, *The Integrated Day in the Primary School*. New York: Agathon Press, 1969.

Bussis, Anne M., and E. A. Chittenden, *Analysis of an Approach to Open Education*. Princeton, N.J.: Educational Testing Service, 1970.

Cazden, Courtney B., *Infant School*. Newton, Mass.: Education Development Center, 1969.

Cazden, Courtney B., "Language Programs for Young Children: Notes from England and Wales," in C. B. Lavatelli (ed.), *Language Training in Early Childhood Education*. Urbana: University of Illinois Press, 1971.

Cort, H. R., Jr., N. H. Henderson, G. G. Justison, R. A. O'Keefe, and C. J. Potter, *An Evaluation of the Innovation Team Program in the D. C. Model School Division*. Washington, D. C.: Educational Studies Department, Washington School of Psychiatry, 1969.

Dennison, G., *The Lives of Children: The Story of the First Street School*. New York: Random House, 1969.

Dewey, J., and Evelyn Dewey, *Schools of Tomorrow*. New York: Dutton, 1915, 1962.

Dreeban, R., *On What Is Learned in School*. Reading, Mass.: Addison-Wesley, 1968.

Featherstone, J., "The Primary School Revolution in Great Britain," *The New Republic*, reprint of articles which first appeared Aug. 10, Sept. 2, and Sept. 9, 1967.

Featherstone, J., *Schools Where Children Learn*. New York: Liveright, 1971.

Gardner, Dorothy E. M., and Joan E. Cass, *The Role of the Teacher in the Infant and Nursery School*. Oxford: Pergamon Press, 1965.

Glasser, W., *Schools Without Failure*. New York: Harper & Row, 1969.

Hawkins, D., "I, Thou, It," paper presented at the primary teachers' residential course, Loughborough, Leicestershire, Apr. 3, 1967. Reprinted in Hawkins, *The Informed Vision*. New York: Agathon Press, 1974.

Hertzberg, Alvin, and Edward F. Stone, *Schools Are for Children: An American Approach to the Open Classroom*. New York: Schocken, 1971.

Holt, J., *How Children Fail.* New York: Pitman, 1964.

Holt, J., *How Children Learn.* New York: Pitman, 1967.

Howard, L. M., *The Developmental Classroom.* Boston: Office of Program Development, 1968 (mimeograph).

Howard, L. M., *Educational Change in a Big City School.* Boston: Office of Program Development, 1971 (mimeograph).

Jackson, P. W., *Life in Classrooms.* New York: Holt, 1968.

Koch, K., *Wishes, Lies, and Dreams.* New York: Chelsea House, 1970.

Kohl, H. R., *Thirty-six Children.* New York: Signet, 1967.

Kohl, H. R., *The Open Classroom.* New York: Random House, 1969.

Langdon, Margaret, *Let the Children Write.* London: Longmans, 1961.

Leonard, G. B., *Education and Ecstasy.* New York: Dell, 1968.

Marshall, Sybil, *An Experiment in Education.* Cambridge, England: Cambridge University Press, 1966.

Murrow, C., and L. Murrow, *Children Come First: The Inspired Work of English Primary Schools.* New York: McGraw-Hill, 1971.

Neill, A. S., *Summerhill.* New York: Hart, 1960.

Oates, Maureen K., *The Pilot Communities' Boston Resource Team: An Evaluation Based on Questionnaire Responses of School Personnel.* Newton, Mass.: Education Development Center, 1970.

Plato, *The Republic,* F. M. Cornford, (translator). New York: Oxford, 1945.

Plowden, Lady B., et al., *Children and Their Primary Schools: A Report of the Central Advisory Council for Education.* London: Her Majesty's Stationery Office, 1967.

Prescott, Jane, and Kathleen Raoul, "Live and Learn," *Shady Hill News,* Cambridge, Mass., Fall 1970.

Rathbone, C. H., *Open Education and the Teacher.* Unpublished doctoral dissertation, Harvard University, 1970.

Richardson, E. S., *In the Early World.* New York: Random House, 1964.

Rousseau, J. J., *Emile,* W. Boyd (ed. and translator). New York: Teachers College Press, 1956.

Rugg, H., and Ann Shumacker, *The Child-Centered School.* Yonkers, N.Y.: World Book, 1928.

Sargent, Betsye, *The Integrated Day in an American School.* Boston: National Association of Independent Schools, 1970.

Sheehy, Emma D., *The Five's and Six's Go to School.* New York: Greenwood; 1954.

Silberman, C. E., *Crisis in the Classroom.* New York: Random House, 1970.

Skidelsky, R., *English Progressive Schools.* Baltimore: Penguin, 1969.

Tolstoy, L., *Tolstoy on Education,* L. Weiner (ed.). Chicago: University of Chicago Press, 1967.

Walberg, Herbert J., and Susan C. Thomas, *Characteristics of Open Education: Toward an Operational Definition.* Newton, Mass.: Education Development Center, 1971.

Walton, J. (ed.), *The Integrated Day in Theory and Practice.* London: Ward Lock, 1971.

Weber, Lilian, *The English Infant School and Informal Education*. Englewood Cliffs, N.J.: Prentice-Hall, 1971.

Wiseman, F., *High school* (film), 1969.

Yeomans, E., *Education for Initiative and Responsibility*. Boston: National Association of Independent Schools, 1969a.

Yeomans, E., *The Wellsprings of Teaching*. Boston: National Association of Independent Schools, 1969b.

PART TWO

Curriculum and Objectives

Chapter 3

Perspective on Open Education:
A Speculative Essay

James B. Macdonald, *University of North Carolina at Greensboro*

THERE is a good deal of nonsense in the air about open education. On one side it is suggested or implied by our rhetoric that open education is the new panacea for our educational ills, created overnight by saviors or communists (or both). Another approach would have us believe that open education is an English primary school phenomenon that we must now imitate if we are to have decent schools. Still others view it as the inevitable weakening of our moral fiber and a symptom of permissiveness in our midst. And so on . . . !

What seems to be lacking for many is a sense of perspective. This is, I suspect, a fundamental problem of our age, for we seem caught in a quickening spiral of events which appear to carry us rapidly along some unpredictable path. Given this sense of uncertainty and dismay, we still must create meaning for our events and lives, and we tend to snatch at simple explanations that help us get on to the next happening. This is quite understandable and perhaps partially unavoidable, but I am reminded of something Aldous Huxley[1] once wrote about education in general, and I believe his advice may help us place open education in a perspective that could make sense for us and also maximize for us the inherent positive aspects of the movement.

What Huxley contended was that nothing should be encountered as a thing or idea in and of itself; one should always have three basic perspective referents in mind. These referents were (1) the history, (2) the contemporary relationships, and (3) the semantic implications of each new phenomenon. Thus, it seems useful here to view open education from the perspective of history, contemporary events, and language.

What we call open education is a form of knowledge about education.

It is a human attempt to utilize and re-create existing knowledge and create new knowledge that can guide educational practices and endeavors. Therefore, as mankind continues to create his own history and to be made over by his own creation, he does so through the fundamental impulses that have generated his past endeavors. History changes with new perspective, cultures change, and language changes as history and culture evolve. New knowledge and interpretations arise.

For example, open education is not progressive education, simply because it exists in a different historical time which projects a changed cultural milieu and new knowledge forms and language terms to talk about education. Thus, our history, our contemporary cultures, and our language must be informed by our understanding of the sociology of knowledge, that is, by our awareness that knowledge grows out of the past but is continually re-created and created by the changing cultural forms that emerge in history. We must look, therefore, not only at the data of the past and present but also at the basic impulses that urge us to continue to develop and inform our knowledge and practice.

Yet history, contemporary events, and language do not provide enough of a framework to guide us. A second kind of concern seems necessary if we are to proceed with any hope of clarity: namely, to reveal the basis of human interest that encourages open education.

Jurgen Habermas[2] has identified three major human interests that appear to be useful explanatory concepts for looking at the development of human knowledge and consequent activity. He calls these three interests (1) control, (2) understanding, and (3) liberation. Habermas sets forth the basic proposition that knowledge cannot be divorced from human interest. He attempts to deal at length with crucial persons and ideas which demonstrate how the scientific aura of the nineteenth and twentieth centuries has resulted in a substitution of concern for a theory of knowledge by the concern for a philosophy of science. Thus, we have come to think that knowledge is derived only by empirical analytical means and that other sources of knowledge are misleading. He reminds us of Nietzsche's remark that what distinguished the nineteenth century from previous ones was not the victory of science but the victory of the scientific method *over* science.

Knowledge, in a scientific sense, has become a product of an empirical-analytic methodology. What is ignored is the circumstances or grounding from which methodology arises. Where did the methodology come from, and why did it arise? Is this an example of pure random, historical trial-and-error learning? Habermas thinks not, and I am inclined to agree with him.

On the contrary, historically people have considered knowledge to have a broad base in what are now known as the arts and sciences.

It is only the positivistic methodology of science that has misled us into denying the knowledge base of the arts. Habermas distinguishes between these two as the *monologic* and *hermeneutic* understanding of meaning.

By monologic he means the abstraction of fact from value and the creation of theory explaining facts in an empirical-analytic fashion. The process of verification is a linear one called variously, for example, deduction, induction, or abduction. A formalized language (e.g., calculus) is utilized to facilitate objectivity.

Hermeneutic understanding of meaning arises in the context of different expressions of cultural life such as ordinary language, human actions, and nonverbal expressions. All these expressions carry symbolic meanings, but they need a dialogic interpretation rather than monologic verification; that is to say, methodology is reciprocal or spiral rather than unidirectional. The interpretation of meaning in hermeneutic understanding depends upon a reciprocal relation between "parts" and a diffusely preunderstood "whole" and the correction of the preliminary concept by means of the parts. It is a method that discovers the empirical content of individuated conditions of life while investigating language structures. Habermas argues that hermeneutic understanding has fallen prey to objectivistic tendencies, in that historians, for example, have labored under the illusion that the facts are/were separate from the values and ground of activity.

The trouble with both the monologic and the hermeneutic modes is that they have divorced themselves from self-reflection, for objectivism deludes the knower by projecting an image of a self-subsistent world of facts structured in a lawlike manner and thus conceals the a priori selection of these facts. The overriding concern for methodology which follows an objectivist stance hides from our self-reflection the ground and sources of the "facts." As Habermas notes: "Representations and descriptions are never independent of standards. And the choice of these standards is based on attitudes that require critical consideration by means of arguments, because they cannot be either logically deduced or empirically demonstrated." (p. 312, Appendix)

Thus, Habermas proposes that an emergence in the twentieth century of a self-reflective science, originating in the late nineteenth century, will begin to transcend the problems of objectivism. He sees psychoanalysis as an exemplar of a process of knowing which transcends the problem of monologic and hermeneutic meaning. I shall return to this in a moment.

Fundamental to the whole argument is the assertion that all knowledge is grounded in human interest. This interest may be fundamental self-preservation, but even self-preservation cannot be defined independently of the cultural condition of *work, language,* and *power.* Thus, self-preservation becomes preservation of whatever fantasy of the "good life" one holds. Thus, the morality of human interest enters as a meaning structure which knowledge serves and which is nicely caught by Bertrand Russell's comment: "Without civic morality communities perish, without personal morality their survival has no value." In either case, knowledge is at the service of our interests.

There are then, if Habermas's analysis is valid, three fundamental cognitive human interests that are the ground for knowledge: (1) a *technical cognitive interest in control* underlying the empirical-analytic approach; (2) a *practical cognitive interest in consensus* underlying the hermeneutic-historical approach; and (3) a *critical cognitive interest in emancipation* or *liberation* underlying the self-reflective approach.

Open education is surely within the basic area of fostering and developing the emancipation and liberation of human potential and expression. It is, I believe, a contemporary educational expression of the desire for human liberation, and I shall try to show that this desire has taken three major directions historically and also in today's world.

These liberating directions in education are fundamentally allied with (1) the liberal (or liberating) arts, especially the freeing of intellectual capacity and intellectual activity; (2) the desire for social reconstruction in terms of justice, equality, and love; and (3) the concern for personal growth and the moral integrity of each person. Thus, what follows is a speculative essay that attempts to provide a perspective on open education which could be looked at, in one sense, as is shown in the diagram below.

Perspective on Open Education

		Historical Roots	Contemporary Context	Semantic Implications
Human interest:	(1) Social change			
Liberation	(2) Liberating the mind			
	(3) Personal growth			

What follows will be an attempt to sketch in some data for the empty squares. This data will reflect my own biases and limitations, but it is offered in the humble spirit that it will provide a perspective upon open education that will allow us to identify its most positive potential and create truly quality programs.

Looking Backward: Creating a History

Whatever one may say about many historical events, it seems clear that open education is not a historical accident. In fact, it has a long, healthy and varied (if sometimes tenuous) line of antecedents. Thus we may dispense with the impression (often reflected by the young) that we have come across an idea that was invented today by persons who have finally evolved to a plane of insight that transcends our history. On the other hand, as I shall try to make clear in the next section, the contemporary forces at work have catalyzed a special "now" quality which is indeed important, but in light of our past as well as our present circumstances.

It is, in fact, the special quality of today's world that may mislead us into feeling that the newness of open education is revolutionary. This is in a sense a great sadness to persons who have struggled for quality in education for many years, for the social significance of open education is not its present revolutionary character but that it is a contemporary manifestation of qualities which hold a promise of radical improvement (basic change) for society. It is in essence another chance for educational reform sparked by our contemporary scene.

The antecedents of open education go back as far as we have documents written about matters of education. Let me caution, however, that the historical antecedents are not additive definitions of open education but presentations of a human spirit and perspective that has existed over time and finds appropriate expression in various times and places.

Socrates[3] is perhaps a good beginning point, although we know very little about him directly. But what has come down to us through Plato as the "Socratic method" of teaching surely reflects the spirit that I am talking about. There is in the Socratic method of questioning a lack of direct instruction, an approach which encourages the student to think and create his own answers to questions. Even though it is usually clear that Socrates had answers he hoped others would arrive at, it is clear also that he valued the act of student participation and active searching for answers to important questions.

It is pointless to argue whether the "Socratic method" is open education or not, but it is surely significant that this method of teaching is a major impetus to what came to be known as the idea of a liberal arts education. I shall try to show that the spirit of the liberal (liberating) arts has provided one major historical thrust in open education. The major concern here has been to free the intellect from the parochialism of the unique families, societies, and cultures that we are born into, to open up new intellectual vistas, and—perhaps yet more centrally—to facilitate the realization of one's self through living a reflective life.

I leap centuries to Jean-Jacques Rousseau[4] for our next look at antecedents, for I write now not as a chronicler of history but as a seeker of historical data to provide perspective. I am aware that many persons and practices between Socrates and Rousseau could be profitably elaborated as influential in this context. (Aristotle, Francis Bacon, and Comenius[5] come to mind, for instance.)* From this long history I chose Rousseau because I believe that he came to symbolize another aspect of liberation in education, the damage that is done to man by a discordant environment.

Rousseau is quite often quoted for his famous statement to the effect that all men are born good, only society makes them evil. The importance that I attach to this idea in the present context is that Rousseau recognized (and came to symbolize educationally) what Sir Thomas More and others before him knew well (also Plato): that education cannot be thought of purely in terms of liberating the intellect or even of personal growth, but must be seen in the total context of the broader social conditions in which it is embedded.

In this perspective the importance of Rousseau, manifested especially in *Emile,* is that he placed the self-development of the individual above society's needs and desires. Thus, one may say that the "romantic" impulse of his times contributed to what later came to be a direction of education as a vehicle for opening up the societies we live in: a desire for social reconstruction stems from a demand that societies become contexts in which men and women can develop fully as persons. May I repeat that I do not necessarily attribute this goal to Rousseau himself but that in educational theory, as opposed to other aspects of intellectual history, Rousseau's romanticisms came to symbolize what later developed as a liberal tradition in education.

The works of Pestalozzi[6] and Froebel[7] were very much influenced by the German idealism of that period and found their expression in convictions such as the moral sacredness of the individual and the natural unfolding of individual development. Froebel, with his "gifts" and "occupations," of course had powerful spiritual overtones in his work, and later such fascinating persons as Rudolf Steiner went further in this direction. It is important to keep this aspect—the spiritual dimension—in mind because there are contemporary forces (which I shall refer to later) tangential to open education that reflect similar interests. But primarily I would like to posit here that a third major trend, which could be interpreted in secular or spiritual terms, was fully present by the early nineteenth century. This was the moral dignity and integrity of the individual.

---

* Comenius, for example, illustrates the use of an inductive process of teaching in an empirical framework growing out of this spirit and impetus. For better or worse (as history), I would like to keep this in the liberal arts tradition, in the sense of adding the inductive dimension to the deductive process.

By the late nineteenth century the American impact on education began to be registered; this came in many forms. Certainly the transcendentalists (e.g., Emerson, Whitman) contributed a romantic impulse, but two major trends seem to have been crystallized between 1880 and 1900: the scientific study of child development and the progressive education movement.

John Dewey[8] came to be identified with progressive education. This was perhaps unfortunate, not because this intellectual giant did not develop both the ideas and practices which came to epitomize progressive schooling, but because by focusing so centrally upon Dewey as an educator we are apt to miss the larger spirit of the progressive movement.

It is my personal reading of history that the three major thrusts of progressive education—(1) the idea of intellectual freedom, (2) the idea of schools and reconstruction in society, and (3) the moral agency of the person—were present and intensely felt throughout the society of that day. Thus, progressive education became one aspect of a progressive movement reflected in such activities as the desire for social justice (e.g., Jane Addams' Hull House) or the "muckrakers' " attempts to expose and right the wrongs of an emerging industrial society.

In this light Dewey as a pragmatic philosopher might be said to have provided some sort of intellectual method for helping the country develop from an agricultural to an industrial nation. As such, Dewey's progressive education was an attempt to synthesize the three major thrusts of progressivism into workable school policies and programs built upon a philosophical method and position which more nearly suited the times.

Dewey's concern for problem solving and reflective thinking provided a major synthesis in educational theory of the deductive and inductive methods of the liberal arts tradition. Thus Dewey, whose major concern for freedom was a freedom of the intellect (freedom of action he saw as desirable to the extent it was needed for intellectual freedom), brought the cognitive aspect of progressive education up to the brink of the contributions later made by Jerome Bruner and Jean Piaget in the new cognitive concerns of open education.

Open education's debt to John Dewey and to a host of other influential and exceptionally able educators of his era (e.g., George Counts, Harold Rugg, L. Thomas Hopkins, Boyd Bode, William Heard Kilpatrick) must be duly recognized, for they contributed a crystallized and complete rationale and a set of possible practices which illustrated how quality education reflecting our historical antecedents could be grounded and integrated in American culture.

And yet progressive education failed to make a major impact on traditional school practice. I suspect this is so for at least three major reasons.

One reason lies in the gradual dominance of the progressive education movement by professional educators. This resulted in a cutting off of education from the broader social and political progressive movements in our society and in the exclusion (probably by choice) of non-educators from the progressive education movement.

A second happening, probably equally disastrous and perhaps related, was the splitting of the movement between those who wished to focus primarily upon the child and those who saw schooling as a form of social reconstruction. Hence progressive educators broke into factions according to the relative emphasis they assigned to two aspects of a totality. Hence they also became more and more divorced from social reality, an effective grasp of which requires a synthesis between persons and the societies they live in and create.

The third major circumstance was the splitting (in the mind of the nonprofessional education scholars and much of the public in general) of the idea of progressive education and the idea of cultural substance (i.e., subject matter). Although Dewey and many other progressives never divorced education from subject matter, the liberal arts tradition came to be seen as antithetical to progressive education. This was partially a reaction to some school practices that also caused Dewey (e.g., in *Experience and Education*) to protest their use of the name "progressive," but it also appears to have been a social and political phenomenon that turned the conservative intellectual community into a "liberal arts" camp and split it from the progressive group already split between radicals (reconstructionists) and sentimentalists (child-centered). All in all, in most minds progressive education came to mean "life adjustment" as opposed to real substantive education.

The legacy of the progressive education movement, however, is extremely important in considering open education, and the following ideas reflect some of the distilled and Americanized spirit of our historical antecedents: (1) the school as a community, (2) the school in the community, (3) the person and his moral right to freedom and choice, (4) concern for individual differences, (5) the method of intelligence (problem solving), (6) building a curriculum through and with the students, (7) seeing the disciplines as potential end points rather than starting points for pedagogy.

Looking Sideways: Peripheral Vision of Contemporary Circumstances and Relationships

The vitality and impact of progressive education had waned by the end of World War II (1945) and survived only as a small spark by the early 1950's. Some say it went to England for a holiday and stayed for twenty years. And I suppose there is some truth in this, for the English movement (or reform in primary [and later in secondary] schooling) of recent decades has strong resemblances to American progressive education. Although it is as dangerous to make such an assumption about the derivation of the English movement as it is to assume that one can transport that movement to the United States *in toto,* unquestionably the English movement *is* a major ally for the resurgence of the human spirit in education in America, which I have tried to illustrate historically.

Perhaps a more interesting and more fundamental question is why many Americans were ready and willing to look toward England for new educational guidance. And I personally believe that, in answering that question, in this country rather than in the English "model" itself may lie the hope of success for open education. I see our search for alternatives such as the English infant school model as part of a contemporary convergence of the three major historical forces mentioned earlier, not only in our search for educational renewal but in our broader social and cultural life also.

To me it is no coincidence that open education should become a significant movement in American education in the mid-1960's. This is intricately related to another contemporary development, namely, that in recent years a sizable portion of the American public has reached a higher level of consciousness about our social system as it affects individuals, as it reflects social justice, and as it exercises social control through its educational practices. I believe that open education is part and parcel of the social spirit and impulse for liberation that is reflected in such diverse phenomena as the counterculture's attempt to escape the dehumanizing and alienating role structure of our society; the New Left's attempt to stimulate participatory democracy to rejuvenate political life; minority-group (including women here) demands for justice and equality; a revulsion toward war and authoritarian power as legitimate social devices; and a dawning recognition that existing American education is not essentially an intellectually liberating experience but a "professionalized" servant of the status quo of social roles.

I would agree with Gibson Winter[9] when he says that the major thrusts of those persons reaching for social justice (the emerging nations of the Third World, blacks, Chicanos, women, the young, the old, etc.) are toward (1) participation, (2) pluralism, and (3) liberation. These forces have provided a social and political alliance and strength which, much in the same spirit of the early progressive era, provide a milieu of social ferment for the social support and consciousness which give a broader urgency and legitimacy to many persons for encouraging "open" programs.

Thus the concern for, and connection to, the Rousseauean idea of the oppressive state (now called "the system") is seen to reappear and be reflected in calls for educational reform. The liberating (liberal) arts and sciences have also had a resurgence, mainly through the work of psychologists such as Abraham Maslow,[10] Jerome Bruner,[11] and Jean Piaget.[12] Broader social readiness to accept the implications of the work of these and many other men and women may well derive from renewed awareness of the sterility of most educational curricula which are now connected with serving the power elite in "the system." Yet the work itself is a continuation of a liberator's concern to discover how intelligence grows and functions in human beings, and how to create a pedagogy which will utilize mental processes for educational goals.

It is the English infant school movement that has adapted most directly to the work of Piaget, and Piaget has been the largest single influence in its resurgence. Primary education in England has adopted the findings of Piaget as a basis for helping children develop their intelligence and mental operations through the engagement of human beings and other cultural resources in the context of schooling. This has meant shifting the focus of education back upon the individual child (as in the progressive movement), but with a concern for intellectual processes that is more precise and directed than the progressive method of problem solving.

Thus contemporary open education, with its interest in cognitive processes rather than in specific content and with its concern for methods of inquiry, has brought a new impetus and strength to the liberal arts traditions suggested here as moving from Socrates to Dewey, and now to Piaget.

The third major contemporary impulse contributing to the spirit of open education is the resurgence of concern for the person in society, which is reminiscent of the progressive concern with the "whole child." Again, the failures of the twentieth century, characterized by war and continually growing material inequities among people, may well have led to the popularity of existential philosophy. The seeds of existentialism go far back in history, but surely are demonstrably present for the modern world at the beginning of the nineteenth century. Yet for America the vigor of industrial society and a frontier psychology resulted in a dominant philosophy of pragmatism. Only after World War II did existentialism begin to make inroads into the consciousness of a sizable number of intellectuals on this side of the Atlantic.

The American response to existentialism has had a more optimistic character than the pessimism, nihilism, or stress on the absurd that characterizes many European writers of this tendency. Perhaps we would have emerged into the new philosophy much sooner had William James,[13] rather than John Dewey, been the educational philosopher of pragmatism, for the seeds of phenomenalism and existentialism are strongly present in James' radical empiricism. The optimism of America is present also. This existential optimism in America has refocused us upon the "choosing to choose" that William James was so fond of. It has refocused us upon the moral agency of the person and the necessity of choosing one's destiny through decisions and the freedom to make them. Allied with this has been a spiritual resurgence in the form of Christian existentialist theology and of Eastern mysticism in a Westernized form. Perhaps Paul Tillich among Christian theologians and Alan Watts in the tradition of Westernized Asiatic religions and mysticism are representative cases.

In any event, the need for finding oneself and experiencing a personal reality beyond that readily available in the materialistic role structure of our technological society has given a spiritual aura to at least some aspects of diverse phenomena ranging from a concern with Eastern meditation to the "Jesus people" and the hippy counterculture. A historical examination of the connection between education and the spiritual might well lead us back to such unique figures as the Austrian social philosopher Rudolf Steiner.[14]

It is these contemporary events which color and stimulate present-day open education proposals and programs. This historically traced triad of thrusts emerging again today becomes the ally and support and deepens the urge for new educational forms under the rubric of "open education."

Seeing the World: The Semantics of Open Education

I have tried to indicate aspects of the historical and contemporary focus and spirit which have fostered open education. The final question for perspective remains, the question of definition: What is open education, and why call it that? In a sense they are really the same question.

It is, of course, clear to all of us that semantic lesson number 1—"The word is not the thing"—is to be kept in mind at all times. Semantic lesson number 2 is also helpful: "Cow 1 is not cow 2 is not cow 3." Thus, before we start we must be aware of the impossibility of defining in any highly specific or any universally generalizable way a complex human activity such as whatever "open education" may appear to be.

This is important to keep in mind beyond a narrowly academic sense of semantics because the very spirit of "open" education would appear to be clearly in tune with the semantic nature of meaning in language.

Ordinary language is an open system, and the language of human pedagogical activity is neither mathematical nor technically precise; if it were
either mathematically or technically precise, it would have to exclude
much of the lived phenomena of the activity.

"Open" education suggests a reality of language communication about
complex human activities. It is potentially more "truthful" and "realistic"
than specifying programmatically in precise ways. It clearly implies the
creative aspects of language in its reality construction.

Neither the term "open education" nor any other examples of ordinary language are meaningless "ink blots" to be interpreted in any way
that the perceiver decides. There is a general idea which pervades the
terminology used. Still, it seems clear that we cannot project an ideal
universal of open education (a kind of eternal verity, exemplified in various forms through history); nor can we project a definite *particular* as
representing open education so that there is only one right model. It
is a *general idea* somewhere between the universal and the particular
that must be pursued if we are to give any meaningful definition to
the term.

It is also probably true that open education is more easily defined
by what it is *not* than by what it is. I think it is far less dangerous
to approach it this way, but shall resist that attraction in an attempt
to explicate the general idea of it. (However, I highly recommend that
anyone interested in open education try to start a dialogue by discussing
what it is not!)

The general notion of open education is allied with the emergence
of the concept of *openness* in a number of fields of inquiry. Thus, biolo-
gists, psychologists, cyberneticists, sociologists, and anthropologists (for
a few) have found some use for the term. I shall illustrate these ideas
on the biological, psychological, and sociopolitical levels.

Biologically the concept of an open system (versus a closed system)
describes, for example, all animal life. Thus, a person is not self-
contained but needs environmental input into the system and also needs
to produce output in order (if for no other reason) to secure needed
input for survival. A human being is thus an open biological system,
and biological systems are *self-regulating*.

Psychologically, there have been a number of persons concerned with
personality who found the concept of openness a useful way of looking
at such phenomena as creativity, self-realization, dogmatism, and prejudice. Generally, the import of these studies would lead one to believe
that reasonable openness to new stimuli and experiences has a strong
positive effect upon growth of personality and learning. Thus, for example, such defense mechanisms as those described by Freudians when

predominant in the behavior of a person seem to adhere to states of neurosis or other mental pathology. Conversely, an open person appears to reflect a healthier person.

On a sociopolitical level, openness means "access to" the environment with "freedom to choose" and to exercise the rights and responsibilities of citizenship. What can be called an "open society" is probably best epitomized by the general notion of democracy.

Given these three illustrations, we see that a number of general notions appear to coalesce around the idea of openness, and since open education certainly involves the biology, psychology, and sociology of human activity we can begin to see some pattern emerging. Open education, then, would reflect the fact that persons are self-regulating open systems who when not psychologically thwarted are curious and seek out stimulation and also creatively order and reorder their ideas, notions, and activities; further, that they are sociable and seek contact with other persons. And, finally, an open society in the school would reflect a respect for the "personness" of each individual by the justice of equal access to self-fulfillment and self-worth through the freedom to make choices and have alternatives.

This is about as far as I would care to go with a general notion of what open education is, for in truth it could not be open if there were no creative options within its general idea for particular persons and places.

Summary

I have tried to provide a speculative background for a perspective on open education. The speculative aspect of this resides in the fact that the statements are entirely interpretative. I have made little effort to quote the original sources. I am convinced that what I have said is valid in outline, even if some specific interpretations should prove untenable.

The perspective I have tried to give provides interpretations of data from a historical, contemporary, and semantic-linguistic framework. This idea I borrowed from Aldous Huxley and combined with the human interest of emancipation or liberation via the work of Habermas.

Essentially I have proposed that three major liberating thrusts (in contrast to controlling human concerns) have existed historically and have reemerged in new colors in today's world. These thrusts are for the freeing of the intellect, the connection of education with broader social concerns for liberating structures and processes, and the moral agency and self-development of each person.

I have suggested that the English open education movement has been an important available model for stimulating our own American development, but also that open education must remain a general idea, neither a universal nor a particular notion, if it is to fulfill its promise of creative emergence.

References

1. Huxley, Aldous, reference no longer known to present author.

2. Habermas, J., *Knowledge and Human Interests* (Boston: Beacon Press, 1971).

3. See, e.g., Broudy, H. S., and Palmer, J. R., *Exemplars of Teaching Method* Chicago: Rand-McNally, 1965).

4. Rousseau, J.-J., *Emile* (New York: E. P. Dutton, 1966).

5. See, e.g., "To Teach All Things to All Men: John Amos Comenius (1592–1670)," in R. Gross (ed.), *The Teacher and the Taught: Education in Theory and Practice from Plato to James B. Conant* (New York: Dell Publishing Company, 1963).

6. See, e.g., references to Johann Heinrich Pestalozzi (1746–1827) in 3 and 5 above.

7. See, e.g., Weber, E., *The Kindergarten: Its Encounter with Educational Thought in America* (New York: Teachers College Press, Columbia University, 1969), for a discussion of Freidrich Froebel (1782–1852).

8. See, e.g., Dewey, J., *Democracy and Education* (New York: Macmillan Co., 1916), or *Experience and Education* (New York: Macmillan, 1938).

9. Winter, G., *Being Free: Reflections on America's Cultural Revolution* (New York: Macmillan, 1970).

10. Maslow, A., "Defense and Growth," *Merrill-Palmer Quarterly*, 1956, *3*, 36–47.

11. See, e.g., Bruner, J., *The Process of Education* (Cambridge: Harvard University Press, 1960), and *On Knowing: Essays for the Left Hand* (Cambridge: Harvard University Press, 1962).

12. See, e.g., Flavell, J. H., *The Developmental Psychology of Jean Piaget* (New York: Van Nostrand-Reinhold Company, 1963).

13. See, e.g., James, W., *Essays in Radical Empiricism and a Pluralistic Universe* (New York: E. P. Dutton, 1971).

14. See, e.g., Steiner, R., *The Essentials of Education* (Spring Valley, N.Y.: Anthroposophic Press, 1968).

CHAPTER 4

Defining Goals in Open Education

Ronald W. Henderson, *University of Arizona*

A WIDESPREAD feeling that our schools are failing to live up to their promise is reflected in an almost mind-boggling array of proposals for reform. Assessments of the causes of inadequacy in our school programs are varied in their emphases, but collectively they signal the growing apprehension that there is a crisis in American education. Open education approaches represent one type of response advocated as a means of overcoming inadequacies in the present system; but implicitly, if not explicitly, open education is in competition with alternative approaches to educational reform. Each alternative makes some claim to being based on knowledge and principles derived from psychology. The uniqueness of the goals and means of open education and their relationship to psychological principles might best be appreciated when considered in contrast to alternative proposals for educational reform.

Perspectives on the Source of the Crisis

Among the critics who agree that there is a crisis in American education, there is a considerable range of opinion concerning the nature of the failure. Many critics characterize the crisis as a *failure in outcomes*. They are likely to emphasize the need for knowledge and skills which are assumed to be required for effective participation in a technologically oriented society. More often than not, concerns about the failure of the educational system focus on "substandard" scores on standardized tests. An implicit assumption in this position is that performance on standardized achievement tests is a good predictor of an individual's success when he leaves school and enters the "cultural mainstream" which awaits him.

A contrasting point of view is that the crisis results less from a failure in outcomes than it does from a *failure in purposes*. This point of view is reflected in Silberman's (1970) oft-quoted statement about mindlessness, which he identifies as the source of many of the ills of American public school systems:

> . . . what is most wrong with the public schools is due not to venality, or indifference or stupidity, but to mindlessness. . . . by and large, teachers, principals, and superintendents do their best by their lights. If they make a botch of it, and an uncomfortably large number do, it is because it simply never occurs to more than a handful to ask *why* they are doing what they are doing—to think seriously or deeply about the purposes or consequences of education. (pp. 10–11)

Critics who assume this position often maintain that our schools have overemphasized content and isolated academic skills, to the neglect of important long-range affective goals and such more complex cognitive outcomes as self-direction, creativity, inquiry, and problem solving, with an emphasis on process rather than product.

Alternative Responses to the Crisis: Assumptions about Learners and Teachers

One reaction to the obvious fact that large numbers of children fail to profit much from the regular programs of the schools may be characterized as the *packaged-curriculum response*. A basic assumption behind this priority seems to be that if discrete curriculum components whose effects have been appropriately demonstrated are combined into larger and more comprehensive packages, exportable programs (products) with known effects will result. According to one recent set of USOE guidelines (1971) for annual budget justifications of educational laboratories and centers, "*Products* are exportable methods and/or materials which, when used as prescribed, will produce *specified* outcomes with designated target populations" (p. 71, italics added). With changes in personnel and with the reorganization of agencies responsible for the funding and monitoring of research and development in education, specific guidelines will undoubtedly change. Nevertheless, the statement quoted above is more significant than a simple administrative fiat. It can be regarded as a bit of sociological data reflecting the widespread attitude that educational problems can be solved in much the same way we have solved the problem of how to get to the moon. If the user will follow the technical manual, desired results will occur.

Several assumptions seem to underline most packaged curricula. One assumption is that learning experiences should be carefully sequenced because important skills and knowledge are structured in a hierarchical fashion. It may also be assumed that there are a given set of skills and a body of knowledge which are important for everyone to learn, although the rate of learning will differ for different individuals.

In addition to assumptions about learners, there are also some assumptions about teachers implicit in priorities which value packaged materials over the training of educational personnel. It is assumed that, left to their own skills and initiative, few teachers will be able to manage an effective learning environment, and therefore the procedures and the organization of content must be prescribed by experts and incorporated into the materials.

A second group of programs might be characterized as an *incentive-program response*. In this type of response it is assumed that a lack of motivation to do well on school-type tasks is a major cause of failure to profit from instruction. Educators in this group may also use programmed instruction or other varieties of packaged curricula, but they often assume that existing materials are adequate, if only students can be influenced to attend to and persist with them. It is noted that many teachers depend heavily on aversive control to influence student behavior, and that they are inconsistent in the use of whatever positive reinforcement they employ to manage classroom behavior. It is assumed that if teachers can be trained in contingency management, students will learn more from whatever reasonably well-designed materials are available. The reinforcers used are often tangible rewards, access to preferred activities, or some form of token system with tangible backup materials which can be purchased with the tokens.

There is a considerable degree of overlap among programs which might generally be categorized in either of the response types mentioned above, and both types of responses are likely to be motivated by the view that the failure of the schools lies in outcomes rather than in purposes. The *open education response* differs considerably from these approaches and is based, in large measure, on the view that the aims of education have been misdirected. According to Walberg and Thomas (1972), the point of view of open education "is far more consonant with developmental, humanistic, and clinical psychology than with the branches that have been most influential in education, connectionism, behaviorism and psychometrics" (p. 198). In an attempt to conceptualize elements which are common to a variety of approaches to open education, Henderson (1973) postulated five kinds of practices which might be considered as criteria of open education:

1. A process rather than a product orientation to learning and instruction.

2. Provision for selection of activities on the part of the children.

3. An attempt to deal with skills and knowledge in an integrated or orchestrated way, in contrast to the traditional compartmentalization of academic "subjects."

4. The random or heterogeneous grouping of children, intended to make it possible for children to learn from one another, in contrast to tracking or other forms of ability grouping.

5. A style of teacher behavior which enables the teacher to respond to the behavioral cues presented by individual children and to use these cues as a basis for building on or extending what a child already knows, and his interests and skills, in contrast to a teacher style in which desired behavior changes are specified in advance by the teacher or the curriculum.materials.

Many spokesmen for open education insist that the teacher is the manager of a rich and complex learning environment. The classroom should not be permissive, and the teacher must plan growth-facilitating experiences for students (Silberman, 1970; Hapgood, 1971). Obviously, the skills required of the teacher to arrange and manage an open and productive educational environment are ones for which few teachers have had appropriate training and experiences. Even in the open education approaches of British infant schools, which have attracted so much attention in this country, good open classroom programs are operating in only a minority of the infant schools (Featherstone, 1971), and those which are good have been a long time in developing.

Unfortunately, when teachers and administrators attempt to abandon traditional practices in favor of a more open and humanistic approach, as often as not the result is a marked discrepancy between the emulated practices of open education and the reality of the classroom. This discrepancy is well characterized by Hapgood (1971). In the better open classrooms which she observed in England,

> There was a quiet hum of children working and talking together, moving carefully and purposefully in the room that was always crowded with children and things to learn from. Work went on all over the school—in the corridors, in the assembly hall, outdoors. The work of each child was his own, unique to him and respected as such. (p. 66)

In contrast to this description, Hapgood (1971) observed that many American attempts to follow suit often result in a poor copy. Her characterization is all too frequently accurate. In such a typical poor copy:

> The class is "activity-centered," but the activity is often aimless and noisy, and sometimes destructive. Books are used very little, and children are allowed to disturb other children with dramatic play, carpentry blocks, or musical instruments. The teacher is so busy trying to maintain some semblance

of order that she has little time to help children individually or to record growth. The order she admired in the British model has become chaos. (p. 66)

There are undoubtedly many reasons for the difficulties which face teachers who set about to implement open education procedures in their classrooms, but issues relating to the definition of appropriate goals for open education and the specification of means for assessing progress toward these ends are central to the problem of implementation.

The Aims of Education: Perspectives on the Mindlessness Issue

Charles Silberman (1970) has written one of the most penetrating and insightful critiques of American public education to appear in recent years. He sees American public education as being afflicted with a mindlessness which results from the lack of sound educational philosophy and from a failure to think deeply and seriously about educational purposes and about the relationships between the things we do and important educational purposes. Certainly such consideration is essential, but if we are to avoid mindlessness, we must attend with total analytic seriousness to more than just philosophy. It is necessary to examine very carefully the relationships between educational means and outcomes and to develop and test techniques that are required to objectify these relationships.

Means-Ends Relationships

Traditional programs, at least as they tend to operate on a day-to-day basis, often give little consideration to important, long-range outcomes for education process. Goals which should be regarded merely as instrumental skills needed to accomplish some more important, long-range objectives have a tendency to become goals for their own sake. The instrumental goals are treated *as if* they were terminal goals. For example, some teachers seem to become obsessed with the importance of certain word attack skills or with the acquisition of a prespecified basic sight vocabulary. Presumably, such skills should enable children to become more and more independent in their reading and, therefore, encourage them to read for pleasure or to find information of interest to them. But if the subordinate skills are the central focus of instruction, a feeling of urgency that these skills be mastered can result in aversive teaching procedures which may defeat the more significant and long-range purposes of reading instruction by *teaching* the child to dislike reading and to avoid it whenever he can. It is often overlooked that we do teach certain emotional responses through simple classical conditioning procedures which are inadvertantly applied in school settings. Thus, if handled with a lack of balance and sensitivity, particular means of accomplishing short-term objectives may defeat the more significant objectives. Much of the appeal of open education undoubtedly derives from the hope of avoiding this kind of means-end dilemma.

Unfortunately, overly zealous rejection of practices which are concerned with discrete skills may lead to equally undesirable results. Often those of us who are interested in promoting more open programs are guilty of focusing excessively upon the more global and long-range educational outcomes, to the neglect of the steps instrumental to getting there. If we are to think seriously about relationships between the things we do and truly significant educational outcomes, it is vital that we be able to demonstrate that the means we advocate do lead to the results we cherish. This cannot be done with any kind of responsible accountability if we point exclusively to expected outcomes which cannot be observed for several years: e.g., the student does not drop out of school at the first opportunity.

Behavioral Objectives: Anathema to the Aims of Open Education?

For some time now, psychologists and educators in the Arizona Center for Educational Research and Development have been attempting to develop ways in which behavioral objectives can be used to relate practice to outcomes in open education programs. Many proponents of open education, including some of our colleagues in the Center, believe that the whole notion of behavioral objectives is anathema to open education. Certainly it is true that the usual procedures of determining what specific behavioral changes should result from a particular instructional activity, under what specific conditions the behavior will occur, and the strength of the behavior (i.e., level of accuracy, proficiency, and so on) would be inappropriate for open education. But without some form of clear definition of goals at a more specific level than "curiosity," "creativity," "openness to change," or "self-direction," we are left little more than our subjective judgments to tell us where we are when we get there. Certainly subjective judgment does play an important role in instructional decisionmaking, but it is a well-established fact that people who are committed to what they are doing are likely to see what they expect to see, and to overlook what they do not anticipate. Ideally, subjective observation and documented empirical observation should provide a set of checks and balances for instructional decisionmaking; but in practice, subjective judgment is too often used to the virtual exclusion of more objective evidence. If there is to be any hope of maintaining open education in the face of growing national concern for accountability in education, it seems essential that new ways of using objectives be developed to guide instruction and monitor pupil progress.

Open education appears to be generally concordant with humanistic philosophy, and that philosophy suggests a reordering of priorities in the goals of education. But as important as a guiding philosophy is, it provides only part of an essential strategy for the specification of worthwhile educational practices. The methods of science provide the missing element in the required strategy, for the methods of science can provide a corrective mechanism to determine if our means do in fact lead to the ends which our philosophy dictates. In this regard, it is often said that teachers in open programs are encouraged to be experimenters. Clearly, a good open classroom provides almost limitless opportunities to experiment —to use roughly the same procedures as those used by scientists to produce and verify knowledge. The teacher can observe the behavior of individual students under a rich range of circumstances. Observations provide the data base for prediction. These insights may be converted into hypotheses, or testable hunches, which might guide the planning of instruction. Given a clear specification of desired outcomes, the effects of a particular strategy for an individual learner may be evaluated. In actual application in open classrooms the weakest steps seem to be in getting reliable observational data, specifying objectives in measurable terms, and obtaining data on the effects of a given strategy. If open education is to survive in any form capable of influencing the lives of more than a few select children, it seems essential that we learn to objectify the relationships between our efforts and our outcomes.

The manner of giving concrete definition to goals must necessarily differ from that which has been characteristic of most packaged-curriculum and incentive-program responses. But given the sociopolitical temperament of these times and lacking some concrete definition of goals and evidence that the goals are being reached, one might predict that open education very likely will meet the same fate as did progressive education. Some of the factors which influence the specification and measurement of objectives are discussed below.

Influences on Goal Definition in Open Education

A number of forces operate simultaneously to influence the definition of goals in any kind of educational program, and this is especially true of open education. Philosophy, psychological theory, and empirical evidence relating to program effects are among the important factors which interact to influence the relationships between goals and means.

Philosophy. Humanistic philosophies, especially phenomenology, have had an increasing influence on psychology and education in recent years. There would be little argument that the goals and methods of open education should be congruent with the values of humanistic philosophy, and most open education advocates would argue that these goals and strategies are quite different from those which would be dictated by positivism and the traditions of empirical psychology which derive from it. Such distinctions may, however, be misleading and detrimental to an attempt to define demonstrable goals for open education. Many educators who are involved with open programs have a very negative view of empirical psychology, and dislike especially that branch known as behaviorism. Behaviorism is often narrowly viewed as the mechanistic application of procedures designed to *control* behavior. It is easy to see how such attitudes have developed when one considers that laboratory procedures first used with animals were initially generalized to institutional situations dealing with persons having quite profound disturbances, and eventually behavior modification was applied in regular classrooms, with little change from the laboratory procedures. Early behavior modification and behavior management programs often failed to follow their own principles by doing a functional analysis of the behavioral influences in the natural environment of the classroom and by using those naturally occurring stimuli and reinforcers to promote an optimally effective learning environment. The most conspicuous uses of behavioral psychology have been in crisis intervention, and perhaps for this reason behaviorism has been considered by many to be synonymous with the external control of behavior. This stereotyped view is as unfortunate as the notion of some behaviorists that humanistically oriented programs are necessarily permissive and chaotic.

Concerning the relationships between humanism and behaviorism, Thoresen (1972) has argued persuasively that

> As many differences . . . exist within heterogeneous groups called behaviorists or humanist as exist between them. The issue is not behaviorism versus humanism—that is a pseudo-issue which has been promoted by caricatures of these positions. Instead, the issue is how best to utilize the concepts and methodologies of both behavioral and humanistic psychology. (p. 2)

Maslow (1966) has asserted that the major task of humanistic psychology is to collaborate with the behavioral sciences to determine how to create environments capable of fostering self-actualization. In a humanistically oriented open classroom situation, the effects of influences on the learning environment would be viewed most appropriately in terms of influences on individual students. In this connection, one of the principal themes which Thoresen (1972) found in the writings of humanistic psychologists and educators was a focus on the individual person rather than on the average performance of groups or populations. While many open education proponents assume that the methods of behavioral psychology are incompatible with the aims of open education, the considerations mentioned above suggest that this may not be the case. Behavioral methods (including those of the social learning group) bear a *possible,* but *not necessary,* incompatible relationship to the goals of open education. The ways in which goals are defined will have a determining influence on the manner in which behavioral principles are applied and, consequently, will determine whether or not the applications are compatible with a humanistic value system.

Psychological Theory.   The knowledge base of psychology has fallen far short of its potential impact on educational practice. In traditional programs, psychological theory has influenced educational practice primarily in the areas of psychological and educational measurement and in the development of curriculum materials which reflect the psychologist's concern with matters such as sequence, small learning increments, management of stimulus load, redundancy, and review. Systematic attention to these factors largely characterizes the packaged-curriculum response mentioned earlier. These matters may not be entirely alien to the goals of open education, but in practice these influences have often been counterproductive because they have been applied mechanistically, targeted on a very circumscribed range of goals and practiced in isolation from the informed use of other psychological knowledge.

As a result of simplistic applications, particular psychological theories and principles are often judged inappropriate to the purposes of open education. The fact that dissatisfaction with a particular set of principles may stem more from the ways in which the principles have been applied than from inherent limitations of the principles is seldom considered by open education proponents. For example, Skinner (1972) favors the use of operant learning principles to ensure that a child will execute "right" or socially appropriate responses automatically. The responsibility of choosing the goal behavior is exercised by someone other than the individual who will do the behaving. No doubt it is possible to use behavioral principles in this manner, but it is *not necessary* to do so. Many of us would reject the notion that someone other than the child always make these decisions. Operating within the framework of a set of values different from Skinner's, one could choose to use the learning principles which he has advanced to help the child to learn to exercise self-direction and self-control. There is already evidence (Bandura and Perloff, 1967; Glynn, 1970) that self-monitored contingencies can be as effective as externally imposed programs. Examples of goals designed to help the learner become increasingly self-governing are proposed later in this paper.

The above remarks suggest the need to reconsider the role of learning principles from empirical psychology in open education. There is also a need for some reconsideration of the application of principles of developmental psychology in open programs. Educational critics such as Silberman and Featherstone have argued that open classroom practices are better articulated to theories of developmental psychology than are more traditional kinds of programs. As a matter of fact, such a point of view is rather provincial in that it seems to include in the category of developmental psychology only those theorists who take an age-stage descriptive approach to the study of psychological development. This view omits a rather sizable group of developmental psychologists whose work is oriented to a learning-theory framework.

That oversight aside, it is often claimed that stage theories of development (especially Piaget's) have had a profound influence on the development of open education. Educators should be aware, however, that when writers claim scientific support for the principles of open education they often overlook an important point. Psychological theories such as Piaget's have been used to generate educational practices, and thereafter the worthiness of the practice has been supported by reference to the theory. (In many cases it is more likely that an existing practice is justified post hoc on the basis of its congru   :e with the theory.) This is a kind of circular reasoning which overlooks some very important aspects of the methods of science. Such a sequence is an all-too-frequent example of how the products of science (i.e., a theory of intellectual development) are translated into ideology. Piaget's observations and theories are singularly perceptive and insightful. They provide a rather broad-gauged way of viewing behavioral change. But to deal with the important question of specific influences of a learning environment on a child's development over shorter periods of time, one would want to test hypotheses about the effects of given experiences on a child's learning and development. An important aspect of the methods of science is brought into play when procedures are initiated to demonstrate in a verifiable way that a given set of events, whatever their genesis, leads to a particular outcome. Open education offers a unique, and as yet largely unrealized, opportunity for a teacher—and even for students themselves—to employ the methods of science to obtain empirical evidence regarding the relationships between specific educational activities and the attainment of educational goals.

Empirical Evidence.   What constitutes acceptable empirical evidence on goal attainment? A year or so ago, a writer and photographer from a national magazine (now defunct) spent several days observing and taking photographs in an open education program with which we had been working. At the end of their visit they remarked that this was what a school should look like—in their words, the "vibes" were right. The writer and the photographer were satisfied, but they needed concrete evidence that the children were doing better than they would have done in a traditional program. Their editor would judge whether their article was publishable on the basis of conventional evidence on program effectiveness. Although philosophically in tune with the program they observed, these journalists needed group achievement scores to justify their story.

This incident is only symptomatic of the dilemma that faces open education programs, because it goes without saying that many of the most important objectives of these programs are not measured with a group achievement test. We have become painfully aware that open programs must incorporate monitoring procedures to determine if the anticipated growth in children's social and intellectual competencies is indeed taking place. But in open education there is a widely held belief that appropriate means for evaluating these programs are not available and that the best measure of a child's work is the work itself. It is also assumed that evaluation must consider cumulative effects over long periods of time if the results are to be relevant (Evans, 1971). Anecdotal records and work samples are commonly used to examine pupil progress in open programs, but the results lack any provision for psychometric qualities such as reliability, and often the goals to be assessed are global and poorly articulated. Thus, at a time when the public and its elected officials are increasingly calling upon educators to be accountable for the effects of their educational programs, open education programs are in a poor position to demonstrate that they are accomplishing what their supporters claim for them.

If standardized tests are not concordant with valued goals of open education and if the existing informal evaluation techniques are unconvincing, what alternatives are left? It has already been suggested that, for purposes of obtaining data relevant to decisionmaking in open education, the appropriate focus for evaluation of behavior growth is the individual student rather than the average performance of some group of students. It may be that what is in order is an unlikely, seemingly paradoxical marriage between humanistically oriented open education and the experimental procedures of behavioral psychology. Before the reader becomes too offended by this suggestion for apparent mismarriage, a quotation from Thoresen's "Behavioral Humanism" (1972) should show where this line of reasoning might lead. Thoresen reminds us:

> Skinner's early work with animal subjects was based on a continuous observing and recording of data over long periods of time. Various interventions were tried, and the results were directly observed. On the basis of these observations interventions were often altered. (p. 10)

Some humanists may be outraged by the suggestion that procedures developed with animal subjects might be applied to children—and in open education of all places. But the emphasis of both Skinner and the humanists is on the effects of the environment on the development of the *individual*. Consider the possibilities which this approach would offer for (a) designating (by teacher, individual student, or student committee) of individualized objectives, (b) determining if a given procedure or activity is helping the individual to move toward designated goals, (c) revising procedures or activities as the data dictate, and (d) providing continuous monitoring of the cumulative growth of the individual over time and under various instructional conditions. Considered in this light, perhaps the real paradox is that so many open education advocates look for direction to precisely those developmental theories which are based on data representing the *average performance* of various populations of children, which may represent individual persons rather poorly.

In a paper entitled "Achieving Humanness: Supporting Research," Robert Soar (1969) summarized research which generally supported the efficacy of indirect teaching as a facilitating condition for student growth. Among the most interesting findings he reported was the fact that there were complex interactions among factors such as degree of indirectness, pupil growth in creativity, and personality or emotional characteristics of students, such as anxiety. The more anxious students were apparently not able to use the freedom of highly indirect classrooms as constructively as were students who were less anxious. The use of single-subject experimentation, appropriately applied within the confines of a humanistic value system, should aid the teacher in finding, or helping the student to find, instructional situations in which he can function most comfortably and effectively and also become capable of functioning under new and changing conditions.

Discussions of the applicability of the single-subject experimental design to humanistic concerns (Thoresen, 1972) and technical procedures for the intensive study of individuals within a behavioral framework (Wolf and Risley, 1971) are available elsewhere. We shall now turn our attention to a consideration of strategies for the definition of educational goals which are appropriate to the broad purposes and philosophy of open education and which can be assessed with defensible data-gathering procedures.

Toward Accountability in Open Education*

The development of a strategy for the use of behavioral objectives for open education poses complex problems which are not encountered in establishing performance criteria for traditional programs, or for most programs characterized here as packaged-curricula or incentive-based programs. The primary reason is that in these latter approaches to education it is usually assumed that all children should learn much the same responses, and that someone other than the child decides in advance what these responses should be. In contrast, in open education one is never quite sure where a particular activity might lead or even what activities children may choose. Bussis and Chittenden (1970) have commented on the unwillingness of teachers in open education to articulate precise goals, and they have underscored that "the need for a clearer conceptualization of the objectives of such programs is critical, both for better communication of the essential components and for more meaningful evaluation of their outcomes" (p. 2). The question is: How can this clearer conceptualization be accomplished without inadvertently destroying the flexibility and spontaneity which are hallmarks of open education? Some educators believe that behavioral objectives are contrary to the basic premises of the approach. This reservation, if not hostility, toward the use of behavioral objectives would be appropriate if one were to follow the usual custom of developing extensive lists of minutely detailed performance objectives and assuming that these objectives should pertain to all children, with allowance for variation in the rate of accomplishment.

In a search for a useful alternative that would be appropriate to open education, we have been exploring procedures that enable the teacher and the students themselves to specify behavioral objectives which are appropriate to a particular individual, in a particular classroom, and under given circumstances. An objective may pertain to more than one student or to a single child, and fundamental skills which all children must eventually master may be acquired in different ways and through different activities. In planning a learning activity, the teacher attempts to anticipate many possible objectives which might be attained, depending on which of several directions are followed as the activity develops (Paul, Smith, and Henderson, 1970).

* Many of the considerations explored in this section have emerged from discussions (sometimes quite heated ones) in staff meetings at the Arizona Center for Educational Research and Development. It would be impossible to identify the contributions of everyone whose ideas have influenced the conceptualization expressed here. Specific acknowledgment, however, is given to the thoughtful contributions of Dr. John R. Bergan, who participated in the preparation of an in-house working paper on the use of behavioral objectives in the Tucson Early Education Model. A detailed exploration of relationships between humanistic values and scientific application may be found in John R. Bergan and James A. Dunn, *Psychology in Contemporary Education: Science for Humanistic Goals* (New York: Wiley, in press).

Defining General Goals

In one attempt to provide a set of procedures to establish behavioral objectives, the first step was to identify categories for general objectives which could serve as the cornerstones of an organizational structure within which more specific goals could be defined. For this purpose, we have taken the four goal categories specified for the Tucson Early Education Model (TEEM; Hughes, Wetzel, and Henderson, 1973): (1) motivation, (2) language, (3) societal arts and skills, and (4) intellectual skills.

Motivation. A primary area of instructional concern in our view is the general goal labeled here as motivation. We assume that responsibility for learning must in the final analysis rest with the student. This does not imply that the educational program should take a laissez-faire position with respect to motivation and expect that the intrinsic interest in activities and materials of the classroom will be sufficient to involve the learner in profitable learning activities. On the contrary, it seems reasonable that the school must provide the student with skills which will assist him in becoming a self-motivated, independent learner. Procedures and materials now extant in the public schools in many instances actually militate against the development of self-motivated students. In many programs the students are implicitly regarded as passive objects to be manipulated by teachers and/or packaged educational materials. Characteristically, in these programs, little is done to teach the student how to set his own goals, how to establish his procedures to achieve those goals, and how to make his own evaluative decisions regarding goal-attainment. Moreover, when goals are set exclusively by teachers or materials, provision for students to obtain the success necessary to instill self-motivation is often lacking.

Language. A second important general goal in the TEEM is that of language skills. Language competence is one of the major technical skills needed to function effectively in a complex technological society. Critical information is transmitted principally in verbal form. Verbal skills deficiencies can hamper or preclude the child's opportunities to receive important information about all aspects of the world in which he must function. The correlation between language skills and intellectual development is well known and suggests that many of the subtle distinctions drawn among abstract concepts without concrete referents cannot be made unless an extensive repertoire of verbal cues is available. Thus, language functions both as an avenue of important information and as a facilitator of higher-level abstract conceptualization. Development of this facility is essential to enable the child to profit from his academic and social milieu.

Societal Arts and Skills.   A third general goal is a broad area composed of a wide range of skills which are important in a complex technological society, one in which relationships among people are especially intricate. Classified here are reading, writing, arithmetic, and other quantitative skills, as well as social skills such as leadership, cooperation, and other capabilities vital to productive group work and satisfying interpersonal relationships. Several of the major subordinate goal areas for this category have been identified as follows.

It scarcely seems necessary to argue the importance of *reading skills,* but while highly formal programs are sometimes seen as overemphasizing reading to the neglect of broader purposes of education, educators favoring less formal approaches have sometimes overreacted by underemphasizing the importance of reading skills. Critics have seized upon this fact as a weak point of open education. Reading skills should constitute a priority area for goals, because reading competence is essential to effective functioning in a modern society and everyday classroom life. Through the written word, experience is translated, explicated, ordered, and stored for a vast variety of purposes. A child's ability to understand the code permits him to profit vicariously from the experiences of others, be they known or unknown.

Because of limitations on the availability of a teacher's time in the classroom, the ability to read is also one avenue to self-instruction and to greater independence for each child who acquires such skill. In open education more than any other form of instruction, the child who has mastered certain reading skills is afforded greater freedom in his selection of available options for learning within the classroom. A child who can read can select instructional materials suited to his own interests and needs, and he can pursue them in an increasingly independent fashion. Mastery of reading skills thus permits increased instructional individualization for the child and permits him to profit more fully from his environment, both inside and outside the school.

The subordinate goal of *quantitative skills* is given high priority because productive functioning in a modern technological society requires a high degree of sophistication in quantitative skills. The utilization of the scientific method, even in most rudimentary form, is dependent upon quantification skills. With the development of these skills, a child can increasingly approach his environment with problem-solving strategies. Through the ability to categorize, order, and quantify, a child is capable of describing, measuring, and drawing inferences about his environment. Quantitative skills can be envisaged as a communication system which enables an individual to categorize and process information about his environment and to reach sound and verifiable conclusions.

Many of the *social skills* which are important in routine social transactions in an interdependent society are overlooked or are haphazardly dealt with in traditional education programs. As matters now stand, skills such as cooperation, leadership, planning, and reinforcement of others or of oneself are primarily influenced by forces outside the classroom. In order for these skills to be mastered by all children, they must be carefully identified and defined and systematically taught. These contacts, in turn, influence the range and quality of experiences to which the child is exposed. The chain of events which may be facilitated through the development of social competence is extensive and obviously has many affective and cognitive implications.

The goal area of *aesthetic skills* is of great significance, but the definition of goals has only begun for it. As a nation we may rapidly be approaching an era in which we shall all have extended amounts of leisure time. If we are to help children to prepare for a more satisfying life under these conditions, we need to pay increased attention to the development of skills and enriching experiences with a wide variety of modes of aesthetic interaction and perception. Within this subordinate goal area, attention should extend beyond such traditional categories as music, visual arts, dance, athletics, hobbies, travel, theatrical production, and art appreciation to include the art forms of ethnic groups.

Intellectual Skills.   A fourth general goal area, intellectual skills, comprises capabilities assumed to be necessary in the process of learning. As yet, these skills are only partially recognized and defined and usually are not formally taught in traditional educational programs; yet the importance of these skills in every learning process is being increasingly recognized. We are beginning to suspect that the success of the child in the educational process is dependent upon his acquisition of several basic intellectual skills. It is hypothesized that these skills may be learned by many children largely outside the classroom.

Consider, for example, learning to learn skills. Typically, if a child wants to learn a list of words relating to a project he is working on and if he takes them home to learn to spell, he is put in the position of having to teach himself. If at home he has parents who are willing to read the words to him or show him how to write and check them against the list, or if he has a sibling who is willing to show him how to go about the task of learning, he will learn the words. If he does not have these resources outside the classroom, he may fail to teach himself. It is clear that as a child progresses through the educational system he is given greater and greater responsibility for teaching himself. At the same time, the traditional educational system does not systematically teach children the skills of self-teaching or learning how to learn.

Some intellectual skills involve the conceptual organization of stimuli in the environment: for example, ordering objects along certain dimensions such as size, color, and form or sequencing events according to time. Other intellectual skills are complex behaviors, which include the ability to attend, to recall significant events, to be able to reorganize one's behavior toward specific goals, to evaluate alternatives, to choose, to plan, to develop expectations, to be able to distinguish significant and important behaviors in others, and to imitate. We hope to focus on such behaviors as these as part of the instructional goals. It is necessary to identify and teach systematically these crucial behaviors, the acquisition of which traditionally has been left to chance.

Using Goals to Guide Instruction

The designation of broad goal categories and a statement of rationale, as illustrated above, is a necessary first step in defining the aims of an open education program. The goal categories are somewhat arbitrary, but they provide the framework for a conceptual structure which may guide the specification of more discrete objectives.

The general goal of motivation may be used to illustrate how a goal structure may help the teacher to maintain a balanced view of pupil growth in self-directed learning and to guide the collection of data samples to demonstrate that progress is taking place. Approach behavior, self-goal-setting, task persistence, and self-evaluation might be considered as components of motivation.

For example, in relation to the subordinate goal of approach behavior, the teacher may be interested in helping individual children to grow in approaching a wider and wider range of classroom resources for learning and support of learning. For a particularly "shy" child, for instance, an appropriate objective may be for him to begin to approach the teacher or other adults and to initiate interaction with them. For the child who customarily does not initiate such interaction, the teacher may be interested in getting him to approach adults in the classroom for any purpose whatsoever. The teacher may feel that it is important for this child to begin to approach adults simply to call their attention to some work he has produced or to seek comfort. On a more complex level of involvement, the teacher may hope to get the child to approach adults as resources: as sources of information or to help in solving a particular problem. These could be significant objectives for individual children, and development could be reliably judged simply by counting such behaviors and noting the change.

Within open classrooms there is also a range of available activities, and the provision for free choice of activities makes a natural situation in which the teacher can observe whether or not a given child is becoming interested in and choosing from an increasingly broad range of activities. On a simple level, an objective may be merely to get a child to approach an activity center and to explore and manipulate the materials there. On a more complex level of involvement, an objective may be for the child to approach the learning center and to involve himself in solving a problem posed there.

The subordinate goal of self-evaluation provides a further illustration of ways in which specific behavioral objectives might be developed within a goal framework. One way of defining evaluation is as the process of judging the extent to which a performance or product meets preestablished criteria. Criteria may be based on broadly accepted cultural standards, such as standards for writing in manuscript. Evaluation may also be based on criteria set by the student himself, on criteria jointly determined by the child and his teacher, or on criteria agreed upon by a group of peers in a committee activity.

Evaluation, as we have considered it, requires the ability to judge performance according to a standard or model. It also requires the capability to measure performance. Measurement may be accomplished with procedures and instruments such as checklists, tallies, or graphs.

Self-evaluation objectives are frequently developmental. Developmentally, both judgment and measurement skills may vary along the dimensions of the amount of adult or peer assistance required and the complexity of the product or performance to be evaluated. For instance, an objective may be that the child, with assistance from his peers, will be able to check the "mechanics" of his written products against classroom references. An example would be that, having written a story to be "published" in a class book, the child will check his punctuation and spelling against standard reference sources in the classroom. He might then submit his story to an editorial committee of peers for further checking. Evaluation in this instance is based on the use of a standard or model.

The kind of measurement appropriate for self-evaluation may take many forms and may be used with increasing degrees of independence. An objective might be for the child to be able to use a graph, developed with the assistance of the teacher, to record the number of new sight words he learns each week. In becoming a self-directed learner, the child may set weekly goals regarding words occurring in his own stories that he wants to learn as sight words.

The definition of goals provided by these few illustrations suggests some of the ways in which clearer specification may be given to open education approaches with minimum threat to the flexibility of the program. The process of goal definition should be an ongoing one, with decisions about the appropriateness of goals and procedures being based on outcomes. By working with a specific objective, which might well be specified by the child himself, the teacher and/or student can collect data of a nature that provides quick feedback, which may confirm a particular activity, procedure, or set of materials or which may suggest revision. The teacher becomes a scientist in the true sense of the term. Moreover, as the student gains independence in setting goals and evaluating outcomes, he should be able increasingly to assume this role himself. Evaluation and decisionmaking are focused upon individual students rather than on performance of groups of students. Furthermore, this framework makes it possible for the teacher to use *all* relevant psychological *principles* which can be made available to her. She is not limited to the mechanistic application of *procedures* selected by a curriculum developer.

Our experience in using this developing framework is limited as yet, but some encouraging outcomes have already been reported. In staff planning and in planning among students and teachers there appears to be a noticeable shift from a concern with selection of "interesting activities" to a focus on "What are some of the things we want to accomplish?"; and *then,* "What interesting activities and materials could be provided for these purposes?"

Both the vision and the promise of open education seem infinitely broader, more exciting, and more relevant to life than competing attempts to improve educational practice. But to realize these hopes requires a responsible attempt to move beyond clichés and slogans. It requires clear specification of intended outcomes and also empirical exploration of techniques for determining whether or not these outcomes are being achieved. At least some of us who support open education believe that "... genuine humanism rests not so much in intentions as in the actual results of efforts to facilitate the growth of children in our charge" (Henderson, 1973, p. 372).

References

Bandura, A., and B. Perloff, "Relative Efficacy of Self-monitored and Externally Imposed Reinforcement Systems," *Journal of Personality and Social Psychology,* 1967, *7,* 111–116.

Bussis, Anne M., and Edward A. Chittenden, *Analysis of an Approach to Open Education.* Princeton, N.J.: Educational Testing Service, 1970.

Evans, Ellis D., *Contemporary Influences in Early Childhood Education.* New York: Holt, Rinehart and Winston, 1971.

Featherstone, Joseph, *Schools Where Children Learn.* New York: Liveright, 1971.

Glynn, E. L., "Classroom Applications of Self-determined Reinforcement," *Journal of Applied Behavior Analysis,* 1970, *3,* 123–132.

Hapgood, Marilyn, "The Open Classroom: Protect It from Its Friends," *Saturday Review,* Sept. 18, 1971, 66–69 and 75.

Henderson, Ronald W. "Accountability and Decision-Making in Open Education," *Childhood Education,* 1973, *49,* 368–372.

Hughes, Marie M., Ralph J. Wetzel, and Ronald W. Henderson, "Tucson Early Education Model," in Bernard Spodek (ed.), *Early Childhood Education.* Englewood Cliffs, N.J.: Prentice Hall, 1973.

Maslow, A. H., *The Psychology of Science.* New York: Harper and Row, 1966. Cited in Carl E. Thoresen, "Behavioral Humanism," Research and Development Memorandum No. 88. Stanford, Cal.; Stanford Center for Research and Development in Teaching, April 1972 (mimeographed).

Paul, Alice A., Alice S. Smith, and Ronald W. Henderson, "Intellectual Kits: Tools for Instruction in the Tucson Early Education Model," Tucson: Arizona Center for Educational Research and Development, University of Arizona, 1970 (mimeographed).

Silberman, Charles, *Crisis in the Classroom.* New York: Random House, 1970.

Skinner, B. F., "Man." *Cumulative Record: A Selection of Papers* (3rd ed.). New York: Appleton-Century-Crofts, 1972.

Soar, Robert S., "Achieving Humanness: Supporting Research," in Norman K. Hamilton and J. Falen Saylor (eds.), *Humanizing the Secondary Schools.* Washington: Association for Supervision and Curriculum Development, 1969.

Thoresen, Carl E., "Behavioral Humanism," Research and Development Memorandum No. 88. Stanford, Cal.: Stanford Center for Research and Development in Teaching, April 1972 (mimeographed).

U. S. Office of Education, Division of Manpower and Institutions, "Draft Guidelines for Annual Budget Justification," Washington, D.C.: U.S. Office of Education, July 17, 1971 (mimeographed).

Walberg, Herbert J., and Susan Christie Thomas, "Open Education: An Operational Definition and Validation in Great Britain and United States," *American Educational Research Journal,* 1972, *9,* 197–208.

Wolf, Montrose, and Ted Risley, "Reinforcement: Applied Research," in Robert Glaser (ed.), *The Nature of Reinforcement.* New York: Academic Press, 1971.

CHAPTER 5

Affective Goals in Open Education

David T. Miles

DECISIONMAKING is a significant part of teaching. Teachers decide what their students ought to learn (goals), how they ought to learn it (procedures), and whether it is learned (evaluation). Teachers who tend to make similar decisions regarding such matters are said to share a particular philosophy of education or approach to teaching; other decisionmaking patterns characterize different types of teaching or education.

The manifestations of teacher decisions are seen in the behavior of students and teachers as they interact within educational environments. Recent research has shown that certain consistencies in behavior and physical events can be observed in classrooms which have been identified with open or informal education (Resnick, 1971; Evans, 1972).

Studies have also demonstrated that differences exist in various patterns of activity and events between so-called open schools and other educational approaches (Walberg and Thomas, 1972; Traub et al., 1973; Tuckman et al., 1973). Thus it seems safe to infer that open school teachers make different decisions than other teachers. But upon what basis are such decisions made? What accounts for these observed differences in decisionmaking patterns? Barth (1972) and Greene et al. (1973) have provided evidence that such differences are at least partially a function of particular beliefs and assumptions which teachers hold regarding motivation, learning, intellectual development, knowledge, and educational evaluation.

Another approach to describing and characterizing particular educational models or practices is through an analysis of the goals or objectives associated with the educational concept of concern. This paper examines open education from the point of view of educational goals, with particular emphasis on affective rather than cognitive or psychomotor goals.

The four major ideas to be explored are:

1. The expression of educational purposes in terms of learning goals
2. The role of educational goals in classroom decisionmaking
3. Affective goal priorities in open education
4. Problems and prospects of evaluating affective goal attainment

The first premise upon which subsequent arguments will be built is that education is a purposive activity, and that its purpose is to have some desirable influence on people which would not otherwise occur. These desirable influences are typically cast in the form of educational goals or objectives. Henceforth the term "goal" will be used instead of "objective," since it is shorter and sounds more pleasant.) Many people use these terms to refer to different levels of outcomes, such as broad general aims ("to produce good citizens") versus specific instructional results ("the student will describe the virtues and limitations of the democratic process of decisionmaking"). However, such use is not consistent, and in this paper "goal" will refer to any level of learning outcome. Thus the particular purposes of a curriculum, educational program, course, or learning activity are conceived of in terms which describe how students should be influenced by the event: that is, what knowledge, skill, or attitudes it is hoped they will acquire. These learnings constitute the purpose or desired ends of educational enterprises.

Student learning, then, is considered the primary criterion for judging the success of such experiences. Such learning outcomes are observed and evaluated at the end of various time periods—entire school programs such as curricula of 4, 6, or 12 years; instructional programs lasting from several months to several years; courses running from a few days to a few months; and learning events which might last a few minutes or a few hours. But, in each case, teachers decide what is to happen to students and assess the success of goal achievement in terms of intended influences on students.

The degree of clarity or objectivity with which teachers state their goals varies considerably, as does the validity and reliability of their measurement of goal attainment. Teachers in open education seem to use rather general traits or competencies to guide their decisions. Critical thinking ability, resourcefulness, open-mindedness, persistence, and ability to express ideas in writing are examples of such general goals. Teachers employing goals such as these typically do not write their goals down and consult them in making decisions; nor do they set particular levels which they wish students to attain, either individually or as a group. Rather, goals are considered as open-ended, and each student is expected to move at a different rate in different ways toward improvement in the particular capability or trait. It is also likely that such teachers who claim to be working toward the same goals have somewhat different conceptions of what the goal means in terms of behavior. This fuzziness is tolerated in part because such teachers often subscribe to a phenomenological viewpoint which suggests that everyone's meanings, or his reality, are personal and private—and are to some degree unknowable by others and naturally different from others.

Educational Goals and Decisionmaking

The use of cognitive goals for decisionmaking in education has had a long history. For the most part, prior to 1960 curriculum goal statements referred to content to be covered or presented to students instead of describing what students should be able to do upon completing instruction. The goals which dealt with learning outcomes employed vague terms such as to "know," "appreciate," or "understand." Examples of such goals would be:

1. To appreciate the historical origins of our present form of government
2. To examine the processes of mitosis and meiosis
3. To study major Western painters of the 18th century
4. To explore concepts of line, form, and shape
5. To understand the parts of a sentence

These types of goals were often written down and had some influence on decisions about instruction and evaluation. Prescribed levels of attainment for all students were rarely set in selecting these goals; all students were expected to attain some level of competence with each goal—those achieving the highest level getting A's, and so on. A common occurrence with teachers employing such goals as these was, and still is, that the content presented by the teacher, the tests given to students, and the goals of the instruction have had little in common. Some attention was paid to affective goals, particularly during the "life adjustment–whole child" education movement; but for the most part, prior to and following the progressive period most educational decisions were based on concern for cognitive and psychomotor learning.

Recent trends beginning in the early sixties have led to more extensive use of goals for planning and evaluating instruction (Popham and Baker, 1970). Programmed instruction and the development of *The Taxonomy of Educational Objectives,* applications of learning psychology, and military training research, among other developments, have led to the present emphasis for specification of goals in precise measurable terms. The following are examples of goals characteristic of this movement:

1. Given a list of some early contributions of desert people to the world, the student will describe how man uses three of these contributions.

2. Given a story containing real-life and make-believe elements, the student will suggest which elements are real and which are make-believe.

3. Given a group of words, the students will classify each group as a sentence or as a phrase—then add words to each phrase to make it a sentence.

4. The student will produce a collage which expresses his personal interpretation of something that recently happened in class. The collage must (a) incorporate at least three collage techniques presented in class, (b) be understood by the majority of the class, and (c) be different from, in both form and content, the collages produced by other students in the class.

Teachers who employ goals such as these often attempt to get all or most students to attain preset standards of achievement specified in the goals. Usually a close match exists between the goals and what is measured, and instruction is designed explicitly to facilitate goal attainment. Since the goals define clearly observable and, often, objectively measurable behavior, little room exists for misinterpretation of desired learning intents.

Common examples of affective goals from this tradition refer to getting a specific percentage of students to attain a certain score or to make a given percentage increase from the beginning to the end of the course on an attitude questionnaire. Some goals also refer to such observable behaviors as the number of unassigned books read, choice of courses taken, and time spent in various free-investigation activities (Mager, 1968).

Accountability, performance contracting, competency-based education, and individually prescribed instruction are the present-day education concepts which have roots in the movement toward measurability of instructional goals. These developments have met with controversy. While some educators are certain that behavioral objectives and instructional technology are comparable to the second coming of Jesus, others are convinced that the major effect of the movement will be a dehumanized "Brave New World."

About this same time open education, which has evolved from different roots—some theoretically based (Piaget, Montessori, phenomenological psychology) and others more pragmatic, such as teacher shortages—has been imported into this country from the British primary schools

(Engstrom, 1970). Although some commonalities can be seen between these two movements, such as the concern for adapting instruction to accommodate individual differences in learners, prominent differences are more characteristic of the comparison. Among the most telling contrasts are the instructional goals which are selected and how these are used.

The two major classes of decisions which goals have an influence upon are: (1) those dealing with learning activities (i.e., What should students do, with what materials and equipment, in what kind of social organizations?), and (2) evaluation decisions (i.e., What ought the student be able to do?, Is the student moving in the right direction?, Did he attain what was intended?). Goals function as the basis upon which such decisions are made. Whenever such decisions are required, either quite deliberately or somewhat intuitively, teachers consult their goals and attempt to make choices which are consistent applications of their goals.

In some forms of instruction most of the decisions about learning activities and evaluation are made before the teacher encounters the students. Such decisions are made at the beginning of either a year, semester, week, day, or hour and are then implemented in the classroom with only minor alterations, if any.

In open education many decisions are also made in advance of student contact. These decisions deal with the general structure of learning activities: i.e., social grouping, who will initiate various activities, the extent to which students will learn similar and different things, types and arrangement of furniture, equipment, and materials, etc. These decisions appear to be made in part according to general beliefs about learning and development, but perhaps more so on the basis of affective and cognitive outcomes which students should attain. Many other decisions are made by open teachers as they interact with students. These "spontaneous" decisions, often made in concert with students, appear to deal more with specific activities or subject matter rather than with the general structure or methodology of learning.

One of the statements frequently encountered regarding open education is that *how* students learn is considered equally, if not more, important than *what* they learn (Rogers, 1970). What is meant by such contentions is *not* that the means of learning and instruction, rather than the ends or effects such activities have for the student, are considered to be the purpose of education. On the contrary, what is meant is that open educators consider the attitudes, values, and beliefs that are learned as a result of the methods of learning and evaluation employed in school to be of more importance than the cognitive content which is taught through using such methods. Thus, open educators have shifted their priorities from a concern for only cognitive outcomes to include affective outcomes as well. They have recognized that the social norms and structure, motivational strategies, physical arrangements, and patterns of activity in the classroom have profound influences on affective outcomes. Moreover they realize that such affective effects are slow to emerge and often difficult to detect with available measurement techniques. As a result, emphasis has been placed on the design and implementation of learning activities which appear to foster desired affective learning outcomes. Goals such as self-directed learning, self-esteem, openness to new experiences, positive attitudes toward reading, aesthetic appreciation and expression, etc., are what open educators desire as learning outcomes. And to achieve such goals, children must have extensive experience in particular learning environments and activities which appear to foster such outcomes. Students must (1) practice directing their own learning, (2) be treated as worthy persons by teachers and peers, (3) have enjoyable new experiences, and (4) get personal reward from reading and aesthetic expression, if they are to acquire such characteristics. Thus, the claim that open teachers are primarily concerned with the *how* of learning is true to the extent that they are aware of the profound effects of the total school experience on the affective characteristics of their students.

A related point of confusion is the claim that purposes or goals in education can be meaningfully cast in terms of a learning experience. Eisner (1969) has proposed the use of "expressive" objectives:

> Expressive objectives differ considerably from instructional objectives. An expressive objective does not specify the behavior the student is to acquire after having engaged in one or more learning activities. An expressive objective describes an educational encounter: it identifies a situation in which children are to work, a problem with which they are to cope, a task they are to engage in—but it does not specify what from the encounter, situation, problem or task they are to learn.

This notion of goal setting and decisionmaking is inconsistent with the purposive nature of education. Learning experiences are encountered by students to accomplish some desired outcome. It just doesn't make sense to say that a goal is to visit a farm or design a birdhouse. These activities will very likely have some influence on students—and are thus selected in preference to other activities precisely because of the desired effects they should have. The proposed evaluation of such expressive goals would be whether they happened, i.e., whether students visited the farm or designed their birdhouses. Such data are not very useful in deciding whether the activity was worthwhile. What happened to the students, how they were affected by the experience, what new concepts, skills, or feelings they acquired—these are what teachers are concerned with. If the teacher had no learning goal in mind for such activities, one might wonder how the particular activities were selected in favor of any other activity. Or more fundamentally, why have any activity at all? It should be noted that the desired outcomes of many learning experiences may differ for each student. Students may acquire different concepts from their farm visit—which is fine if that was one of the reasons the teacher chose the activity. But if some students did not acquire any new concepts, then the activity was a flop for them. Likewise, each student may use different material and design a different type of birdhouse, which would be viewed favorably if the goal was to foster individuality and attitudes associated with originality and resourcefulness. The orientation proposed by Eisner places no responsibility on the teacher for evaluating outcomes of learning activities. Such practices can foster the "mindlessness" of focusing on means without concern for ends or purpose which Silberman (1970) found so prevalent in his investigation of American schools.

Affective Goal Priorities

In most "conventional education," cognitive objectives are given highest priority, whereas affective goals are rarely stated and even more rarely used in making decisions about instruction and evaluation. Affective goals have had some attention in areas dealing with music and art appreciation, politics, and religion. But most affective learning in schools has been treated as incidental outcomes—unplanned results of instructional methods, social grouping, or evaluation and grading practices. Affective constructs are also found on some grade cards (e.g., citizenship, gets along with others, completes work on time, etc.); however, little serious effort is expended to foster such behavior deliberately or to measure such performance objectively.

It should be emphasized that the notion of goal priorities does not refer to a list of objectives in a curriculum catalog which have little relation to what actually goes on in the classroom. In this context, goal priorities refers to the basis on which decisions are made regarding classroom learning activities. As mentioned earlier, the results of teacher decisions can be seen in the physical and behavioral events of the classroom. The amount of time and energy allotted to particular activities—how students encounter each other and learning materials—how they receive guidance and feedback—permits inferences to be made regarding the priorities of educational goals.

To further clarify the concept of goal priorities in open schools, a gross comparison between open and "traditional" evaluation might be useful. Figure 1 illustrates a gross contrast between these two approaches in terms of goal priorities, using the behavioral domains and taxonomy classifications of educational objectives from Bloom and Krathwohl (Miles, 1972).

Figure 1.

Comparison of Goal Priorities of Traditional and Open Education

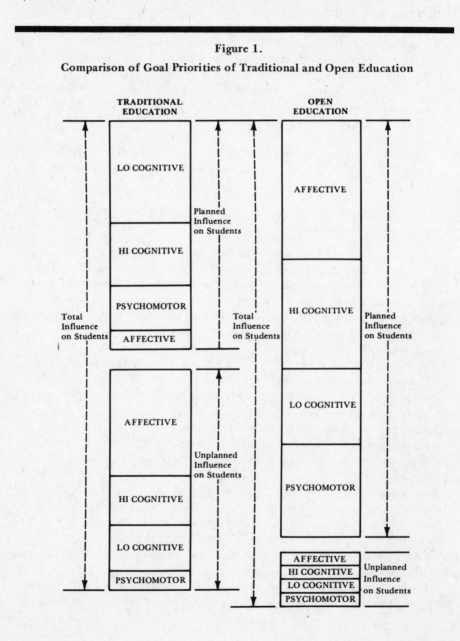

One major difference between open and traditional education shown in the figure is that a much larger proportion of the total influence of the school on the students is *planned* in the open school. In many traditional schools, little effort is expended and few instructional decisions are made on the basis of producing affective outcomes. Nevertheless, students acquire attitudes about themselves, learning and society, plus personal values and motivational styles, many of which are considered less than desirable. Open schools, on the other hand, typically place such affective goals as self-concept, self-directedness, curiosity, resourcefulness, creativity, responsibility, and sensitivity in a position of highest priority, and thus plan much of the educational procedure to facilitate achieving these outcomes. Similarly, open schools place considerable emphasis on high-level cognitive skills such as learning to learn, problem solving, critical thinking, and social and communication skills. Traditional schools appear to place a great deal more emphasis on low-level cognitive outcomes such as the acquisition of knowledge.

Another important feature of open schools which may have confused many people is that students appear to make the major decisions regarding what they learn. In part, this is true: students do make most of the decisions about what specific activities they will engage in during school. However, the decisions regarding the affective and high-level cognitive goals are made by teachers and others. The student does *not* have a choice of whether he will acquire a healthy self-concept, become self-directing, learn to enjoy school, or acquire creative problem-solving skills. In fact, it is these priority decisions by teachers that result in procedures in which students are given considerable freedom and responsibility to select what they will pursue each day. Of course, these decisions by students are also influenced by higher-priority goals of the school. The arrangement of the environment, the availability of various materials, the powerful influence of older children joyfully engaged in productive learning, the teacher's style of inquiry and interaction, all these exert a strong influence on what students do and how they do it. Certainly, different open schools emphasize different objectives in all domains, but the major arrangement of priorities appears to be fairly consistent.

Additional support for the affective priority position has been offered by Hoetker (1970), who suggests that:

> ... there has to be some relationship between what we do every day and what we finally achieve. At the very least, we cannot shape one sort of behavior day after day, year after year, and expect that at the end of their educations students will manifest precisely the opposite behavior. We cannot teach critical independence by insisting on the mechanical application of memorized critical formulas. We cannot teach respect for thought by attending

only to mechanics and forms of expression. We cannot teach honest self-expression by punishing disagreements with established opinions. We cannot teach students to be free citizens by treating students to honor the common humanity of all men by expressing contempt for the student's own humanity in our every word and gesture.

Although there are numerous theoretical explanations, varying in sophistication, of how learning takes place, this rather commonsensical approach of inferring what is learned from examining what people do would be compatible with the following assumptions:

1. People learn to do what they do often and enjoy.
2. People learn to avoid doing what they do and dislike.
3. People do *not* learn to do what they do infrequently or not at all.

Encouraging students to make decisions regarding their own learning was mentioned earlier as a high-priority practice and a desired outcome of open education. The standard of evaluation employed in classrooms also reveals educational values. For example, the student who receives C's and D's in most of his courses for twelve or more years must have a hard time ignoring the message about his relative competence. Other messages about the competitive, win-lose, scarcity-of-success interpretation of a society cannot be ignored by students who experience the evaluation and grading system employed in most conventional schools. Open educators have questioned whether the extensive emphasis on ranking and classifying students regarding their relative achievement might not interfere with learning. Some competition may be motivating, but most people give up in the face of continued failure, and the comparative evaluation of students (the grading system) ensures that the majority will fail (where an A grade is success). It is also well known that continued failure often has deleterious effects on self-esteem.

Some of the recent work on mastery-learning and criterion-referenced evaluation has shown that one of the major factors contributing to varying levels of achievement in school is that of holding the amount of time to learn constant. Since students learn at different rates, it is hardly surprising that some will learn more than others in a set amount of time. When time is *not* fixed, but certain levels of achievement are, it is found that nearly all students can achieve the desired level. It's just that some take a little longer to get there than others.

Open educators have even gone further in questioning whether it is necessary or desirable ever to employ comparative evaluation standards in school. Since every human being is different, with different aptitudes and inclinations, these educators question the intent of continually comparing students on the criterion of how fast they learn things. They have also questioned the justification for requiring all students to learn the same things (other than some basic skills and attitudes) or to attempt to achieve the same levels of mastery. Underlying such questions appears to be a high-priority concern for the self-esteem of students. Open educators contend that if a student doesn't feel proud of himself about something, if he doesn't have some feelings of self-worth and competence, if he isn't significant in his own eyes, he just isn't going to make out very well in anything.

Affective goal priorities can be observed in such classroom functions as:

1. *Activity decisions*—the percentage of time teachers, the class, student groups, individual students, or someone else decides to spend and what learning activities to engage in, and how to conduct the activities

2. *Motivation*—the percentage of time students engage in learning activities for different purposes or motives (e.g., curiosity, extrinsic rewards, etc.)

3. *Activity differentiation, participation, and pacing*—the percentage of time students spend in total class activities, small group activities, or individual activities, and progress in their learning as a class, as groups, or individually

4. *Evaluation source*—the percentage of time students obtain feedback regarding their success in learning from the teacher, other students, or themselves (i.e., self-evaluation)

5. *Evaluation standard*—the percentage of time the feedback students receive regarding their success in learning is based on a comparison with other students as opposed to a comparison with some other standard (e.g., individual improvement)

6. *Participative governance*—the percentage of nonacademic rules and regulations of the classroom and school which students, teachers, and others (e.g., principal, superintendent) participate in deciding upon

7. *Activity mood*—the percentage of time that the general mood or atmosphere of activities is: *(a)* orderly and businesslike, *(b)* enthusiastic and exciting, *(c)* informal and relaxed, etc.

8. *Student feelings*—the percentage of time students have various feelings about themselves regarding their experiences in learning activities, (e.g., accepted and appreciated, inadequate and inferior)

A careful, or even casual, examination of how each of these eight variables is expressed in a school or classroom can usually clarify the learning priorities of the people responsible for the education provided therein (Miles, in press). Such a systematic analysis of open classrooms has not been performed to date. However, casual examinations from the goal priority perspective prompted the hierarchical arrangement depicted in Figure 1. Example goals illustrating the affective priority position found in many open classrooms are shown in Figure 2.

Figure 2. Goal Priorities in Open Education

1. Affective Goals

Self-esteem	*2. High Cognitive Goals*	
Resourcefulness		*3. Low Cognitive &*
Curiosity	Critical thinking	*Psychomotor Goals*
Self-direction	Problem solving	
Openness	Learning skills	
Self-awareness	Communication skills	Xylophone playing
etc.	Creativity	Subtraction
	Quantitative reasoning	Haiku poetry
	etc.	Worm anatomy
		Paragraph writing
		Economic theory
		etc.

1. Affective goals, which are the highest-priority goals, are teacher-determined and are the basis for such decisions as the physical and social arrangements of the classroom as well as motivational, learning, and evaluation strategies.

2. High-level cognitive goals, which are given second priority, are also determined by teachers and guide decisions regarding alternative learning activities, plus equipment and materials to be made available. These decisions are made in light of and must conform to those decisions made regarding the affective goals.

3. Low-level cognitive and psychomotor goals are selected by students alone, or by students and teachers together, and include various specific subjects. These goals are selected within the context of both sets of higher-level goals and are based in part on a student's current interest or concern and in part on the teacher's and student's perception of what would be useful to know and be able to do.

Evaluation and Affective Goals

Open education is not the only movement today in which affective goals are given the highest priority. The numerous programs associated with humanistic education (Weinstein, and Fantini, 1970), psychological education ("Psychological Humanistic Education," 1969), participative education (Wight, 1970), free schools (Gross and Gross, 1969), and cross-cultural training (Wight and Hammons, 1970), as well as the expanding array of short-term courses and workshops dealing with parental skills (Gordon), sexual behavior (Institute for Advanced Study), interpersonal competencies, mental health, etc., are also examples of educational efforts in which feelings, attitudes, and values are the prime concern.

These programs as well as open education face the common demand that they must prove their worth. For education, the age of accountability appears to be dawning. The traditional pragmatic values of our culture, combined with emerging attitudes of responsible citizenship, demand that educational as well as other social institutions demonstrate their value or else be replaced or eliminated. Performance contracting, voucher systems, alternative schools, and competency-based training and certification are examples of this movement.

One of the problems facing the affective priority movements is that of evaluation philosophy and methodology. At the heart of much humanistic educational philosophy is a phenomenological psychology—a point of view which emphasizes the unique personal meanings of each individual. For example, the following items selected from Barth's list of assumptions (Barth, 1972), which open educators strongly agree with, illustrate such beliefs:

20. Those qualities of a person's learning which can be carefully measured are not necessarily the most important.
21. Objective measures of performance may have a negative effect upon learning.
29. It is possible, even likely, that an individual may learn and possess knowledge of a phenomenon and yet be unable to display it publicly. Knowledge resides with the knower, not in its public expression.

Such learnings influence how goals are employed. For the phenomenologist, feelings and thoughts are real, and overt behavior is but a gross, often inaccurate indication of the internal reality—a symptom of the private mental and emotional life of persons. On the other hand, the behaviorist contends that overt behavior is all that the teacher or psychologist can ever deal with, so it is this rather than mental and visceral events which is of concern.

Applications of such viewpoints are apparent in open educators' use of goals which have wide interpretation versus behavioristic teachers' specification of goals which refer to performance upon which most everyone can agree. Although teachers with both orientations base generalizations about learning upon observations of behavior, open educators seem to be less convinced about the validity of such data. In other words, they ascribe different meanings to the behavior they observe. Open school teachers appear to have little interest in paper-pencil tests of affective traits or cognitive capabilities, and they rely more on direct observation of students over long periods of time. In the current evaluation jargon, open school teachers are more interested in frequent formative evaluation rather than in occasional summative evaluation. Goal statements which provide general but purposeful direction to teachers' decisionmaking may provide the optimum level of guidance for many teachers. More narrow and short-term goal statements may "overguide" teachers and result in their losing sight of general goals or purposes. Broader goals also appear to be more consistent with the open education notion of maximizing the contribution of both students *and* teachers to educational decisions.

Currently state education departments are establishing value priorities in terms of affective and cognitive goals for which schools will be expected to demonstrate attainment (Welsh, 1971; *Action Goals*, 1972). Behavioral objectives are also being written into legislation. If educators opposing their strict and rigid use are to be heard, they must produce equally viable objectives and/or alternatives which show other ways to be accountable for educational outcomes. Unfortunately, the small number of existing acceptable measures of the affective domain make assessment, and thus accountability, difficult. There is a recognized need to develop more and better measures.

Extensive work has been invested in the development of instruments and procedures for assessing affective behavior in the various behavioral science disciplines. However, the great majority of assessment tools and techniques have been developed for purposes of formal research or clinical diagnosis of mental deviancy. Sociologists and social psychologists have produced a wide range of paper-pencil instruments for measuring attitudes and values (Shaw and Wright, 1967). Personality theorists have also generated numerous tests for measuring various personality traits. Research by operant psychologists as well as by social and educational psychologists has recently stimulated development of systematic observation and recording techniques for measuring such phenomena as teacher-student interaction (Amidon and Hough, 1967), classroom climate (Stern, 1963), and individual deviant behavior (Sulzer and Mayer, 1972).

Although these developments have made enormous contributions to behavioral science, they have contributed little to educators concerned with affective educational goals. The prime reason for this is that these tools and techniques were developed for different purposes. Affective goals defined in terms of performance on paper-pencil instruments are of little use to teachers in making classroom decisions. Extensive knowledge of the traits purportedly measured by such tests, how such traits are influenced by experience and how to recognize various manifestations of the traits, is what teachers need to make decisions. Educational administrators and teachers have distinctly different needs and concerns from those of researchers and clinical psychologists. While some behavior observation techniques could be quite useful for assessing affective behavior in the school, the time and money required to employ such techniques on a broad scale are prohibitive for most public schools.

Considerable literature and materials are available for the classroom teacher to guide and facilitate the development of so-called "teacher-made tests" for assessing cognitive achievement. Little if any comparable literature or materials dealing with affective behavior is available. If teachers are to be expected to direct more of their attention to affective education, then valid, reliable, and practical instruments and procedures must be developed for it.

Publication of *The Taxonomy of Educational Objectives* in 1964 (Krathwohl et al.) was met with great interest by educators. But the contribution of this work has been exceedingly disappointing over the past eight years. Many reasons for its limited impact have been proposed, but perhaps the most telling is the lack of valid, reliable, and practical instruments for measuring the various classes of affective behavior delineated in the taxonomy.

Some professional testing companies have begun to concern themselves with problems of affective behavior assessment (Bussis and Chittenden, 1970). But, unfortunately, these companies may limit their efforts to the production of standardized, paper-pencil instruments which can be sold and for which they can provide scoring and interpretation services. Such products will be welcomed, but they still may not provide the kind of data which teachers will require to continuously monitor and assess various affective processes and outcomes in public schools.

Psychometry has been dominated for sixty years by the theory and methodology originated for measuring human intelligence by Binet, Cattell, Terman, and Wechsler. Educational and psychological tests and testing today are almost solely concerned with paper-pencil, multiple-choice, norm-referenced testing activities.

The movement toward specifying and measuring attainment of precise educational objectives, as well as recent trends toward individualization, have made some alterations in the philosophy and practice of evaluation in schools. As many educators have decided that their primary task is not to determine who are the fast and slow learners but to see that all students acquire particular capabilities, the criterion-referenced evaluation philosophy has grown in popularity. Again the major efforts in this trend have been in assessing cognitive learning. One exception is the work done at the Instructional Objectives Exchange of the Center for the Study of Evaluation (UCLA), which has recently produced several instruments for measuring self-concept and attitudes toward various subject matters. These tests are useful for periodic group evaluation of these two affective areas. More recent works which give clear indications of the needs and some initial steps toward meeting the needs of affective evaluation include: *Handbook of Formative and Summative Evaluation of Student Learning* (Bloom et al., 1971), various publications of the Association for Supervision and Curriculum Development (Beatty, 1969), and the current "Affective Education Project" (Wight and Doxsey, 1972), in which affective goals and measures for public schools in eight Western states are being developed. The encouraging work in values clarification (Raths et al., 1966), although not directed specifically at problems of assessment, has evolved several techniques for individuals and groups to examine and clarify their values and attitudes to themselves. Most of these techniques appear to be a direct extension of some elements of humanistic educational philosophy.

Another promising direction involves the use of available or easily obtainable data which reflects particular behaviors: for example, attendance records, patterns of choice within classes, elective courses taken, frequency of student-initiated contacts with teachers, number of students voting, etc. Although the variety of interpretations of what is meant by "humanistic" is nearly limitless, the notion that individuals should be treated as unique, worthy, and capable of directing much of their own lives would at least be considered related to humanism by many people. In keeping with this premise, evaluation tools and techniques should be designed for individuals to use in self-evaluation; and when individuals are evaluated by others, they should have complete knowledge of for what, how, and why they are being evalauted, as well as the opportunity to choose not to be evaluated. If trust and honesty in human relations are also germane to most people's conceptions of humanizing experiences, many of the thorny psychometric problems of deception and responding in a socially desirable manner can possibly be reduced. For example, if a teacher can create an environment in which students feel they are respected and trusted, they should be more likely to accept requests to be evaluated and to exhibit attitudes and behaviors indicative of their true feelings, interests, or values. If a student is aware that (1) his teacher is recording the amount of time he spends in independent reading, (2) that she desires that he spend more time in this activity, (3) that she only wants him to read more if he feels it is personally enjoyable or satisfying, and (4) that she will in no way punish or treat him differently if he does not engage in more reading, then the data she collects on this student's independent reading habits should approximate the level of validity necessary for making meaningful inferences.

One final notion which may hold some prospect for affective measurement involves direct use of self-assessment. Perhaps students can be taught about affective traits and behavior and learn to sample their own feelings and behavior periodically (Mahoney and Thoresen, 1972). Such a procedure is similar to the values-clarification techniques. For example, students might learn what is meant by self-esteem or aesthetic sensitivity, including how such traits are acquired, extinguished, and expressed internally and externally as well as how to observe and record such expressions. Such a procedure is similar to that employed in teaching achievement motivation, in which students are taught to have achievement fantasies, set moderate goals, obtain and react to concrete feedback, and express positive ideas about themselves (Alschuler and Ivey, 1972).

If certain attitudes or values are considered so essential for students to acquire, should not students learn about them so that they can make informed decisions about their own affective learning? A capability such as this might be the highest-priority goal of all in affective education.

References

Alschuler, A. S., and A. Ivey, "The Human Side of Competency-Based Education," *Educational Technology*, November 1972, 53–55.

Amidon, E. J., and J. B. Hough (eds.), *Interaction Analysis: Theory, Research and Application*, Reading, Mass.: Addison-Wesley, 1967.

Barth, Roland S., *Open Education and the American School*. New York: Agathon Press, 1972.

Beatty, W. H. (ed.), *Improving Educational Assessment and an Inventory of Measures of Affective Behavior*, Washington, D.C.: Association for Supervision and Curriculum Development, NEA, 1969.

Bloom, B. S., J. T. Hastings, and G. F. Madaus, "Evaluation Techniques for Affective Objectives," Chapter 10 in *Handbook of Formative and Summative Evaluation of Student Learning*. New York: McGraw-Hill, 1971.

Bussis, A. M., and E. A. Chittenden, *Analysis of an Approach to Open Education*, Interim Report. Princeton, N.J.: Educational Testing Service, 1970.

Eisner, E., "Instructional and Expressive Objectives: Their Formulation and Use in Curriculum," in *AERA Monograph Series on Curriculum Evaluation*, vol. 3, *Instructional Objectives*. Chicago: Rand-McNally, 1969.

Engstrom, G. (ed.), *Open Education: The Legacy of the Progressive Movement*. National Association for the Education of Young Children, 1834 Connecticut Avenue, N.W., Washington, D. C. 20009, 1970.

Evans, J. T., "An Activity Analysis of U. S. Traditional, U. S. Open, and British Open Classrooms," paper presented at the American Educational Research Association meeting, Chicago, April 1972.

Gordon, T., *A New Model for Humanizing Families and Schools*. Effectiveness Training Associates, 110 S. Euclid Ave., Pasadena, Cal. (n.d.).

Greene, J. F., J. Keilty, and S. Rothman, "The Open Curriculum and Selection of Qualified Staff: Instrument Validation," paper presented at American Educational Research Association meeting, New Orleans, February 1973.

Gross, R., and B. Gross (eds.), *Radical School Reform*. New York: Simon and Schuster, 1969.

Hoetker, J., "Limitations and Advantages of Behavioral Objectives in the Arts and Humanities," in J. Maxwell and A. Tovatt (eds.), *On Writing Behavioral Objectives for English*. Commission on the English Curriculum, National Council of Teachers of English, Urbana, Ill., 1970.

Krathwohl, D. R., B. S. Bloom, and B. B. Masia, *Taxonomy of Educational Objectives, Handbook II: Affective Domain*. New York: David McKay, 1964.

Mager, R. F., *Developing Attitude Toward Learning*. Palo Alto, Cal.: Fearson Press, 1968.

Mahoney, M. J., and C. E. Thoresen, "Behavioral Self-control: Power to the Person," *Educational Researcher,* October 1972, 5–7.

Miles, D. T., "Affective Priorities and Educational Objectives," *Educational Technology,* December 1972, 33–35.

Miles, D. T., "Clarifying Learning Priorities in Education," *Educational Technology,* in press.

Popham, W. J., and E. L. Baker, *Systematic Instruction*. Englewood Cliffs, N.J.: Prentice-Hall, 1970.

Raths, L. E., M. Harmin, and S. B. Simon, *Values and Teaching: Working with Values in the Classroom*. Columbus, Ohio: Charles E. Merril Publishing Co., 1966.

Resnick, L. B., "Teacher Behavior in an Informal British Infant School," paper presented at the American Educational Research Association meeting, New York, February 1971.

Rogers, V. R., *Teaching in the British Primary School*. New York: Macmillan, 1970.

Shaw, M. E., and J. M. Wright, *Scales for the Measurement of Attitudes*. New York: McGraw-Hill, 1967.

Silberman, C. E., *Crisis in the Classroom*. New York: Random House, 1970.

Stern, G. G., "Measuring Non-cognitive Variables in Research and Teaching," in N. L. Gage (ed.), *Handbook of Research on Teaching*. Chicago: Rand-McNally, 1963, 398–447.

Sulzer B., and G. R. Mayer, *Behavior Modification Procedures for School Personnel*. Hinsdale, Ill.: The Dryden Press, 1972, 261–286.

Traub, R. E., J. Weiss, C. W. Fisher, and D. Musella, "Closure on Openness in Education," paper presented at the American Educational Research Association meeting, New Orleans, February 1973.

Tuckman, B. W., D. W. Cochran, and E. J. Travers, "Evaluating the Open Classroom," paper presented at the American Educational Research Association meeting, New Orleans, February 1973.

Walberg, H. J., and S. C. Thomas, "Open Education: An Operational Definition and Validation in Great Britain and United States," *American Educational Research Journal*, Spring 1972, 9:2, 197–208.

Weinstein, G., and M. Fantini (eds.), *Toward Humanistic Education: A Curriculum of Affect*. New York: Praeger, 1970.

Welsh, J., *Educational Quality Assessment: Pennsylvania Looks at its Schools*. Harrisburg, Pa.: Pennsylvania Dept. of Education, 1971.

Wight, A. R., and A. Hammons, *Guidelines for Peace Corps Training*. Estes Park, Colo.: Center for Research and Education, 1970.

Wight, A. R., "Participative Education and the Inevitable Revolution," *The Journal of Creative Behavior*, Fall 1970, *4:4*, 234–282.

Wight, A. R., and J. R. Doxsey, *Measurement in Support of Affective Education*. Monograph of the Interstate Resource Service Center, 710 E. 2nd South St., Salt Lake City, Utah 84102, 1972.

"Psychological Humanistic Education," *Educational Opportunity Forum*, Fall 1969, *1:4*.

Institute for Advanced Study in Rational Psychotherapy, 1973 Programs/Publications/Newsletter, 45 East 65th Street, New York, N.Y.

Action Goals for the Seventies: An Agenda for Illinois Education. Springfield, Ill.: The Office of the Superintendent of Public Instruction, May 1972.

PART THREE
Studying Classrooms

CHAPTER 6

An Observational Portrait
of a British Infant School

Richard M. Brandt, *University of Virginia*

IN HIS searching critique of the American classroom, Silberman (1970) strongly endorsed the British infant school as one model for improving it. The contents of the present volume represent the latest in a long list of publications which attempt to recommend and explain the "open classroom" style of teaching in general, and the British infant school pattern in particular. Despite this extensive body of literature, however, only limited objective information exists regarding the precise nature of instructional processes and learning activities in such a school.

Resnick (1972) made a start at gathering objective data on infant school life but limited her focus to the nature of teacher behavior in one school. What has been sorely needed is a full, empirically derived description of the daily activities, teacher expectancies, pupil tasks and outcomes, organizational variations from one classroom to another, and other distinguishing features of this much heralded educational model.

In the present study a comprehensive assortment of descriptive data on an infant school was gathered in an effort to understand the nature of ongoing instructional processes and pupil experiences. Although teacher behavior was included, considerable information was obtained on pupils also and on the types of contacts they had with adults, peers, and materials. In addition, many situational data were produced, and recordings of certain teacher-led class discussions were made.

Method of Observation

The investigator spent three weeks during the spring of 1971 in an infant school in Northwest London. During this time I visited all six regular classrooms, made anecdotal notes of ongoing activities, and filled out a teacher interaction checklist in several rooms in order to have some basis of comparison with the two classes I chose for in-depth study. With the checklist, each teacher-child interaction was coded according to who initiated the interaction (teacher or child) and what type of approval (physical contact, verbal, or gesture) or disapproval (physical contact, verbal, or gesture) the teacher displayed.* I also questioned teachers frequently, especially the head teacher, during lunch periods or at other unobtrusive moments, about general organizational features of the school, the community, specific materials and activities, and other such matters. I briefed teachers generally on the kinds of data to be gathered and allowed them to see and react to some of the data after they had been collected. All teachers saw the teacher interaction data I collected, and both teachers in whose rooms audio taping was done listened to the tapes afterward.

I was allowed not only to roam freely and record whatever I observed but also, after teachers had seen the kinds of data being collected, to use the information for research analyses and even teaching purposes as long as names would not appear in print. I wish to thank these unidentified teachers for granting such permission and for being so open to such close inspection by an outsider.

The two classrooms which provided the greatest amount of data were chosen for intensive study after initial visitation to all rooms because the teachers (A and B) were the most experienced (5 to 10 years) in the building and seemed especially receptive to an observer's presence.

The primary observational instrument used was PROSE (i.e., Personal Record of School Experience), developed by Medley, Schluck, and Ames (1968).† This instrument consists of a recording sheet for each child and a manual of instructions describing 148 behavior and setting categories to be used by an observer in coding ongoing classroom activity. With PROSE, the observer focuses on one child at a time for approximately two minutes each; using a timing device, he codes whatever categories of behavior he sees occurring at each 25-second point-in-time for five consecutive intervals (see Figure 1). After each cycle of five such behavioral events, the observer ignores the timing signal and, turning the PROSE sheet over (see Figure 2), codes various contextual and behavioral variables to reflect conditions and happenings during the en-

* Appreciation is expressed to my colleagues Richard Abidin and Wendy Golladay for the development of this action checklist.

† Revised editions of this instrument have subsequently been produced by Medley, Quirk, Schluck, and Ames (1971) and by Carrico and Massey (1973).

tire cycle (approximately a 100-second period). He then focuses on another child, uses a new recording sheet, and repeats the entire process. Even in an open classroom, where children may be moving around, he can readily code a cycle of behavior for 8 to 12 children an hour.

Figure 1. Modified PROSE Recording Sheet for Behavior Categories*

CYCLE A Child-Adult Contacts (C–A)

1. INIT	1 2 3 4 5	C initiating contact
STAR	1 2 3 4 5	C getting individual attention
PART	1 2 3 4 5	C part of group getting attention
LSWT	1 2 3 4 5	C listens-watches; A focuses on others

Who Adult Is

2. TCHR	1 2 3 4 5	teacher
AA	1 2 3 4 5	adult aide
TAA	1 2 3 4 5	teenage aide
IBS	1 2 3 4 5	observer
OTH	1 2 3 4 5	other

What Adult is Doing

3. POS	1 2 3 4 5	giving praise or positive attention
PRM	1 2 3 4 5	giving C permission or choice
SHTL	1 2 3 4 5	showing or telling something
LSQUW	1 2 3 4 5	listening, questioning, or watching
DO4	1 2 3 4 5	doing something for C
CNTR	1 2 3 4 5	controlling C or group
NEG	1 2 3 4 5	indicating disapproval

Child-Child Contacts (Target C)

4. AGR	1 2 3 4 5	aggressive toward peer
INIT	1 2 3 4 5	initiating peer contact
COOP	1 2 3 4 5	cooperating with peer
WTHD	1 2 3 4 5	withdrawing from peer contact
RST	1 2 3 4 5	resisting peer contact

Child-Child Contacts (Other C)

5. AGR	1 2 3 4 5	aggressive toward target C
INIT	1 2 3 4 5	initiating contact with target C
COOP	1 2 3 4 5	cooperating with target C
WTHD	1 2 3 4 5	withdrawing from target C contact
RST	1 2 3 4 5	resisting target C contact

CYCLE A Tape of Adult or Peer Contact

6. CNTC	1 2 3 4 5	Physical contact
MTL	1 2 3 4 5	material involved in contact
VRB	1 2 3 4 5	verbal
		(leave blank if none of above)

Sex, Ethnic Group of Contact

7. OSOG	1 2 3 4 5	opposite sex, opposite group
OSSG	1 2 3 4 5	opposite sex, same group
SSOG	1 2 3 4 5	same sex, opposite group
SSSG	1 2 3 4 5	same sex, same group

Appropriateness of Child's Activity

8. COOP	1 2 3 4 5	cooperating, paying attention, task involved
DSTR	1 2 3 4 5	distracted
RIS	1 2 3 4 5	responding to internal stimuli
WOA	1 2 3 4 5	working on other activity
DSRP	1 2 3 4 5	disrupting class or individuals

Physical Movement

9. HIWL	1 2 3 4 5	high activity with locomotion
MDWL	1 2 3 4 5	moderate activity with locomotion
HINL	1 2 3 4 5	high activity, no locomotion
MDNL	1 2 3 4 5	moderate activity, no locomotion
LOW	1 2 3 4 5	low activity
		(leave blank if C is still)

Type of Activity

10. FANT	1 2 3 4 5	fantasy
DVG	1 2 3 4 5	divergent
CVG	1 2 3 4 5	convergent
WRK	1 2 3 4 5	socially useful work (e.g., sweeps floor)
KIN	1 2 3 4 5	kinesthetic, repetitive activity

Expressed Affect of Child

11. POS	1 2 3 4 5	positive (e.g., smiles, laughs)
NEG	1 2 3 4 5	negative (e.g., frowns)

*Brief category descriptors and category set names appear in place of Cycle B and Cycle C recording numbers and spaces. Consult PROSE Manuals for complete category descriptions and relevant examples.

Categories covering the behavioral events (Figure 1) relate to the nature of contacts the child has with adults, peers, and materials. For adult contacts, the observer codes who the adult is; what the adult is doing; who initiates the contact; whether the child is contacted as an individual or as part of a group; whether the contact is primarily physical, through materials, verbal, or nonverbal; and the sex and ethnic group of the contacted person in relation to the child. For peer contacts, the observer codes who initiated the contact; the nature of both the target child's behavior and that of the peer; whether the contact is physical, through materials, verbal, or nonverbal; and the sex and ethnic group of the peer. He codes the nature of the tasks confronted (divergent, convergent, etc.) whenever the child is in contact with materials and tasks rather than people. In addition, he codes the amount of child mobility and physical activity, as well as any positive or negative affect if it is apparent.

Setting conditions to be noted during a cycle (Figure 2) include the instructional content area, the role of the teacher and other adults, the location of the child in relation to the teacher, the size of the group he is in, and the general noise level of the class. The observer also records, if they occur, (a) such specific behaviors of the target child as using words or numbers, asking a peer for help, disobeying, and a host of other particular behaviors that sometimes take place during a cycle and (b) the child's use of various kinds of materials, such as food, puzzles, games, or musical instruments. The instructional manual must be consulted for the operational definitions of the various categories (Medley et al., 1968).

Except for the lunch period, the observer used PROSE rather continuously throughout the school day for three or four days in each of two classrooms. As children ranged from ages five through seven in each room, in accordance with the general principle of "family grouping" followed in many infant schools, a stratified random sample (by age and sex) was chosen from each room: i.e., two boys and two girls from each of three age levels. A total of 24 children were observed (12 in each classroom).* I observed each child in preselected order for one cycle of five events, covering approximately two minutes per child. As soon as the record sheet was completed following a cycle and the next child in the sample could be spotted, recording was begun again. In this fashion I continued observing children throughout the school day, with between two and three cycles (10 to 15 behavioral events) completed for each child. I was able to record a total of 9 cycles and 45 events on each of the 24 children during seven days of concen-

---

* These children, hereafter, will be referred to as target children.

Figure 2. Modified PROSE Recording Sheet for Cycle Categories*

Class Activity

1. ARITH	A	Arithmetic
ARTCRF	A	Arts and crafts
EXGM	A	Exercise, group games
FRPL	A	Free play, independent activity
HYTHYG	A	Health, hygiene
LANG	A	Language
MUSRTH	A	Music, rhythm
RSTSNK	A	Rest, snack
RINTRN	A	Routine, transition
SCI	A	Science
SENS	A	Sensation
SOSK	A	Social Skills
SOST	A	Social studies

Adult Roles

	A	(T, teacher; O, Others)
2. SHOW	T O	Showing, demonstrating
TELL	T O	Telling
LEAD	T O	Leading an activity
DSCS	T O	Conducting discussion
PEER	T O	Acting as a pupil
MNG	T O	Managing, giving directions
SPVS	T O	Supervising, checking work
RSRCE	T O	Serving as resource
HSKP	T O	Housekeeping
INDATT	T O	Individual Attention to one C
LSWT	T O	Listening, watching only
NCNT	T O	No contact with children

C's Proximity to Group

3. NEXT	A	Next to Adult
NEAR	A	Near but not next to A
MID	A	Middle of group
FRNG	A	Fringe, edge of group
OUT	A	Outside group

Group Size, Adult Presence
[adult in (Ad); not in (NA) group]

	A		B		C	
4. ONE	Ad	NA	Ad	NA	Ad	NA
TWO	Ad	NA	Ad	NA	Ad	NA
3–5	Ad	NA	Ad	NA	Ad	NA
6+	Ad	NA	Ad	NA	Ad	NA
ALL	Ad	NA	Ad	NA	Ad	NA

Classroom Climate

5. ATT EXC	A	Attentive and excited
ATT TNS	A	Attentive and tense
NSY EXC	A	Noisy and excited
NSY BSY	A	Noisy and busy
QU BSY	A	Quiet and busy
QU IDL	A	Quiet and idle

Special Adult Behaviors
[C part of target (P); only watching (W)]

	A		B	C	
7. Called for quiet	P W		P W	P W	
Threatened	P W		P W	P W	
Lost temper	P W		P W	P W	
Laughed with child(ren)	P W		P W	P W	
Used physical restraint	P W		P W	P W	

Special Happenings to Child

6. Used numbers	A	B	C
Used words	A	B	C
Sang, talked to self	A	B	C
Helped other peer	A	B	C
Comforted peer	A	B	C
Showed affection to peer	A	B	C
Asked peer for help	A	B	C
Received help, affection	A	B	C
Rejected by group	A	B	C
Accident, hurt	A	B	C
Showed fear	A	B	C
Cried	A	B	C
Lost temper	A	B	C
Tattled	A	B	C
Led other peer	A	B	C
Bossed other peer	A	B	C
Wrecked something	A	B	C
Refused help	A	B	C
Resisted adult	A	B	C
Disobeyed	A	B	C
Showed hostility to adult	A	B	C
Ridiculed	A	B	C
Cited as bas example	A	B	C
Cited as good example	A	B	C
Chore, errand	A	B	C
Showed affection to adult	A	B	C
Waited	A	B	C

Materials Used by Child (M)
[Location of child (L)]

8. Art materials (paint, clay)	M L	M L	M L
Craft	M L	M L	M L
Musical instruments	M L	M L	M L
Books, writing materials	M L	M L	M L
Puzzles, quiet games	M L	M L	M L
Blocks	M L	M L	M L
Wheel toys	M L	M L	M L
Tools, work bench	M L	M L	M L
Sand	M L	M L	M L
Gym, exercise	M L	M L	M L
Pet	M L	M L	M L
Clothes, jewelry	M L	M L	M L
Food, water	M L	M L	M L
Dolls	M L	M L	M L
Homemaking	M L	M L	M L
Cleanup tools	M L	M L	M L
Audiovisual device	M L	M L	M L
Special instruction device	M L	M L	M L
Science equipment	M L	M L	M L
Assigned seat	L	L	L
Teacher's desk	L	L	L
Open area	L	L	L
Toilet	L	L	L
Playground	L	L	L
Out of room	L	L	L

*Cycle category set names appear above each set. To make the various category symbols appearing in the left-hand columns meaningful, short category descriptors are presented in the spaces ordinarily used for recording cycle B and C data for #1, #2, #3, and #5 category sets. For sets #6, #7, and #8, the category abbreviations have been expanded into words for presentation here. Set #4 appears in the same form as is used on a regular recording sheet.

trated use of PROSE. While initiation of observation of children did not follow a precise schedule of predetermined times, the procedure used was rather continuous, and children were observed in whatever activity they happened to be engaged in whenever their turn came up. Thus, it can be argued that I obtained a representative sample of events covering the entire school day and that a particular child's nine cycles approximated a random assortment of his total school experiences on these days.

I could not determine interobserver reliability in the infant school because of the lack of a second trained observer. However, Sherman (1971) reported 92 to 98 percent agreement between two observers with similar amounts of training when they used PROSE to code children's behavior simultaneously in an American classroom.

I analyzed the audio tapes of teacher-led class discussions by developing a list of teacher statement categories and tallying the types of statements made in particular recorded episodes. A Pearson coefficient of 0.87 resulted from correlating the classification frequencies obtained from my own categorization of teacher statements with those obtained from an independent coder. Two independent codings of the same material by the same person also resulted in a 0.87 correlation coefficient.

Findings

Numerous findings must be presented in order to provide a relatively complete picture of all that was observed. These are organized under a dozen subheadings. An introductory section covering general organizational patterns portrays the types of activities that were often going on simultaneously, the kinds of tasks children faced, and some features of the daily schedule. Several sections which focus on teacher behavior follow this introduction: the overall style of teaching observed and the expectancies that were most apparent in the remarks they made to children, the kinds of questions they asked, particular instructional patterns and content emphases, and their manifest affect. A half-dozen sections then report directly on pupils: pupil behavior, adult contacts, peer contacts, task involvements (including the nature of the tasks they faced), manifest affect, and differences among pupils. A final section of the findings presents some of the differences between the teachers and classrooms.

General Organizational Patterns

Certain similarities prevailed from one room to the other in types of activities, grouping patterns, and teaching styles. At least half of each day was spent in informal, self-selected activities, during which time children worked independently, in pairs, or in small groups on tasks they chose to perform. At any particular moment one might find: *(a)* three or four youngsters (more frequently boys) at the workbench with hammers and saws making boats, planes, or something else of their choosing; *(b)* several girls and maybe a boy in the playhouse area engaging in fantasy activity with dolls, dress-up clothes, toy kitchen equipment and supplies; *(c)* several children finger-painting on a large table covered with newspapers; *(d)* three or four looking at or reading books taken from the library corner; *(e)* two or three brush-painting at easels in the hall or outside the building on nice days; *(f)* several playing quiet games at a table, an activity which might require the use of numbers or written words; *(g)* one child putting word puzzles together; *(h)* three youngsters modeling clay objects; *(i)* two others filling bottles at the water box and faucet; *(j)* five children copying items, writing, or illustrating stories in their personal notebooks; and *(k)* three youngsters making structures with building blocks on the floor. This range of materials and activities is typical of those described in a number of books about the British infant schools (Cushen, 1966; Howson, 1969; Ridgway and Lawton, 1968; Rogers, 1970). During these independent activity periods the teacher moved from one child or group to another, inspecting closely what was going on, raising questions about what the children were doing, occasionally making suggestions or lending assistance, and generally monitoring the entire group. She often used this time also to listen to children read or to go over written work in their notebooks. She called one child at a time to her side from whatever activity he was currently engaged in and tried to spend some time with each child individually in this manner each day.

Many of the tasks possessed intrinsic instructional value. For example, several children might be seated at a table with bags of shells, acorns, and other objects. Several balance-type scales might also be located on the table, and the children's task would be to make up simple equations, which they would write in their notebooks, by weighing various objects in relation to other objects. After performing this task for a few minutes, for instance, a child might have written:

$$4 \text{ acorns} = 5 \text{ shells}$$
$$4 \text{ acorns} = 3 \text{ marbles}$$
$$2 \text{ acorns} = 9 \text{ raisins}$$

Sometimes the tasks might take the form of structured problems which the child was to write and answer in his notebook while using the scales, such as:

1. Do 5 shells weigh more than 12 raisins?
2. Do 7 acorns weigh more than 5 marbles?

The teacher would often ask children to show products they had created and tell the class what they had done. Then, if they were capable, the teacher would suggest they write stories in their notebooks about their creation. If they were not able to write, the teacher might write their stories for them, then let the children illustrate these passages with pictures or drawings, and later have them "read" their stories to the class. Thus, many direct experiences children had with class materials and equipment became the stimuli for their talking, writing, and reading at later times.

The remainder of the school day was taken up with (a) games and physical play or movement activities, in outside areas when the weather permitted or in the large multipurpose room when it did not; (b) group stories and discussions; (c) "show-and-tell" periods when accomplishments and experiences from other periods were shared, as well as out-of-school experiences; and (d) brief, school-wide assemblies. Frequently, groups from several classes might be combined for particular purposes so that all children had some direct contact with teachers other than their own. Also, several groups might be combined to watch an educational television show on some particular subject. I saw several such lessons during my visit—one dealing with different kinds of time units, for example.

During independent activity periods, children were usually free to engage in whatever activities they wished, to shift from one activity to another when they desired a change, to move about the room and even the building as they saw fit, to talk with other children or watch them at work, and in general to determine how they would spend their time. This apparent freedom had certain general limits, however. Children were expected to put back materials and equipment they had been using and usually were not permitted to disrupt the ongoing activity of others. Before climbing on playground equipment they were supposed to put on special soft-sole shoes, and before painting or working with clay they were required to put on smocks to protect their clothes.

Teaching Style and General Expectancies

As already indicated, much of the teacher's behavior consisted of brief encounters with one child or a small group of children as she inspected their work, monitored their play, and listened to them read. Her questions, directions, suggestions, and reinforcements usually related directly to the specific tasks with which children were occupied. Because of this rather informal style of teaching, I kept track of the particular nature of directions given and behaviors reinforced, in order to discern whatever teacher expectancies seemed to be expressed most often. Several became apparent:

1. Children were generally expected to *have something to do*. The teacher would usually ask a child what he was doing if she noticed him wandering aimlessly around the room or holding an extended conversation with another child who was busy at his own task. At the beginning of independent activity periods the teacher almost always asked if anyone did not know what he planned to do, and then she discussed the options with him until one was selected.

2. Children were generally expected to *finish something already started before starting something else*. If a child showed the teacher a picture he was painting of some flowers, for instance, she might ask him what color he wanted for the sky or what other kinds of things grew in his garden. Although questions were raised in this fashion, the teacher did not insist on particular details being added; but the child of his own volition often added to his picture items he had mentioned in response to her questions.

3. Children were expected to *have something tangible to show or tell to account for time spent*. Notebooks were inspected frequently, and creative products were displayed before the group, with the teacher usually remarking about the progress made.

4. Children were expected to *take care of materials being used and return items to their proper place and condition after using them*. Since it was late in the school year, I saw children already habituated to proper cleanup patterns; but occasionally, as a reminder of this expectancy, I heard the teacher ask who had been using something that was left out.

5. Children were expected to *participate in group discussion and permit others to talk*. Many times when one child was telling about an experience that others had shared, the teacher would stop others from talking until the target child was finished.

Brown and Precious (1968) and Silberman (1970), among others, have commented on the highly active role of the British infant school teacher, especially as it contrasts with the laissez-faire manner advocated by Holt (1967), Kohl (1969), and many other educational critics or as it was portrayed in the American child-centered schools of the 1920's and 1930's. Resnick's data (1972) generally confirm this high teacher activity rate in the school she studied, with teachers having approximately one extended interaction (usually teacher-initiated) and from four to eight brief interactions (usually child-initiated) with various children every 3 minutes.

I tallied teacher interaction patterns for two 10-minute periods in each of four classrooms and found a slightly higher rate of teacher activity than Resnick did: i.e., approximately three per minute during regular independent-activity periods. During group discussions, when teachers were eliciting news, reactions, and experience-sharing from children, this rate was usually even greater (see the analysis of teacher questioning patterns below).

I recorded teacher behavior much more extensively on the PROSE instrument in two classrooms *(a)* at the end of each 100-second cycle in which a child was observed (Figure 2: cycle category set 2) and *(b)* at those moments when a target child was observed in contact with the teacher (Figure 1: behavior category set 3). For the two teachers combined, over three out of five observations found the teacher in a relatively nondirective role, supervising children's activities, acting as a resource person when children initiated contact, and being concerned with behavior management if necessary. Another 11 percent of the time she was not even in contact with the children, for she was either out of the room or busy with other matters. She was involved only about one-fourth of the time either in discussion leadership or in showing, telling, or leading a large segment of the class in some group activity. Both the PROSE data and the teacher interaction tallies made in three classrooms confirmed the fact that children initiated contact with teachers more often than teachers initiated contact with children. In one classroom, C-initiated was over three times as frequent as T-initiated interaction. These findings support the general notion that children had a great deal of independence of action.

The precise teacher behavior exhibited in classrooms A and B was recorded more explicitly on behavior category set 3 (Figure 1). Overall, *listening and questioning* was the most frequently occurring type, accounting for approximately three out of every five of teacher A's actions and one out of every four of teacher B's actions. A significant difference (p .05) was found between the two teachers, with teacher B making somewhat greater use of *showing-telling* and *controlling* categories and less use of the *listening-questioning* type of behavior.

The PROSE instrument provides space for coding a child's contacts not only with his regular teacher but with other adults as well. On many days a teacher trainee or a teen-age aide was also present in most classrooms. Occasionally, classes or parts of classes were combined for particular purposes under the direction of another teacher in the same building. The head teacher often conducted assembly programs, for instance, involving the entire school. Not infrequently the narrator of a radio or television program represented the adult instructional director of a class, with the regular teachers in a subsidiary role. In all, 57 contacts with other such adults (38.3 percent of all adult contacts) were observed for target children in teacher A's class, and 38 contacts (24.1 percent of all adult contacts) in teacher B's class. The predominant nature of these other adult contacts was of the *showing-telling* and *controlling* varieties (84.3 percent with teacher A's class, and 89.5 percent with teacher B's class). This finding was not surprising, since the primary purpose for regrouping classes or exposing them to other teachers was to conduct instruction for particular purposes.

Teacher Questioning

As indicated above, the dominant teacher activity in classroom A was the *listening-questioning* pattern. Often this took the form of a child's showing his teacher something he was working on; asking for assistance, information, or permission; or telling about an experience he had. Although the teacher occasionally provided information, reaction, or direction, more often her response consisted of raising questions designed to draw the child out further with respect to his feelings, plans, or experiences. Hughes (1959) maintains that such eliciting of additional thinking in response to students' bringing up potential instructional content represents the essence of good teaching. In the classrooms she studied, however, she found it occurred infrequently and accounted for less than 20 percent of most teachers'.behavior.

Because of the greater evidence for this type of behavior in the British infant school, it seemed important to study the specific types of questions teachers raised. I made a tape recording, therefore, of a "show-and-tell" class discussion that teacher A conducted one Monday morning. Although weekend experiences constituted a major portion of the discussion, children were permitted to bring up anything that seemed important to them. Opening questions such as "Who has something he wants to tell us?" encouraged them to talk. The teacher would ask the child responding a number of questions about the experience, until a rather full elaboration of its details was forthcoming. Typically, this listening and questioning on the teacher's part took the form of an open dialogue between child and teacher; other children were permitted to ask questions, furnish additional details (if they had been involved also), and make related comments only after the responding child seemed to have completed his story. The teacher would often hush another child momentarily with such remarks as "We are listening to John now; your turn will come." At other times she would purposefully bring other children into the discussion by asking such questions as "Who else has been to see the Cutty Sark?" (i.e., the item being described).

This particular morning the show-and-tell period was kept going for over an hour, until almost all forty children had shared one or more experiences and until obvious restlessness appeared.* The types and frequency of questions and comments made by the teacher during one interval of 10 minutes, 18 seconds and a second interval of 8 minutes, 15 seconds are presented in Table 1.

Table 1. Types of Questions and Comments of Teacher A
during Two Approximately 10-Minute Intervals
within a "Show-and-Tell" Discussion

Type of Question or Comment		First Interval		Second Interval	
No.	Description	f	%	f	%
1	asks child for news	4	5	4	6
2	repeats C's statement or feeling, or again asks child what he said	13	15	13	19
3	asks for specific information about the event, child, or family	33	38	21	30
4	asks open-endedly for more detail	0	0	0	0
5	asks for C's reaction or feeling	3	4	3	4
6	asks other children whether they've had similar experiences	3	4	3	4
7	makes evaluation of events	2	2	6	9
8	gives information herself	3	4	11	16
9	speculates on event details	8	9	0	0
10	gives spontaneous reaction	9	10	6	9
11	other T comments	8	9	2	3
	Total no. of audible comments	86	100	69	100

It is apparent that, although the greatest number of questions asked were *requests for more specific details* (No. 3) about the event being described or related information regarding the child or his family, the teacher posed a considerable variety of questions and comments in the course of this discussion. Quite often (15 and 19 percent) she merely asked the child to *repeat what he had said* (No. 2; "What did you say?") or asked automatically for reaffirmation of a statement or feeling expressed ("Did you?" "Was she?"). Spontaneous evaluative reactions (No. 10; "I see." "How lovely!") constituted 9 to 10 percent of her remarks and tended to keep the child talking, probably by providing reinforcement for what he was saying. Speculating on event details (No. 9) oc-

* The teacher kept this session going considerably longer than usual in order to provide me with a full record. Despite this dissimilarity from her usual pattern of questioning, no other differences were apparent. A high consistency of teacher questioning patterns (r .80) was found between two separate 10-minute periods during the hour, even though topics and children reporting were different.

curred more frequently in the first than in the second discussion sequence, most likely reflecting differences in the storytelling abilities of children. With one rather slow-speaking child particularly, the teacher tended to anticipate words or phrases before they were uttered. ("You fell in the water." "You didn't dare tell your mother.") This anticipation did not seem to cause the child to stop telling his story; he merely nodded yes or no, or corrected the teacher if she were wrong, and then continued.

The rather low percentage of *comments directed toward other children* (No. 11, excluding No. 6 to which they were supposed to respond) exemplifies the dialogue quality of the interaction with the one child who was speaking at the time. This also reflects the general attention other children had in this dialogue, since statements directing other children to listen or wait their turn to speak were classified here.

One other finding with regard to the teacher's questioning was its high rate of occurrence. An average of 8.3 teacher comments or questions was made per minute during both show-and-tell episodes analyzed, which was over twice the rate of overall teacher interaction reported earlier for independent-activity periods.

Instructional Teaching and Content

Much has already been said in regard to the informal nature of teaching and the manner in which teachers often allowed and encouraged pupils to choose what they would do or talk about. Some of the time, however, more formal instruction and control prevailed, in which teachers or other adults presented the children with information, read stories, led group discussions, or otherwise directed class activities closely.

Additional data reporting instructional patterns and emphasis were recorded on appropriate PROSE cycle categories (Figure 2). These categories were designed to cover some of the classroom setting variables and the kinds of materials and equipment used by the child. Particularly relevant were notations made regarding the instructional content area receiving general emphasis. Table 2 presents these data as recorded in the two classrooms for 108 cycles each.

The most obvious finding was further documentation of statements made earlier that *independent activity* (i.e., *free play)* accounted for half of the daily schedule.* This fact emphasizes one of the weaknesses of PROSE, however, as a recording instrument for full content coverage in an open school. During independent activity, children select from among the many options available those which they will attempt. Most of these options, of course, lie within other content areas. Therefore

*Exclusive of the 1½-hour lunch and recreation period.

Table 2. Number of Cycles Characterized Predominantly by
Particular Content Areas
(Based on cycle category set 1 of PROSE)

Content Area	Teacher A	Teacher B
Arithmetic	0	2
Art or Craft	1	0
Exercise or physical games	5	1
Free play (independent activity)	53	55
Health, hygiene	1	0
Language	20	23
Music, rhythm	0	10
Rest of snack*	0	0
Routine, transition	14	10
Science	11	0
Sensation	0	0
Social skills	0	0
Social studies	1	0
Assembly†	1	3
Not recorded†	1	4
Total no. of cycles	108	108

* Children drank milk or otherwise snacked whenever they chose after milk or food was delivered to the room during independent-activity periods. The observer did not record behavior during the 1½-hour lunch and recreation period because many children went home during this time.

† Added categories to account for all cycles

a particular child may choose to make a painting (*art* or *craft* category), while another may choose some number games (*arithmetic* category). For a more complete assessment of content emphasis, an observer would have to record the areas each child was engaged in, rather than the overall instructional area which the PROSE manual suggests.

In spite of this limitation, certain generalizations can be drawn from Table 2. *Language* was the area which received greatest emphasis during formal class instruction. Generally I classified class discussions as language-usage periods unless they were clearly related to specific content areas. I also classified story reading, word games, and show-and-tell periods, where the emphasis was primarily on eliciting child verbalization, as language activities. Overall, I found language usage occupying approximately one-fifth of the total time in each room. *Science* received greater formal instructional emphasis than other particular subject matter fields in one class, at least on the days observed, and *music* or *rhythm* in the other. It should be obvious, however, that because of the PROSE limitations indicated above, the figures reported in Table 2 underestimate the amount of time children actually spent on various types of traditional subject matter.

Further elaboration of the content emphases can be found in the sections below which relate to pupil behavior and the nature of tasks, equipment, and materials to which children were exposed. Even there, however, a complete inventory of tasks and materials was not attempted.

Manifest Teacher Affect

The final analysis of teacher behavior related to classroom climate in general and to expressed teacher affect in particular. Although much can be surmised already from the preceding reports of classroom organization and teaching patterns, several additional sets of data are particularly relevant.

Following each 100-second behavior cycle, I rated the emotional and motivational state of the class as a whole during that cycle (Figure 2, No. 5). The main generalization to be drawn from these ratings was the predominance of a *noisy and busy* atmosphere over other categories. I used this category for 61 percent and the *quiet and busy* category for 23 percent of the classifications, so that in the eyes of the observer, children seemed to be busy and task-oriented most of the time, even though considerable talking or other sounds were also in evidence. The children, as a group, were almost never idle; nor did they display any observable tension. Admittedly, this set of judgments requires a more quantitative type of rating than probably any other PROSE scale. The validity of these estimates, however, was substantially established by some of the pupil behavior findings described below, which report the amount of behavior characterized as *distracted, responding to internal stimuli* and *disrupting* (Figure 1, No. 8) and the quality of peer interaction occurring (Figure 1, Nos. 4, 5).

Cycle category set 7 (Figure 2) requires checking any instances of teachers *calling for quiet, threatening children, losing their tempers, laughing with pupils,* or *using physical restraint*. In all 216 behavioral cycles, I saw teacher A calling for quiet five times and none of the other behaviors from either teacher. Overall signs of class disorganization or turmoil seemed almost neglible.

The first and last categories of behavior set 3 (Figure 1) proved rather useless, even though one might expect these to be among the best indicators of classroom climate. At no time during the 212 moments when I saw a target child in contact with his teacher was she exhibiting *positive* affect toward him or her, and only twice did I observe a teacher exhibiting *negative* affect—even though these two categories, according to the PROSE instructions, were to be given recording precedence over other categories when observed. Other users of PROSE have also reported very little display of teacher affect at those particular instants when a target child was in contact with his teacher.

Perhaps the most discriminating data with respect to teaching climate came from the teacher interaction checklist which was used in four classrooms. The means of teacher reinforcement was primarily verbal, with three-fourths of the positive and 20 of the 21 negative reinforcements being direct comments to children. Contact and gestures accounted for the remaining reinforcements coded. Overall, more than twice as much *approval* as *disapproval* was observed. Teacher A provided more than three times as much approval as disapproval, and teacher B exhibited no evidence whatever of disapproval. Only one teacher provided more disapproval than approval during the relatively brief period of observation.

Pupil Behavior

Sufficient descriptive data are available from the PROSE notations to provide a reasonably full picture of how target pupils spent their time. A total of 45 observations (9 cycles of 5 behaviors) were recorded in the manner described earlier for each of the 24 children.

At a given moment, four mutually exclusive possibilities existed for the overall classification of a child's behavior: (a) he was in contact with an adult (No. 1); (b) he was in contact with a peer (No. 4); (c) he was involved with an appropriate task; or (d) he was distracted, responding to internal stimuli, working on an inappropriate task, or actively disrupting others (No. 8, exclusive of the cooperating category). Table 3 presents the number of behaviors classified for each child for each of these possibilities.

Over the entire group of 1,080 observations, children were found to be (a) in contact with an adult 29 percent of the time; (b) in contact with a peer 20 percent; (c) involved with an appropriate task 28 percent; and (d) distracted, responding to internal stimuli (i.e., wandering aimlessly or daydreaming), or working on an inappropriate task 22 percent of the time. No significant differences (p .05) were found between the two classrooms in the general distribution of behavior among these four general types of behavior, although considerable variation was apparent among the individual children. Obviously, any attempt to explain learning outcomes must take into account these differences in children's school experiences as well as the fact that the types of tasks they face and, to a somewhat lesser extent, the quality of their peer interactions are probably influences as important as the nature of their contacts with teachers.

Table 3. The Number of Classifications
of Each General Type of Behavior for
Each Target Child

Child	Adult Contact	Peer Contact	Task Involved	Distracted Etc.
A—B1*	19	5	7	14
A—B2	19	0	8	18
A—B3	8	15	11	11
A—B4	13	4	15	13
A—B5	15	11	12	7
A—B6	9	16	14	6
A—G1	5	13	21	6
A—G2	12	8	17	8
A—G3	8	11	16	10
A—G4	18	10	9	8
A—G5	14	4	20	7
A—G6	19	3	4	19
Subtotals Class A	159	100	154	127
B—B1	33	2	2	8
B—B2	4	15	13	13
B—B3	13	5	11	16
B—B4	9	19	0	17
B—B5	11	11	12	11
B—B6	11	3	23	8
B—G1	2	16	22	5
B—G2	8	11	20	6
B—G3	21	2	18	4
B—G4	23	7	4	11
B—G5	18	7	15	5
B—G6	5	22	11	7
Subtotals Class B	158	120	151	111
Totals both classes	317 (29.3)	220 (20.4)	305 (28.2) (Grand T)	238 (22.1) 1080

*The first row of entries relates to boy 1 in teacher A's classroom.

While directly comparable data on similar-age children are not yet available from other schools, PROSE data are beginning to appear in various research reports which suggest that major differences between schools or programs may be uncovered through such information. The amount of peer interaction found in the British school (i.e., 20.4 percent) was almost twice that reported in two sets of data covering a rather substantial number of preschool classrooms for four- and five-year-old American children (Griffith et al., 1971; ETS, 1969). Also, a rather brief set of PROSE observations made recently by Massey (1972) in second- and eighth-grade Russian classrooms indicated almost no peer interaction. Obviously, differences in the ages of children and perhaps some differences in the use of PROSE preclude stating strong inferences regarding program differences at this time, but the possibilities for solid comparative research in the future would seem promising.

Adult Contacts

Behavior category 1 (Figure 1) data revealed that almost two-thirds of the pupil-adult contacts were made as the adult was attending to a group of children of which the target child was a member. This could have been only a two-person group, a larger group, or the entire class. The target child was singled out in less than 5 percent of the observations with the adult attending to him differently from any other child (STAR category). This finding is not surprising when one considers the rather large number of children present in the classrooms (37–40). Either a target child was trying to initiate adult contact, or an adult was already responding to his initiated contact, during 10 percent of the observations. The remaining category—i.e., *listening* or *watching*—accounted for the other 20 percent of adult contacts.

Peer Contacts

Target children initiated approximately one-third of the peer contacts, and well over half were categorized as *cooperative* behaviors in relation to the actions of the peers involved. The general harmonious nature of these relationships was further borne out by the very small amount of *aggressiveness, withdrawing,* or *resisting* observed. The combined totals for these latter three categories accounted for less than 7 percent of all pupil-pupil contacts.

Task Involvement and the Nature of Tasks

Several category sets provided data relevant to the nature of tasks and related pupil involvement. As indicated above, pupils were not in direct contact with peers or adults during approximately half of the observations. I observed them in some type of appropriate behavior, either self-selected or teacher-designated, for over half of this latter amount (28 percent of the total). I coded the children as engaged in inappropriate behavior or, at least, as not actively working on what was expected of them during 22 percent of all observations.

The vast majority of observations in which category set 8 (Figure 1) was not used were pupil-pupil contacts. The manual requires the use of this category for adult-contact and material-contact situations only.

Overall, children were observed to be *cooperating* 71 percent of the times in which category set 8 was used. *Disrupting* behavior was nonexistent, and *working on other activities* was almost neglible. Being *distracted* (13 percent), often momentarily, and *responding to internal stimuli* (15 percent) accounted for almost all the inattention to tasks and ongoing activities. The relatively high amount of attention to tasks and ongoing activities provides additional documentation for the generalization made earlier that, despite considerable noise, pupils were usually busily engaged in appropriate behavior and the classroom climate was that of purposeful industry.

Consistent with the notion that considerable freedom of expression prevails in infant schools, tasks and activities permitting *divergent* responses were the most frequently observed type in each of the classrooms. Overall, they accounted for 38 percent of the task categorizations, whereas *convergent* tasks represented 29 percent of the classifications; *kinesthetic,* 14 percent; *useful work,* 13 percent; and *fantasy,* 6 percent. In the two previously mentioned studies of American preschool classrooms (Griffith et al., 1971; ETS, 1969), convergent tasks were most frequently observed. In one study children were involved with divergent tasks an average of 25 percent of the time in eight "basic" classrooms and, as might be expected, only 9 percent of the time in two Montessori classes (same teacher). In the other study of 30 to 40 classes, they were involved with divergent tasks an average of 34 percent of the time—only slightly less than in the British school. Again dissimilarities in research methodology, program objectives, and ages of the children suggest caution in interpretation of these various differences.

A more recent study (1973) of four kindergarten classes in two Montessori schools produced highly discrepant findings in regard to task emphasis (Brandt, Carrico, and Massey, unpublished). In one school children were occupied with divergent tasks only 23 percent of the time observed, but in the other school 84 percent of the observations revealed divergent activity. Apparently the latter teachers permitted considerable use of Montessori materials in other than the tightly prescribed ways for which they had been designed. Such inconsistencies between one school and another, despite similar program labels, dramatize the importance of empirical monitoring in order to identify the true nature of a school program.

Primary-age youngsters are noted for their high rate of activity and energy expenditure. PROSE category set 9 (Figure 1) provided data with respect to the locomotion and estimated physical-activity levels of target pupils. Surprisingly perhaps, physical activity was not so great as anticipated. I saw *no activity* (i.e., no movement) at all during 59 percent of the time that target children's behavior was being recorded. I saw actual *locomotion* only 16 percent of the time. Undoubtedly these figures reflect the extensive task involvement mentioned earlier, since there was no general expectancy that children remain inactive or not move around.

Two sets of cycle categories provided additional information relevant to the types of activities pupils experienced. For one of these (Figure 2, No. 6), I merely checked whichever of the 27 specific behaviors listed I had observed for the target pupil during the 100-second interval I had been watching him. None, one, or several categories might have been noted. Although most behaviors listed in cycle category set 6 had to do with either the child's own behavior patterns or happenings to him, several reflected in part the types of activities he was engaged in. For example, I observed target pupils *using words* in approximately one-third of the total 216 cycles. I saw them *using numbers* during only seven cycles, and performing chores or running errands just once.

The other relevant cycle category (No. 8) provided considerably more task information. On an extensive list of equipment and materials, I checked those which target pupils made use of during observation cycles. *Books* and *writing materials* were the most frequently used items in both classrooms; they were used half as much as all other types of materials combined. Clay, paint, and other art materials were the next most frequently used items. Perhaps the most sweeping generalization to be made from cycle category set 8 data is that children made use of a great variety of materials and equipment during the several days of observation. The only type of equipment listed that I did not see target children use at all during the observation cycles was *wheel toys*.

Manifest Affect of Pupils

Silberman (1970), among others, waxed greatly enthusiastic over the happiness and joy he found British pupils displaying in the course of their infant school activity. PROSE category set 11 (Figure 1) provided information about children's spontaneous reactions to some of their experiences. In addition, many of the specific behaviors contained in cycle category set 6 (Figure 2) also produced affective notations *(cried, sang or talked to self, showed affection to adults or peers,* for example).

Although my observations generally supported Silberman's evaluation, I made rather limited use of these categories overall. I saw and recorded only 20 manifestations of strong feelings on category set 11 for target children, all of them positive. This is not a large number when one considers the total number of behavioral episodes covered (namely, 1,080), but what affect was expressed was clearly positive. In addition, I recorded *sang or talked to self* in 8 out of the 216 cycles. During these cycles, furthermore, I observed no instances of a target child *crying, losing his temper, showing fear,* or otherwise expressing hostile or negative feelings.

Differences among Pupils

Differences among children were quite evident. The inverse factor analysis performed on 38 pupil behavior variables is too technical to present here, but it appears in the original report (Brandt, 1972). Some generalizations seem warranted, however, especially those related to the "family grouping" practice, in which five-, six-, and seven-year-olds were placed in the same classrooms. Those children who had most contact with adults tended to be older and more cooperative in relation to what they were supposed to be doing; and yet, paradoxically perhaps, less task-involved overall. The greatest amount of their adult contact was as part of a group and in a listening-watching role. Compared with other children, they had less overall peer interaction; less involvement with numbers, puzzles, or arts and crafts; and less activity with divergent tasks generally.

Some children had considerably more peer interaction than others. Quite understandably, these same children were more distracted generally and less task-involved, cooperative, or attentive overall.

Some children tended rather consistently to be less active than others. I observed them sitting or standing still more often, displaying less kinesthetic activity, playing on gym equipment less often, and even drinking or eating less frequently during the day (excluding lunchtime). In brief, the extensive freedom and informal nature of the school apparently encouraged, or at least permitted, a wide range of pupil behavior patterns. The uniqueness of each child was quite detectable.

Differences between Classrooms

Just as no two children were alike, differences were found in teaching style and emphasis and in the way classrooms were organized. While the findings reported earlier represent central tendency descriptions of infant school life, as I saw it, considerable variation was also noted from day to day and class to class. The two classes studied closely may have been more alike than different overall; yet differences between them were clearly evident for both teachers and pupils. Statistically significant teacher and class differences are presented in Table 4, hopefully to dispel the simplistic notion that there is only one instructional pattern which characterizes infant school teaching. Although certain activity patterns probably distinguish many British infant schools from other types of schools, some departure from these modal characteristics is only to be expected.

Table 4. Differences between Classroom A and Classroom B

Classroom A	Data Source	Classroom B
General pace of activity & interaction:		
T rate of reinforcement*	Interaction Checklist	
T use of gesture & contact reinforcement	Interaction Checklist	
C movement & locomotion	Fig. 1—No. 9	C in quiet activity
C in kinesthetic & work tasks	Fig. 1—No. 10	C in fantasy activity
Exercise & games activity	Fig. 2—No. 1	
C use of gym equipment	Fig. 2—No. 8	C use of musical instruments
Style of teaching:		
C-initiated & individual adult contact	Fig. 1—No. 1	
T listens & questions	Fig. 1—No. 3	T shows—tells
T supervises, manages is resource person	Fig. 2—No. 2	T shows—tells— controls
Science activity	Fig. 2—No. 1	Music & rhythm activity

*Characteristics listed are those in which significant classroom differences were found. For example, teacher A exhibited a higher rate of reinforcement than teacher B as recorded on the Interaction Checklist, whereas Classroom B children engaged in quiet activity and fantasy play more often as measured by PROSE categories 9 and 10.

The main differences represented in the Table 4 summary of findings center around *(a)* the rate of activity and interchange and *(b)* general teaching style. The pace of activity was somewhat faster in classroom A, with children moving about the room more frequently, playing on gym equipment and taking part in physical games more often, and engaging in a greater amount of kinesthetic activity and routine work (e.g., sweeping the floor). The average noise level was also higher, even to the point where teacher A called for quiet five times. (Teacher B never did this during an observation cycle.) Undoubtedly the greater activity level in classroom A reflected this teacher's own high rate of activity, especially her reactivity to children as they initiated contact with her. My tallies on the teacher interaction checklist indicated that she provided almost as much reinforcement during a 20-minute period as the other three teachers combined, including B (31 compared with 42 instances).

In matters of teaching style, teacher A spent more time listening to children and questioning them about their work. She was a supervisor, class manager, and resource person two-thirds of the time, while children took part in various individual and small-group activities. Although teacher B assumed the same roles about half the time, she did spend more time than teacher A showing and telling children something. Perhaps one reason teacher A did so little showing and telling herself is that she made greater use of other adults (other teachers, aides, etc.) for this purpose.

Thus, classroom A utilized team-teaching patterns to a somewhat greater extent than classroom B. More individualized instruction also occurred in classroom A, as evidenced by more child-initiated adult contact and more individual adult attention to the target child. Such differences, however, were primarily in degree rather than kind, and most other comparisons indicated the two classrooms were quite similar with respect to the general findings already noted.

Summary

Three weeks of data gathering with a variety of observational procedures provided an extensive empirical description of many instructional and learning activities. Both teacher and pupil behaviors were observed in considerable detail. The greatest amount of data came from two classrooms and from stratified random samples of children in these rooms. Thus, it was possible to compare teacher and pupil behaviors in these rooms and to examine similarities and differences among children, as well as age, sex, and classroom differences.

Several findings seem especially noteworthy: (1) Certain teacher expectancies were apparent in directions given and behavior reinforced. For example, children were generally expected to have something to do; to finish one task before starting another; to have something tangible for showing or telling about as a result of time spent; to care for materials and return them to their proper places after use; and to participate in group discussions. (2) For approximately half of each school day, children were involved in projects and activities of their own choosing, while their teachers provided general supervisory and tutorial assistance.

(3) Overall, listening to children and raising questions about their activities and progress on various tasks was the most dominant type of teacher activity during these periods, although (4) some teacher differences were apparent in the amount of showing-telling and controlling behavior they exhibited in contrast to listening and questioning. The specific style of questioning by teacher A was analyzed in some detail. The pace of class activity was also somewhat faster in teacher A's than in teacher B's room.

Among the several findings reported about pupil behavior, perhaps the most important pertains to the distribution of their interactions with adults, peers, and tasks. (5) Over the entire school day they interacted or were involved with an adult 29 percent of the time, on the average; with a peer, 20 percent; with appropriate tasks, 28 percent; and they were distracted, responded to internal stimuli, or worked on inappropriate tasks 22 percent of the time. (6) In each classroom they were involved with tasks which permitted divergent responses to be made more than with any other type of task. (7) Considerable variation in behavior patterns was evident among the children.

Discussion of these and other findings is presented in the main body of the paper. Determining how typical this particular infant school is of other British primary schools or how different it is from other types of early childhood schools remains an important question for future research.

References

Brandt, R. M., "An Observational Investigation of Instruction and Behavior in an Informal British Infant School," paper presented at the meeting of the American Educational Research Association, Chicago, April 1972.

Brandt, R. M., M. F. Carrico, and D. G. Massey, *Study of Montessori Schools.* (Unpublished.)

Brown, M., and N. Precious, *The Integrated Day in the Primary School.* London: Ward Lock Educational, 1968; New York: Agathon Press, 1969.

Carrico, M. F., and D. G. Massey, *PROSE II* (revision of D. M. Medley et al., *The Personal Record of School Experiences: A Manual for PROSE Recorders).* Charlottesville: University of Virginia, January 1973 (photocopied).

Cushen, M. E., *Educational Aids in the Infant School.* London: Matthews, Drew & Shelbourne Ltd., 1966.

ETS—Head Start Longitudinal Study of Disadvantaged Children and Their First School Experiences, *From Theory to Operations,* Progress report ETS-69-12. Princeton, N.J.: Educational Testing Service, 1969.

Griffith, L. W., F. W. Neff, and W. M. Ahlstrom, *Evaluation of Early Childhood Education, a Model Cities-Supported Preschool Program.* Kansas City, Mo.: Institute for Community Studies, September 1971.

Holt, J., *How Children Learn.* New York: Pitman, 1967.

Howson, G. (ed.), *Children at School: Primary Education in Britain Today.* London:

Heineman Educational Books, Ltd.; New York: Teachers College Press, 1969.

Hughes, M. M., and associates. *The Assessment of the Quality of Teaching: A Research Report.* U. S. Office of Education Research Project No. 353. Salt Lake City: University of Utah, 1959.

Kohl, H. R., *The Open Classroom.* New York: The New York Review, 1969.

Massey, D. G., "Education in the Soviet Union," unpublished, 1972 (mimeographed).

Medley, D. M., T. J. Quirk, C. G. Schluck, and N. P. Ames, *The Personal Record of School Experiences: A Manual for PROSE Recorders.* Princeton, N.J.: Educational Testing Service, June 1971.

Medley, D. M., C. G. Schluck, and N. P. Ames, *Recording Individual Pupil Experiences in the Classroom: A Manual for PROSE Recorders.* Princeton, N.J.: Educational Testing Service, December 1968.

Resnick, L. B., "Teacher Behavior in an Informal British Infant School," *The School Review,* 1972, *81,* 63–83.

Ridgway, L., and I. Lawton, *Family Grouping in the Primary Schools.* London: Ward Lock Educational, 1968; New York: Agathon Press, 1969.

Rogers, V. R., (ed.), *Teaching in the British Primary School.* London: Collier-Macmillan Ltd., 1970.

Sherman, D. A., *The Relationship of Teacher Behavior and Child Behavior of Four and Five Year Old Black Disadvantaged Children During Distar and Non-Distar Sessions.* Unpublished doctoral dissertation, University of Virginia, 1971.

Silberman, C. E., *Crisis in the Classroom.* New York: Random House, 1970.

CHAPTER 7

Assessment of Openness in Program Structures

John Dopyera, *Pacific Oaks College*
Margaret Lay, *Syracuse University*

THE PURPOSES of this chapter are threefold: (1) to propose that dimensional analysis of programs is necessary to eventual understanding of program effects; (2) to describe one useful dimension, program openness, which may be particularly pertinent to proponents of open education programs; (3) to describe a particular instrument useful in measuring the dimension of program openness, the Open Program Structure Index (OPSI), and to report on its uses to date.

Need for Dimensionalization

Researchers seem generally to have taken the approach that each program type (such as the open education program or the Montessori program or other prototypic models) has a particular differentiating configuration. As a corollary, the most parsimonious approach to program research is thus, first, to carefully delineate the particular configuration and, second, to measure and classify programs on the basis of their closeness to that configuration or their deviation from it. According to this approach, those programs which have all the specified features within a certain delimited range can qualify to be designated as the program in focus. Any others outside the delimited range or with missing configural features do not qualify. These latter, despite the degree to which they may be very like the prototype in many respects, could only be considered as controls or comparison groups in the research undertaken on program effects. The studies typically conducted lump child achievement or other outcome data according to the global program designation. There is often thus as much *within* program variation as there is *between* program variation on a host of potentially influential dimensions in programs being compared. With this potential confounding, it is not surprising that so little evidence exists in support of the relative advantages of one program over another. When global comparisons are made, it is often the case that "different" programs are in fact *not* being compared at all.

The authors of this paper concur with the utility of identifying parameters of prototypic program configurations. We further agree that a program's claims to "openness," for example, require examination to show whether the program essentially models the consensual definition of an "open program." We doubt, however, the final utility of viewing programs globally as an approach to evaluation of program effects. We believe a more productive strategy will be to dimensionalize, or to identify aspects of programming that can serve as effective dimensions for differentiation and that are equally applicable to examining *any* operating program.

There are several basic premises which underlie our efforts. We hold that it is impossible to draw any conclusions about program outcomes for child participants unless there is assessment of the program as it is actually encountered by children. We would strive for examination of differential effects as functions of difference of what is encountered. Second, we view openness as a dimension which can be quantitatively assessed within any program, and we would not assume that a program is "open" or "closed" unless we actually indexed the extent of openness on specific criteria. And, third, we tend to view the assessment of openness as relevant in *any* program context, not only in those especially set up for experimental comparison of "open" versus another kind of program.

As noted, we accept the classification of programs by identifiable configurations. Additionally, we assert that it is possible to dimensionalize and quantitatively assess program components. We anticipate that eventual understanding of program influences on participants will be a function of this kind of assessment. Dimensionalization and assessment alone, it should be remarked, are not sufficient to produce that understanding. Rather, we see their use as a necessary stage in gaining fuller awareness of program effects.

Nature of Program Openness

We are proposing "openness" as a real, identifiable characteristic of programs that is possible and important to dimensionalize and assess. The concept of openness which seems most appropriate for program assessment involves delineation of the degrees of freedom and/or options available to the program participant. Degrees of freedom or options a child participant has within a program refer, in our view, to the relationship between the child's needs hypothetically present at any point in time and the program's accommodation of those needs. The question we ask is "If a child has a need, what is the probability that the program can or will accommodate that need without censure or contingency?"

Degrees of freedom and options may, of course, vary from child to child within a program. On the other hand, regardless of child-to-child variation, there is a point beyond which no further degrees of freedom or options exist *for any child within a given program*. We refer to this point as the *ceiling factor*. There may be variation within this ceiling effect, from child to child, in degrees of freedom and options, but not beyond this point. We assume that this ceiling factor on the dimension of openness is knowable and assessable and that it relates to and influences child learning outcomes.

Although we recognize the contributions of other factors (e.g., material richness, teacher repertoire, consistency, participant density) and although we strongly advocate the inclusion of these components in program evaluation efforts, our immediate concern has been with an examination of the ceiling factor imposed by the teacher on children's options or degrees of freedom. This single component of openness is the focus of the remainder of this study.

The Influence of Teachers' Assumptions

The basis of the work we have done to date in assessing ceiling factor stems from our concepts of the stable influences of assumptions. This focus is within the frame of reference of sociopsychological "cognitive congruence" or "balance" models. Since this is not a common approach to research on programs, there is a need to elaborate why assumption and congruence theory is useful in relating how the teacher manages the dynamics of classroom structure and processes.

Assumptions, as we use this concept, refer to standards of appropriateness which have been internalized by an individual. These standards of appropriateness vary in intensity; may refer to any behavior of self or others, events, activities, or phenomena; and vary from individual to individual and within an individual over time and across situations. As we conceive them, assumptions do, however, function in a stabilizing manner for individuals. In a sense an individual's assumptions are his or her "gyroscope." Assumptions refer to the way "the world" ought to be. When an individual perceives a behavior or an event which is discrepant from the way he or she assumes "things" ought to be, an emotional or motivational state is aroused which is goal-directed. The goal is to reduce the discrepancy between what is perceived and the standards or assumptions held.

Examples abound in personal and professional lives. Teacher A in a preschool situation sees a child go to the jungle gym and begin to climb up, yelling "Look at me!" The teacher stops current activity, runs over to the child, extracts him or her from the apparatus, and says, "You shouldn't climb so high. You'll hurt yourself." Teacher B watches a child under similar circumstances climb to the top, yells out, etc., and then smiles at the child and waves back. Teachers A and B are both concerned about the child's safety or possible harm. However, they have different thresholds for what constitutes a potentially harmful situation; that is, they hold different assumptions or standards. For teacher A, a child who was a few feet off the ground was behaving in a manner discrepant with an assumption regarding "safe." For teacher B, this child's behavior was not discrepant. On the other hand, were the child walking toward a whirling propeller of an airplane, his or her behavior would in all probability be considered discrepant by both teachers, and each of them would intervene.

The use of the concept of assumptions within a cognitive-discrepancy or balance model allows for an examination and cataloguing of a great variety of behaviors shown by adults working with children. At the same time, application of this concept helps to begin to make sense out of a wide array of teacher behaviors related to understanding what children encounter as options.

The teacher who has very strong convictions about the exact ways that children ought to behave during most of a program day will provide one kind of program environment. Another teacher who assumes that a large number of different child behaviors are appropriate during most of the program day will provide a quite different environment. The stability of any individual's assumptions regarding appropriate classroom behavior permits the assessment, with considerable reliability, of what constitutes a ceiling factor on options or an index of openness for individual child participants.

We hold that program openness can be dimensionalized and assessed for any program setting and that openness, though a joint function of a number of factors, is in large part a function of the teacher's assumptions about which child behaviors are appropriate and when. These perspectives on the role that teacher assumptions have in program stability provide the rationale for a procedure for assessing openness.

Description of the Open Program Structure Index (OPSI)

The procedure used in the Open Program Structure Index is a general one that is applicable to the examination of options or degrees of freedom for program participants for a variety of criterion behaviors, activities, or events which might be of interest to an investigator. The criteria used in our work to date are fifteen behaviors. These fifteen items, such as getting a drink of water, running, or playing with other children, have typically appeared in the authors' experiences of conducting and observing programs. The concern of the OPSI procedure is to characterize the extent to which it is possible for the specified behaviors to occur in a program setting, without censoring intervention. The question addressed is: What is the probability that if a child had a need for or interest in manifesting any of these behaviors, it could be accommodated by the program? The fifteen items which have been the actual behavior and activity criteria indexed by the OPSI are as follows:

Go to the bathroom
Get a drink of water
Rest, be left alone, have privacy
Move freely around the room
Practice large-muscle coordination (except running)
Practice fine-muscle (eye-hand) coordination (other than
with pencil or crayon)
Run, play with, tease, chase other children
Talk informally with other children
Receive responsive, undivided individual attention
from the teacher regarding something important enough
for student to initiate contact

Informal involvement* in dramatic play
Informal involvement in music (singing, dancing, rhythm)
Informal involvement with art (painting, clay modeling,
woodworking)
Informal involvement in math, science, nature study
Informal writing
Informal reading

* "Informal" means that there are options present and that children may choose from these options. "Involvement" implies that space and materials which facilitate participation are provided and are accessible.

Data for the OPSI may be provided by any teacher, administrator, or program planner or developer thoroughly familiar with a given program. The respondent is first asked to provide a description of the program as it is typically organized in time or as it occurs on a given day. This description is obtained in a format which specifies the time boundaries within the program. "Boundary" here refers to the expectations of the teacher for what may, will, or should occur and when. The format usually used for this is shown in the three columns to the left in Figure 1. The respondent is asked to indicate three things about the program being described in these spaces: What occurs? When does it occur? For how long does it occur? For each portion of the program day the respondent thus provides a brief label, indicates the time interval during which it occurs, and the total amount of time spent on the program activity.

The respondent is then asked to thoughtfully characterize whether or not each of the behaviors or activities which serve as the criterion items, and which are listed along the top right of the Program Structure Index form, are possible or likely to occur without sanction within the specified time segments throughout the day. The symbol (+) is used to indicate that it is generally O.K. for the behavior or activity to occur during the time period and 0 (zero) is used to indicate that the behaviors would be viewed as inappropriate.

The completed Program Structure Index is scored by converting all ratings to the time they represent. The time during which the behavior is viewed as appropriate during the day is then added, and its total becomes the numerator for the determination of a percentage. The denominator is the total time in the entire program day. The percentage computed reflects, from the respondent's view, the extent to which the specified behavior can occur during a typical or a given program day without sanction. These are the essential steps in using the OPSI.

The percentages produced may be viewed as probability statements: that is, they express the probability that a child's need or interest, were it to occur, to engage in the particular behavior would be accommodated by the program. In the example provided by Figure 1, interest in running or the need to run is accommodated by the program less than 20 percent of the time, talking informally with peers is accommodated approximately 58 percent, and working with math materials 25 percent of the time. The probability that a child would be negatively sanctioned were he to engage in running behavior is very high—83 percent of the time. While these characterizations are only illustrative, they show generally how the procedure works and some possible interpretations.

To summarize, what is indexed by this procedure is the extent to which the teacher would accept, without negative sanction, the occur-

Figure 1. **Illustration of Program Structure Index Procedure**

TIME	PROGRAM DESCRIPTION	Total Time, min	Bathroom	Drink	Rent	Move Freely	Large-Muscle	Fine-Muscle	Run–Play–Tease	Talk Informally	Receive Attention	Dramatic Play	Music	Art	Math-Science-Nature	Writing	Reading
8:30– 8:40	Arrival	10	+	+	0	+	0	+	0	+	+	0	0	0	0	0	0
8:40– 9:00	News/Sharing	20	0	0	0	0	0	0	0	0	0	0	0	0	0	0	0
9:00– 9:45	Activity Period	45	+	0	0	+	0	+	0	+	+	+	+	+	+	+	+
9:45–10:00	Discuss/Share	15	0	0	0	0	0	0	0	0	0	0	0	0	0	0	0
10:00–10:15	Snack	15	+	+	+	0	0	+	0	+	0	0	0	0	0	0	0
10:15–10:45	Outdoor Play	30	+	+	0	+	+	+	+	+	+	+	0	0	0	0	0
10:45–11:05	Story	20	0	0	0	0	0	0	0	0	0	0	0	0	0	0	+
11:05–11:25	Music, Rhythm	20	+	0	0	0	0	+	0	0	0	+	+	0	0	0	0
11:25–11:30	Dismissal	5	+	+	0	+	0	+	0	+	+	0	0	0	0	0	0
	Time Behavior Appropriate		125	60	15	90	30	125	30	105	90	85	65	45	45	45	65
	Total Program Time		180	180	180	180	180	180	180	180	180	180	180	180	180	180	180
	Percentage		79	33	8	50	17	69	17	58	50	47	36	25	25	25	36

KEY TO RATINGS: + generally OK for behavior, activity, or event to occur
0 generally not OK

rence of a behavior were it to occur. The procedure documents possibility or potential, not actuality. That is, when used in the present "self-report" form, the OPSI provides the respondent with a format for recording assumptions held about appropriateness of child behavior in the various activity segments of the program he or she provides. The OPSI does not document the actual occurrence of child behaviors. Rather, through an objectification of the respondent's assumptions, it documents the probability that *if* a child behavior were to occur, it would be viewed as appropriate and therefore accepted without sanction. This acceptance without sanction provides the basis for our view of openness.

Analysis of the Characteristics of the OPSI

Scope

While the scope of the OPSI is limited to assessing the teacher's assumptions regarding behaviors appropriate in a classroom setting, these data encompass a major portion of the activity occurring within that classroom. Whatever the teacher believes to be appropriate behavior becomes a major influence in determining the experiences of the pupils.

Although much research has been conducted on attitudes and values of teachers in classrooms, the focus has typically not included those aspects of attitude or value systems which directly influence the management of the classroom program. The OPSI, on the other hand, facilitates examination of the consequences of a teacher's "belief" system.

Some of the promising investigations of the relationship of the teacher's conceptual level, classroom atmosphere, and student behaviors have relevance in regard to the OPSI. Harvey et al. (1966) reported relationships between the concrete-abstract dimensions of a teacher's belief or conceptual system and the kind of classroom atmosphere that was maintained. A concrete system was represented by a tendency for the teacher's instructional approach to be more structured, more invariant, and less flexible than that of a teacher manifesting an abstract system. A subsequent study (Harvey et al., 1968) demonstrated the relationship between these factors and student cooperation, participation, and initiative. It seems very likely that the data obtained on the OPSI are similar in derivation to the observational ratings obtained by Harvey and his colleagues. If this were indeed the case, one would anticipate similar positive consequences for children in programs described as open by the OPSI scores. Were it empirically established, a direct linkage between a teacher's assumptions regarding children's behavior in his or her own classroom and outcomes for children might afford a clearer direction for teacher education and/or selection of teachers. Further research is needed to investigate these possibilities.

Data Collection

One of the advantages of the OPSI as an instrument is that significant data about a program can be collected with minimal effort and minimal expense. Any respondent who knows a program well can provide the necessary information within a brief time span. This is in considerable contrast to the expensive observational or naturalistic assessment procedures which are otherwise necessary to obtain comparable data on the ceiling factor for children's involvement in program settings.

Form of the Data

The data obtained on the OPSI are descriptive rather than evaluative. How much openness is present in a program is indexed in a percentage form which facilitates comparative analysis. Whether a given amount of openness is good, bad, or indifferent can thus be dealt with as an empirical question. These percentages obtained may be analyzed separately for each behavior criterion in regard to particular outcome measures, or a total score or profile analysis can be used.

Scoring and Interpretation

The scoring process is so readily understandable and the resultant percentages are so directly related to the realities of the classroom situation that the interpretation of the index scores is easily accomplished. Unlike the figures obtained in rating scales, descriptive scales, or most observational schema, the data obtained by the OPSI make sense to anyone with some knowledge of classroom structure. The index thus is directly useful in providing worthwhile perspectives for preservice teacher training, insights to practitioners, easily interpreted profiles for administrators, and other practical applications.

Reliability

Several kinds of reliability may be considered in the use of the OPSI. The first is the extent to which the same program is described and rated in similar ways on subsequent occasions by a given respondent. The second is whether different respondents in rating the same program have relatively high agreement. Although our accumulation of data is not great, an informal examination of this kind of ratings indicates adequate agreement.

More formal assessments of reliability have been determined with the Pearson product-moment correlation between split halves (one half of the day versus the other half) and been adjusted according to the Spearman-Brown formula. The reliability coefficient was determined to be a .78 for 42 protocols.

Validity

In a recent unpublished study by Dopyera and Ribble (1973) the extent to which self-report program descriptions matched actual program implementation was examined. Fourteen early-childhood programs, including Head Start, private nursery schools, public kindergartens, and day-care programs, were studied. Two different teachers in each program were asked on separate days to fill out the OPSI form on the morning prior to that day's observations. Observers then noted the extent to which what the teacher had indicated would occur actually did occur—both in terms of the schedule for the day and for the acceptance of child criterion behaviors. Results showed that although there was some slippage between what was scheduled and when the activities occurred, it was minor. For given activity segments, however, there was major agreement, approximately 95 percent, between what a teacher said she would accept on the OPSI self-report and what she actually was observed to accept without sanction.

Two other findings, however, qualify the validity of the study. Agreement between the two teachers in the *same* program varied considerably. In some programs both teachers agreed on schedules as well as appropriateness of child behaviors during time segments. In other programs, it was difficult to imagine that the OPSI descriptions obtained from different staff members referred to the same program. Upon closer examination of the data, two factors provided clarification: i.e., newness of the teacher to the program, and total size and scope of the program.

The half-day private nursery schools and public kindergartens had good agreement on the OPSI. Teachers had worked together for longer periods and had agreed upon routines and ground rules. The longer, full-day child-care centers and Head Start centers had overall schedules but operated very casually, and much of the adult intervention sanctioning children's behavior was dependent on the particular adult's personal criteria and thresholds. It should be noted, in addition, that reliability between the two observers on 40 separate 10-minute observations of individual teacher sanctioning was very high, exceeding 90 percent. Validity findings are further discussed below, in the "Application" section of this paper.

Limitations

There are the following limitations to the use of OPSI procedures. First, it is most suitable for assessing self-contained program situations. Obtaining ratings for any particular group of children becomes more difficult if they are in a departmentalized situation with several different teachers. It has been interesting to note, however, that when these ratings can be obtained it is found that children have less openness generally in the departmentalized programs than in the self-contained.

Second, when used as a self-report procedure where the respondent is the classroom teacher, both the descriptions and the ratings are subject to the "fake-good" or social desirability bias in reporting. All other self-report measures share this bias, especially when the respondent knows what the researcher or teacher trainer wishes to hear. The above-cited validity data lend support to the contention that faking with the OPSI, though clearly possible, was only minimally present.

Third, the ratings may be subject to some distortion because of the respondent's uncertainty about such things as what the term "generally" may mean in a specific instance or what is the meaning of other terms, such as "informal involvement."

Fourth, the OPSI as described in this chapter is limited to the assessment of the fifteen listed behaviors. Other activities or events or behaviors may be of more relevance in some instances. The procedure can, of course, be expanded to include any criterion a particular researcher, program developer, monitor, or teacher wishes to index. One example would be to use the procedure to index child access to activity areas and materials in the classroom.

Application: Actual and Potential

The OPSI was initially designed as a research instrument and was first employed by the senior author as a dependent measure in a study of classroom planning performed by preservice teachers under contrasting organizational climates (Dopyera, 1971). The climates were simulated through letters for the new teacher from a fellow teacher, building principal, and district superintendent. Those students who read letters simulating a traditional organizational climate were found to plan for considerably less openness than did students who were assigned to schools simulating a British infant school approach. There was also an unexpected finding that, regardless of the simulated assignment, the students who had actual practice teaching placements in more innovative school settings planned for more openness on the OPSI than did those students who had done their practice teaching in more conventional schools. The implications for teacher education seem obvious, and use of the OPSI can serve well to assess directly the differential effects of alternative training procedures on the kind of classroom structure provided for pupils by teacher trainees. There are also innumerable other situations in which OPSI scores might serve as dependent measures in research undertakings.

The OPSI may, under other conditions, serve as an independent measure or as a quality-control measure in program research and evaluation. If one is to assess the effects of openness on children, the extent to which openness actually exists must be known. As one example, Earnshaw (1972) used OPSI scores as independent measures to establish the degree of difference between the classroom structure of second-grade experimental teachers who were trying to implement "open" classrooms and a group of control teachers who were conducting "traditional" classrooms. The four experimental teachers' OPSI mean across the fifteen behavioral criteria was 74.4 (S.D. = 6.6), and the four control teachers' OPSI mean was 51.5 (S.D. = 8.3). This difference was found to be significant at the .005 level. The students in the "open" classroom were found to exhibit more resourcefulness, creativity, initiative, self-reliance, and enjoyment of school on a combination of standardized and experimental measures. Although both groups were well above normal grade level on achievement tests, the children in control classes were performing at a significantly higher level at the end of the one-year experimental period. This study demonstrated the use of the OPSI as an independent measure. There seems little doubt that the experimental treatment was indeed different from the control in the openness provided for children.

In another situation the OPSI was used to indicate contrast between the degree of openness of an innovative day-care program and more traditional day-care arrangements. The two day-care programs are characterized with the OPSI criteria in Figure 2. The innovative program, labeled "responsive day-care," was developed and implemented by the second author at Syracuse University under the auspices of the U.S. Office of Education. The other program, labeled "traditional," was a rather typical suburban day-care program. The programs both ran for ten hours a day. Although there were similarities, some differences were also obvious. Even a cursory examination of the graph shows that the probability of the program's accommodating a child's interest or need, were such an interest or need to occur, was much higher in the responsive day-care than in the traditional day-care model. In the near future, the OPSI will be repeatedly employed as one kind of quality-control indicator.

The OPSI has also been used by both authors in a variety of preservice and in-service teacher education settings. The major outcome of utilizing the OPSI in these settings has been that teachers obtain insights into the relationships between their own assumptions and the classroom practices which follow from these assumptions. Discussions about the various ways to do so also often develop between teachers who wish to provide more options for children. As indicated previously, teachers in these training settings find little difficulty in making sense of the scores derived from the OPSI.

As a recently developed device, the OPSI has not yet had extensive use in determining the range of openness provided in varieties of situations. Our accumulation of data to date, however, indicates that children encounter less openness as they get older. That is, the probability

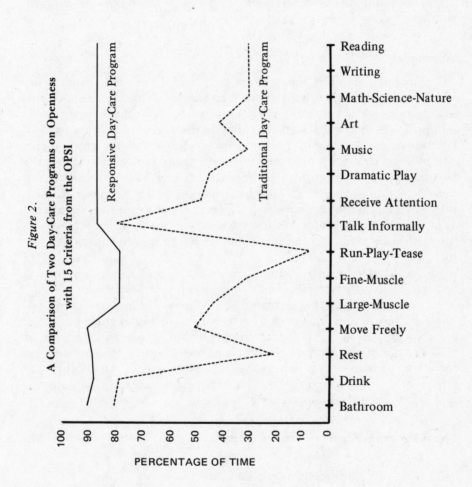

Figure 2.

A Comparison of Two Day-Care Programs on Openness
with 15 Criteria from the OPSI

that an interest or need would be accommodated by the program is much less if the child is a sixth-grader than if he or she is a kindergartener. This finding is not surprising; it does, however, provide additional confirmation of the validity of the OPSI. It also points out one seeming paradox in education in America today. As children grow older and are presumably more able to take advantage of more options, they encounter fewer.

Summary

It is proposed in this chapter that little useful knowledge will be derived from program evaluation until the several influential components of programs are identified and dimensionalized. At that point any existent program can be assessed according to the extent to which a particular component is present. The authors recognize that the components determining children's program experience and, hence, controlling the benefits from the program may include material richness, participant density, child repertoire, and teacher repertoire. One component, identified as ceiling factor imposed by teacher assumptions regarding appropriateness of children's behavior, is proposed as particularly influential in determining the classroom structure and dynamics. Assessment of teachers' assumptions in relation to the program day and a set of selected criteria for this are suggested, and the instrument to be used, called the *Open Program Structure Index,* is described.

In general, the OPSI is characterized as easy and inexpensive to administer, score, and interpret. It is viewed as being highly useful for a range of purposes, including teacher training, assessing effects of teacher training, and as dependent and independent measures in research or as quality-control measures. The specificity of the OPSI procedure is one of its strongest assets. That specificity facilitates communication in both practical and research settings.

Open Program Structure Index (OPSI)

Instruction
The task you are to complete consists of three parts, as follows:

1. Identify in your thinking the preschool, kindergarten, or elementary class you wish to assess for openness. Think about how a typical class day was organized, from the time the children arrived in the morning to when they left. Use the blank sheet of paper to draft out how this typical or representative day was organized in time.

For example: Sharing 8:30–8:45
              Reading 8:45–9:45, etc.

2. After you have drafted out a description of this more or less representative class day, transfer the information to the Recording Sheet. You do not have to record a detailed description; the major concern is that *you* know what the times you've indicated refer to. Brief descriptors and "from-to" time periods will be sufficient.

Be sure, however, that the times are accurate in the sense that they "add up" to the total amount of time in the representative day you have described. You can check this by totaling the time for each segment you describe. Also, if a time segment is used concurrently for more than one purpose (e.g., you might be working with a reading group while the remaining children are doing seat work independently), indicate this with a slash (/): for example, reading/seatwork.

3. After you have transferred your description of a representative class day to the Recording Sheet, read the following list of child behaviors (and note that these are the same behaviors which are listed at the top of the Rating Sheet). (See p. 133):

A Go to the bathroom
B Get a drink of water
C Rest, be left alone, have privacy
D Move freely around the room
E Practice large-muscle coordination (except running)
F Practice fine-muscle (eye-hand) coordination (other
       than with pencil or crayon)
G Run, play with, tease, chase other children
H Talk informally with other children
I   Receive responsive, undivided individual attention from you
       (as a teacher) regarding something important enough for the
       student to initiate contact with you
J Informal involvement* in dramatic play
K Informal involvement with music (singing, dancing, rhythm, etc.)
L Informal involvement with art (painting, clay modeling, woodworking, etc.)
M Informal involvement in math, science, nature study
N Informal writing
O Informal reading

Now, for each time segment you have indicated on the Program Description Sheet you are to make a judgment regarding each of these fifteen behaviors. The question you are to ask yourself is, "Within a given time segment would I generally accept the behavior, were it to occur, or would I think of it as generally inappropriate during that time?" If, from your point of view, the behavior would be generally acceptable during the specific time segment, then rate it with a plus (+). If, on the other hand, you would view the behavior as generally inappropriate during the time segment, then rate it with a zero (0). Continue through the time segments you have described until you have rated each of the fifteen behaviors.

* *Note* that informal involvement means that (1) space and materials which facilitate participation are provided; (2) there are options present; and (3) children may choose from these options.

142 John Dopyera and Margaret Lay

References

Dopyera, John E., *The Influence of Organizational Climate and Teacher Trainee Conceptual Level on Planning for Openness in a Simulated Classroom Planning Task.* Unpublished doctoral dissertation, Syracuse University, 1971.

Dopyera, John E., and Lucile Ribble, *Validity Studies of the OPSI in Day Care and Other Early Childhood Settings.* Unpublished study, 1973.

Earnshaw, George L., *Open Education As a Humanistic Intervention Strategy.* Doctoral dissertation, Syracuse University, 1972.

Harvey, O. J., M. Prather, B. J. White, and J. K. Hoffmeister, "Teachers' Beliefs, Classroom Atmosphere, and Student Behavior," *American Educational Research Journal*, 1968, *5*, 151–166.

Lay, Margaret Z., *The Responsive Care Model: A Program Manual and Report of Implementation.* Syracuse, N.Y.: Syracuse University Early Childhood Education Center, 1972.

CHAPTER 8

An Analysis of American and British Open Education*

Herbert J. Walberg, *University of Illinois*
Susan Christie Thomas, *Education Development Corporation*

THE PURPOSE of this chapter is to describe an observational study of open education as practiced in Great Britain and United States. Our initial hope in conducting the research was that convenient and valid instruments could be developed to enable independent observers, trained in the use of the instruments but not trained to be open educators, to identify objectively the distinguishing characteristics of authentic open classrooms. The conceptual framework of the study is derived from our literature review in Chapter 2. Here we test the hypothesis that open education practice reflects its written characterization by practitioners and sensitive observers.

Before we turn to the study, our continuing concern should be expressed that open education is being confused with "free schools" and laissez-faire teaching ("Let the child do what he likes without the teacher's guidance"). A glance at Figure 1 and a reading of Chapter 2 makes the distinction clear: Open education differs from traditional, laissez-faire, and programmed education in that the teacher and the child cooperate in shaping the goals and means of the child's learning. Thus an authentic open approach makes great demands on the teacher's talents and resources to guide the children in his or her classroom. A major consideration in designing the research below was to construct an instrument to distinguish open education from other forms of education.

* Material from a prior version of this chapter, published in the *American Educational Research Journal,* 1972, no. 9, pp. 197–208, is included with permission of the American Educational Research Association.

Method

Instrument Development

Nineteen major works on open education were scanned for concrete examples of the eight themes described in Chapter 2. Those found were recorded verbatim under each theme (Walberg and Thomas, 1971, Appendix A, pp. 1–76). Based on the quotations, 106 specific statements were drafted which were intended to define explicitly open classroom characteristics (see Table 1 for examples). A total of 29 nationally prominent open educators responded to a request to agree or disagree with statements and to criticize and suggest changes for any they found defi-

---

Figure 1.

Double Classification Scheme Based on Extent to Which (1) Individual Teacher and (2) Individual Child Is An Active Contributor to Decisions Regarding Content and Process of Learning *(from Bussis and Chittenden, 1970)*

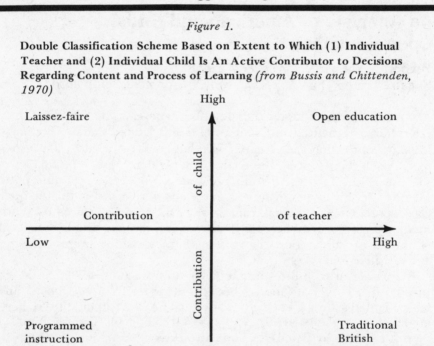

cient. From their reactions, the original list was revised and fifty items were selected for inclusion on an Observation Rating Scale and parallel Teacher Questionnaire. The number of items for each theme reflects the attention given to the theme in the original writers and the extent of agreement by the panel of experts, as well as meeting the criterion of possible observability; for example, half the items are related to provisioning because it is so strongly emphasized by open educators and also because it can be more readily observed. To diminish response set in drafting the final set of scales, some items were stated negatively so that agreement would imply traditional classroom characteristics.

Observers

The observations in the United States were done by fourteen college-educated women ranging in age from early twenties to mid-thirties. Eleven of them had applied for part-time work at the Educational Development Center or had responded to an advertisement posted on a job bulletin board frequented by wives of Harvard graduate students. The other three were already working on the project which led up to this data collection. One of these three, who had been responsible for the design and pilot testing of the instruments, trained the other thirteen observers in the use of the Observation Rating Scale.

The training covered a total of two days. All observers were gathered for the first full-day session; they were apprised of the kinds of situations they would be entering and were instructed in what behavior was expected of them. However, they were not informed of the differences between open and traditional education; nor were they told which classes were designated open or traditional, and an effort was made throughout their training and actual observing to inculcate objective attention to explicit, specific, concrete indicators of classroom phenomena. The trainees completed the Observation Rating Scale after viewing a mathematics project training film in which an exceptional teacher instructs an eager class using a traditional lesson format. After all observers completed the Observation Rating Scale, the same observer/leader provided feedback training through group examination of each item, checking for aberrant choices and misinterpretations, entertaining questions, and bringing the group to a general consensus on each item. In the afternoon session, the observers watched a 60-minute film of an open classroom and then marked the Observation Rating Scale and participated in a similar feedback session. During the following two days, each trainee completed the instrument twice more. Each made a practice observation in a traditional classroom and an open classroom specifically selected as training sites. Inspection of the training and site data revealed no tendency for the "naïve raters" to be less accurate than the three who knew the purpose of the study.

Two additional observers were trained in London during the last two weeks of the data collection. They corresponded to their U.S. counterparts, except that one of them was British. They spent an afternoon with one of the experienced observers who had worked on the project from its inception. Together they went through the instrument carefully and talked at length about the kinds of circumstances they might run into or have difficulty coding, based on the experienced observer's four weeks of observing U.S. sites. A check on these two observers was obtained by comparing their ratings with those of the two experienced American observers with whom they shared the task of making the British observations.

Table 1. Eight Open Education Themes and Their Item Representation on the Rating Scale and Questionnaire

Sample Items	Number of Items	Correlation between Questionnaire and Observation
1. **Provisioning for learning:** Manipulative materials are supplied in great diversity and range with little replication, i.e., not class sets. Children move freely about the room without asking permission. Talking among children is encouraged. The teaches does group children by ability according to tests or norms.* Children generally group and regroup themselves through their own choices.	25	.81***
2. **Humaneness, respect, openness, and warmth:** Children use "books" written by their classmates as part of their reading and reference materials. The environment includes materials developed or supplied by the children. Teacher takes care of dealing with conflicts and disruptive behavior without involving the group.* Children's activities, products, and ideas are reflected abundantly about the classroom.	4	.46***
3. **Diagnosis of learning events:** Teacher uses test results to group children for reading and/or math.* Children expect the teacher to correct all their work.* Teacher gives children tests to find out what they know.* To obtain diagnostic information, the teacher closely observes the specific work or concern of a child and asks immediate, experience-based questions.	4	.48***
4. **Instruction, guidance, and extension of learning:** Teacher bases her instruction on each individual child and his interaction with materials and equipment. The work children do is divided into subject-matter areas.* The teacher's lessons and assignments are given to the class as a whole.* Teacher bases her instruction on curriculum guides or textbooks for the grade level she teaches.* Before suggesting any	5	.60***

Table 1 (continued)

Sample Items	Number of Items	Correlation between Questionnaire and Observation
extension or redirection of activity, teacher gives diagnostic attention to the particular child and his particular activity.		
5. **Evaluation of diagnostic information:** Teacher keeps notes and writes individual histories of each child's intellectual, emotional, physical development. Teacher has children for a period of just one year.* Teachers uses tests to evaluate children and rate them in comparison with their peers.* Teacher keeps a collection of each child's work for use in evaluating his development. Teacher views evaluation as information to guide her instruction and provisioning for the classroom.	5	.48***
6. **Seeking opportunities for professional growth:** Teacher uses the assistance of someone in a supportive, advisory capacity. Teacher has helpful colleagues with whome she discusses teaching.	2	.18
7. **Self-perception of teacher:** Teacher tries to keep all children within sight so that she can make sure they are doing what they are supposed to do.*	1	.42***
8. **Assumptions about children and learning process:** The emotional climate is warm and accepting. The class operates within clear guidelines made explicit. Academic achievement is the teacher's top priority for the children.* Children are deeply involved in what they are doing.	4	.11
Total and canonical correlation	50	.86***

*Reverse coding: throughout this paper 1, 2, and 3 asterisks, respectively, indicate statistical significance levels of .05, 0.1, and .001.

Sites and Procedure

The sites for observations were selected on the basis of reputation and also through the personal knowledge of the investigators. The sample was by no means random but represented urban and suburban public and private schools with administrators and teachers cooperative enough to permit the intrusion of observers. An effort was made to gain access to both open and traditional classes with teachers regarded as excellent by outside experts and their principals, and the sample was further restricted to classes of five- to seven-year-old children in their first three years of school.

About twenty classes each of the U.S. open, U.S. traditional, and British open types (see Table 2 for exact figures) were selected. In the United States, classrooms were observed in three major cities (Boston, Chicago, and New York), one small city (Cambridge, Massachusetts), several suburban towns, and one university town. In Great Britain, classes were visited in two major cities (London and Bristol), one university town (Cambridge), and two villages in Leicestershire.

Table 2. Cell Sizes for Analysis

Socioeconomic Status	Group			
	Traditional	Open	Great Britain Open	Total
Higher	12	11	11	34
Lower	9	10	9	28
Total	21	21	20	62

The selection of sites was made to balance roughly the number of disadvantaged to lower-class schools with the number of middle- to upper-class schools within each of the three groups (see Table 2). As would be expected from demographic data, the disadvantaged schools were concentrated in U.S. and British inner cities. This selection was guided by informants familiar with potential sites. The socioeconomic levels were later verified during interviews with principals and teachers during the observation period.

At least two different observers visited each classroom at least three times in the U.S. schools. For economy reasons, only two observations were made in each British classroom. In both countries, a questionnaire which paralleled the observation scales was left with teachers during the first visit and was picked up during the second visit.

The questionnaires were scored by summing the coded item responses for each scale. Each observer rating was scored the same way, and then the means of the two (for Great Britain) or three (for the U.S.) ratings were computed for the analyses. The questionnaire format was a 4-point format (strongly disagree, disagree, agree, strongly agree); and the observation rating was also a 4-point scale (no evidence; weak, infrequent evidence; moderate, occasional; and strong, frequent evidence).

Results and Discussion

Cross-Method Correlations

A canonical correlation was computed between the 8 observation scales and the 8 questionnaire scales. The canonical correlation was .86 ($p <$ .001), and 6 of the 8 simple correlations between corresponding scales were significant ($p < .05$; see Table 1). With the exception of the substantial correlation (.81) for the provisioning scale, the significant correlations between measurement methods for corresponding scales were moderate (from .42 to .60). Moderate cross-method correlations probably resulted not from lower validities but from lower reliabilities, because all scales but provisioning had few items per scale. As might be expected under this inference, these corresponding scale correlations, when corrected for unreliability (see Table 3 for internal consistencies), are substantial (above .8). Thus on 6 of the 8 themes, the observers' perceptions appear to agree quite well with the way the teacher views her own behavior and that of her pupils. The two scales that are nonsignificantly correlated across methods—seeking and assumptions—are relatively unreliable (see Table 3); from the item content (see Table 1), one suspects that observers could not rate these themes very easily; they are professional traits or attitudes and, important though they are, cannot be easily observed and rated objectively.

Multivariate and SES Effects

Table 3 shows the multivariate and univariate F-ratios for the effects of socioeconomic status (SES), educational group, and the interaction. In a multivariate sense, SES is significant for the questionnaire variables, whereas educational group (U.S. open and traditional and British open) and its interaction with SES are significant on both the questionnaire and observation variables. Both the multivariate and univariate F-ratios indicate that educational group has far larger effects than SES and its interaction with group. Inspection of the means reveals that teachers in higher SES schools tended to agree more often with five open education themes on the questionnaire, and on four of these (provisioning, instruction, self-perception, and assumptions) the observers also rated these teachers higher than teachers in lower SES schools. Since SES did not interact strongly with educational group on these four variables, it may be inferred that classes in higher SES schools, whether British or American, open or traditional, tend to be more "open" (as operationalized here) than the counterpart classes in lower SES schools. Indeed, since the interactions are ordinal and comparatively small and were not hypothesized, they are not reported here.

Open versus Traditional Classes

Inspection of Table 3 reveals the very great differences between educational groups on the questionnaire and observation criteria. The group differences were significant for all eight themes on both methods, with one exception—observation ratings on seeking opportunities for professional growth. This more than the other themes might be difficult to rate because it may not be manifest in obvious ways in the classroom.

Aside from this exception, the scales clearly distinguish open from traditional classes. Figure 2 is a plot of the standardized contrasts of U.S. and British open with U.S. traditional classes; these are the esti-

Table 3. F-Tests for Two Effects and Their interaction on Two Sets of Criteria

Criterion		Socioeconomic Status	Group	Interaction
Observation multivariate:		1.5	9.4***	1.8*
Provisioning	(.97)	5.7*	79.3***	1.2
Humaneness	(.68)	2.3	30.0***	1.1
Diagnosis	(.77)	1.9	50.0***	1.5
Instruction	(.88)	4.0*	51.5***	.0
Evaluation	(.57)	.7	29.7***	3.1*
Seeking	(.59)	.4	1.2	2.4
Self-percention	(....)	3.3*	22.4***	3.3*
Assumptions	(.41)	10.0**	7.6***	1.0
Questionnaire multivariate:		4.0***	8.7***	2.0*
Provisioning	(.90)	16.1***	48.7***	1.5
Humaneness	(.33)	1.9	25.1***	6.6**
Diagnosis	(.34)	2.8	8.0***	.2
Instruction	(.71)	13.5***	20.9***	2.3
Evaluation	(.41)	.0	22.3***	.3
Seeking	(.44)	7.2**	5.4**	3.0
Self-perception	(....)	14.3***	14.0***	.7
Assumptions	(.22)	9.8**	3.1*	1.0

Note: Alpha internal-consistency reliabilities of criteria given in parentheses; since self-perception has only one item, internal consistencies could not be computed for this scale; 1, 2, and 3 asterisks indicate, respectively, the .05, .01, and .001 significance levels.

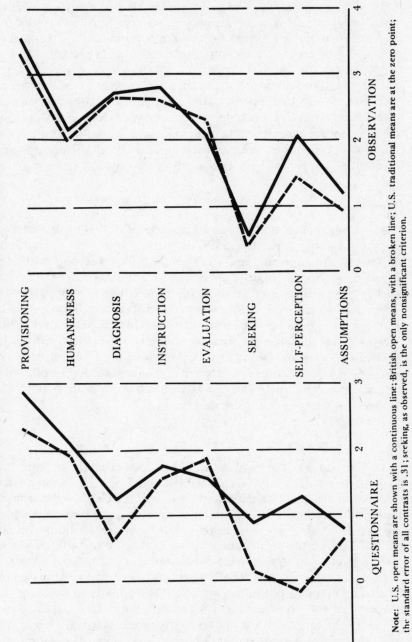

Figure 2. Standardized Contrasts of U.S. and British Open with U.S. Traditional Classes

Note: U.S. open means are shown with a continuous line; British open means, with a broken line; U.S. traditional means are at the zero point; the standard error of all contrasts is .31; seeking, as observed, is the only nonsignificant criterion.

mates of the raw differences in means divided by the within-cells standard deviations of the corresponding criteria (see Bock, 1966); thus, they measure the differences between means in units of standard deviation, and the contrasts are comparable across all criteria. It can be seen that open classes differ sharply from traditional on 5 of the 8 criteria: provisioning, humaneness, diagnosis, instruction, and evaluation. Moreover, British and U.S. open classes are highly similar, especially on the observation criteria. British open teachers were close to U.S. traditional teachers on the questionnaire scales for seeking and assumptions, but both open groups are similar to each other and well-differentiated from traditional groups on the corresponding observation scales.

Conclusion

An earlier report (Walberg and Thomas, 1971) demonstrated a consistency among major analytic and descriptive writings on open education with respect to eight themes. Here we have found strong evidence that the themes also distinguish open from traditional teachers whether a teacher questionnaire or an observer scale is used to measure the differences between groups. Moreover, the differences between open and traditional teachers are far larger than the differences found either between schools of different socioeconomic strata or between schools in the United States and Great Britain. Thus we have found further consistencies between the conceptualization and anecdotal descriptions of open education, on the one hand, and its classroom operation as viewed by insiders and outsiders, on the other.

What the Analyses Miss

The measures of the eight themes developed from the specific descriptive statements defining 105 characteristics of open education classrooms obviously leave much unexamined. Over half the characteristics on which we found agreement in the literature and among prominent educators are not covered in the instruments. Furthermore, it should be kept in mind that even the 105 characteristics cannot be considered definitive. They depict an approach to teaching characterized by adaptability, flexibility, and responsiveness. While attempts to recognize variations consistent with the open education approach were made in drafting the descriptors, all the possible practices and opinions which might be encompassed in the approach cannot be represented. What these instruments miss, therefore, is richness, variety, and flexibility. Too much that we have already identified is not measured or measurable by this means, not to mention that which has yet to be so identified and described.

Those characteristics difficult to measure through an observation-rating scale suffer most exclusion here. Especially noticeable by its limited representation is the theme "self-perception of the teacher," although at least ten distinct characteristics were conceptualized to describe this theme. Similarly, the many agreed-upon general beliefs we drafted to define the theme "assumptions about children and the learning process" are only lightly touched upon. One necessary criterion for selection of items was the likelihood of observability. As a result, the nine-tenths of the iceberg that lies beneath the water and supports what can be observed remains unmeasured in this study.

Another important aspect of any classroom's functioning is the organizational relationships which facilitate (or impede) its success. Although this study tried to tap two crucial characteristics of this aspect of the teacher's existence (the two items based on descriptors from the theme "seeking opportunities for professional growth"), much needs further exploration. For instance, the heads of schools in many of the British schools visited seemed to exert more subtle, pervasive leadership than we observed in traditional or open schools in America. One wonders what difference it may make that these headmasters and headmistresses drift unobtrusively into a classroom, where they blend into the ongoing activities. They act almost as an experienced aide or exceptional student teacher would in an American school, yet bring all the expertise and importance of their position into their informal interactions with children. The instrument does not, of course, tap this frequent friendly presence of the head of the school, who is constantly in touch with the little everyday experiences of teachers and children, not as "principal" or authority figure but as a participant in the pleasure, problems, and process of learning. Is the participant-principal a key? What other organizational relationships may be important?

The scales were not designed for looking at classrooms over time; yet flexibility and responsiveness suggest changes which occur as time passes. This important aspect of open education could not be examined through these instruments. Nor, of course, were indices of student achievement or emotional and social growth a part of this study.

We hope that these eight scales and the 105 characteristics will provide a stimulating source of material for teacher education, research, and evaluation. More than 100 university and school colleagues have written us for copies of the scales, and others have obtained them from the U.S. Office of Education's Educational Research Information Center, where they have been microfilmed.

In teacher-training classrooms and teacher-team gatherings, the items can be used as the basis for lively discussion. We hope teachers and educators in general will find them provocative and helpful, will use them in the spirit of inquiry and respect for teacher variety with which they were developed, and will avoid any behavioral orthodoxy.

There are many additional conceptual and empirical questions to ask about the concept of open education (Walberg, 1972). Here perhaps we have identified some of the crucial elements of these questions. As pointed out at the outset, the concept has been the subject of very little evaluation and research, aside from testimonials by proponents. If it is to be expanded from the limited number of existent experimental settings in this country, administrators, teachers, and parents quite properly should know if it leads to more learning, to higher levels of performance in reading, to greater self-esteem and self-determination, to the good life. We have developed some exploratory instruments that are indicative of presumably important aspects of open classroom processes. Seeing whether these processes are related to valued educational outcomes is an obvious next step for those who wish to evaluate open education.

References

Barth, Roland S., *Open Education and the American School*. New York: Agathon Press, 1972.

Bock, R. D., "Contributions of Multivariate Experimental Designs to Educational Research, in Cattell, R. B. (ed.), *Multivariate Experimental Psychology*. Chicago: Rand-McNally, 1966, pp. 820–840.

Bussis, Anne M., and E. S. Chittenden, *Analysis of an Approach to Open Education*. Princeton, N.J.: Educational Testing Service, 1970.

Gardner, Dorothy E. M., and Joan E. Cass, *The Role of the Teacher in the Infant and Nursery School*. Oxford: Pergamon Press, 1965.

Plowden, Lady B., et al., *Children and Their Primary Schools: A Report of the Central Advisory Council for Education*. London: Her Majesty's Stationery Office, 1967.

Rathbone, C. H., *Open Education and the Teacher*. Unpublished doctoral dissertation, Harvard University, 1970.

Silberman, C. E., *Crisis in the Classroom*. New York: Random House, 1970.

Walberg, H. J., "Optimizing and Individualizing Instruction: Some Traditions, Domains, and Models," *Interchange, 2*, 1972, pp. 15–27.

Walberg, H. J., and Susan C. Thomas, *Characteristics of Open Education: Toward an Operational Definition*. Newton, Mass.: TDR Associates, Inc. (375 Elliot St.), 1971.

CHAPTER 9

An Activity Analysis of U.S. Traditional, U.S. Open, and British Open Classrooms

Judith T. Evans, *Harvard University*

"OPEN EDUCATION," "integrated day," "Leicestershire model," "informal education," and "activity-centered learning" are terms used to describe an educational approach which is established in Great Britain and which is gaining recognition in the United States, especially among elementary school practitioners. This investigation was conducted to provide empirical data to clarify different conceptions about this growing, popular education movement at the primary grade level. An exploratory survey approach based on naturalistic classroom observations was chosen to answer three broad questions: (1) Do students in open classrooms have different learning activities than students in traditional classrooms? (2) How do American open classrooms compare with British open classrooms in terms of learning activities? (3) Are there differences among the three groups in the stability of the activities?

First, it was expected that a greater diversity of student learning activities would be found in open classrooms. Second, no expectations were held of specific differences between American and British open classrooms. Third, it was expected that traditional classrooms would have more stable activities than either British open or U.S. open classrooms.

Background and Methodology

Current Descriptions and Theory

Two recent reviews of the open classroom literature (Weber, 1971; Walberg and Thomas, 1971) and one bibliography (Barth and Rathbone, 1971) have highlighted the lack of empirical research studies about open education. Barth and Rathbone's 265-item annotated bibliography, for example, lists only five open education research studies. There are, however, many descriptive studies and anecdotal reports in the literature (Sargent, 1970; Brown and Precious, 1969; Blackie, 1967; Clegg, 1969; Cazden, 1970; Rogers, 1970; Barth, 1972; Rathbone, 1970; Cook and Mack, 1969).

In reading current articles and books about open education, one is left with uneasy feelings. First, it often seems that an unobtainable ideal of classroom learnings is being presented. Second, confusion is caused by the frequent use of the term "open" for anything that is an innovation, i.e., adoption of a new school program, individual instruction, team teaching, affective education, or architectural changes. Third, American open classroom advocates often stress that British open classrooms are the prototypes of open education and suggest that open classrooms in the United States have a long way to go before they are truly "open." Fourth, assumptions about open education (Barth, 1972) sound quite similar to what psychologists investigating discovery learning, curiosity, and intrinsic motivation have explicated and, furthermore, to what students have been studying in psychology courses. Fifth, not everyone who speaks for or against open education agrees to a common concept of what open education is. Critics call open education vague (Etzioni, 1970; Pagen, 1971) or worry that it will jeopardize academic standards (Cox and Dyson, 1969), while its adherents continue to write about it at an increasing rate (Silberman, 1970, 1973; Barth, 1972, Rathbone, 1971; Featherstone, 1971; Hertzberg and Stone, 1971; Murrow and Murrow, 1971; Weber, 1971).

Therefore, a descriptive study of open education was considered important in order to add more precision to our understanding of what practices actually constitute open or traditional education.

The Sample

For this study three comparison groups of 20 U.S. traditional, 20 U.S. open, and 20 British open classrooms were drawn from a wide socioeconomic range. Children in these classrooms were between the ages of five and eight. U.S. traditional classrooms were matched against U.S. open classrooms on the basis of students' age, locale, socioeconomic status, racial and ethnic composition, and public or private school status. The same criteria were used for selecting classrooms in England. U.S. classrooms were selected from one Midwestern and two Eastern cities; British classrooms, from four major cities in England. To ensure that there was a comparable esprit de corps for the traditional classrooms, school administrators and educational consultants recommended classrooms which they considered exemplary traditional ones. First-year teachers were not included in the study; and open classroom teachers were selected only if they had used an open classroom teaching style for at least one year.

Approximately half of each comparison group was drawn from a working- and lower-class population and half from a middle- to upper-middle-class population. For overall comparisons, the U.S. sample represented a greater socioeconomic range than the British sample because upper-middle-class private schools were used in the two U.S. groups, whereas no private school classrooms were used in the British sample.

In the United States, each classroom was visited by an individual observer three times; in England, because of time constraints and economic considerations, each classroom was visited only twice. At least two different observers visited each classroom. In the United States, classrooms were visited during the latter part of March and the entire month of April, 1971. The English open classrooms were visited at the end of April and during the first week of May, 1971.

Classroom Observation Methodology

There are three basic ways to look at a classroom environment: (1) low-inference categorical systems, (2) high-inference rating scales, and (3) naturalistic observations. The first method, low-inference categorical systems, is generally preferred by researchers (Simon and Boyer, 1966) because it is easier to systematically count specific, discrete units of behavior: for example, the number of open-ended questions the teacher asked or the number of directions given. The second method, rating scales, stresses more global characteristics such as enthusiasm, creativity, and intellectual stimulation. While these characteristics are difficult to define operationally, rating scales can effectively discriminate among groups (Rosenshine, 1970). A third method, naturalistic observations, is useful during the early stages of research. This method requires observers to record as quickly and as objectively as possible what they see. These data are later categorized into thematic units. This method has been effectively used by a number of researchers for gaining baseline data about classroom environments (Gump, 1969; Gardner and Case, 1965; Minuchin et al., 1969; Jackson, 1968). Naturalistic observations were used for this study because the newness of open classrooms in the United States suggested that an exploratory approach would be desirable to gain original knowledge without imposing constraints.

Selecting and Training Classroom Observers

There were differences in the selection, training, and composition of classroom observers for the United States and England. The U.S. training sessions were more rigorous than those conducted in England because the research staff had better training facilities, convenient access to schools, and more contacts for attracting temporary classroom observers. In the United States an intensive three-day training and screening program was conducted for thirteen individuals who applied for temporary classroom observer positions. Two part-time researchers, who were familiar with the study, were trained along with the thirteen applicants. All of the individuals trained were white, college-educated women between the ages of twenty-two and forty-five.

Care was taken during the training period not to reveal the purpose of the study. Observers were told that the research staff was withholding information in order not to bias their perceptions and to avoid having them discuss details of the study with participating teachers. If questioned by the teachers, they were told to say that they were participating in a study of contemporary classroom practices of excellent teachers. The words, "experimental," "control," "traditional," and "open" were not used by the research staff during the training period or in the actual study.

In the United States, films of open and traditional classrooms were shown the first day of the training session. Observers rapidly recorded what students were doing at points in the film when they were instructed by the research staff. After practicing and discussing the observation techniques, the trainees in pairs visited an open classroom and a traditional classroom and made observations of students under actual classroom conditions. Observer records for the two films and two field visits were collected for purposes of screening applicants and for gathering preliminary observer-reliability data.

Eleven of the thirteen applicants and five members of the research staff were used in the study. Two applicants were eliminated from the study because of unreliable or careless records. About one-fourth of the observations in the United States were made by the researchers familiar with the purpose of the study, and the remaining three-quarters by the observers who were hired and trained to do just observations.

In England, one research staff member trained two observers during a one-day training session by carefully reviewing the classroom observation techniques. Neither films nor field visits were used. The two trainees, both women, were recommended by British officials and educators as being perceptive, conscientious individuals familiar with open education concepts. Because the British observers were chosen on the basis of their familiarity with the open education approach, the purpose of the study was not disguised for them as it was for the U.S. trained observers. The British observers were told that documenting differences and similarities between open and traditional classrooms was the purpose of the study, but they were not informed about specific features of classroom practices that the research staff expected to find. A total of two research staff observers from the United States and the two observers trained in England visited all the British classrooms.

Research Procedures

There were significantly more students in the British open classrooms than found in U.S. traditional or U.S. open classrooms: i.e., 19.8 students in U.S. traditional, 20.8 in U.S. open, and 31.8 in British open classrooms. To control for the statistical difference, the percentage of students displaying a particular behavior was considered a more unbiased unit of analysis than the mean number of students. Thus, the statistical unit of analysis was the percentage for each variable, rather than the frequency mean.

Observers made two observations of the students. First, observers made a brief 15-minute observation of each of the students, and then followed this with a more detailed description of what each of the students was doing for a 45-minute observation. The analyses for student activities are based upon the brief 15-minute observations. For stability of student activity, analyses are based upon a comparison of the 15-minute observations with the 45-minute observations.

Categories for student activity and stability of student activity were constructed on the basis of a content analysis of the student observations by three members of the research staff. Spot checks for coder agreement were done to ensure consistency in coding the data into major categories. The percentage of coder agreements was derived by having one researcher code part of a major portion of the data and having another researcher code the same part. An estimate of the number of times there was agreement for the two coders was then made for the entire section. For student activity, there was 95 percent coder agreement; and for stability of student activity, 80 percent agreement. The agreement was not so high for stability of student activity because it required a high-inference rating based upon two different observations, whereas the other category depended upon only one observation and was of a less-inferential nature.

The Findings

Comparisons for the activities of students and the stability of these activities for the three classroom groups are presented in this section. Each table provides a formula which explains how the mean and the percentage were calculated. Essentially, the figures represent what would be seen during a single observation period for an "average" U.S. traditional, U.S. open, or British open classroom.

Student Activities

Seventeen categories of student activities, constructed from the obser-

Table 1. Means, Standard Deviations, Percentages, and F-ratios Based upon Percentages for Student Activities by Groups

Student Activities	U.S. Traditional (N = 20)		U.S. Open (N = 20)		British Open (N = 20)		F-ratio
	Mean, %	S.D.	Mean, %	S.D.	Mean, %	S.D.	
1. Reading: language experience	0.55 2.6%	1.50 7.4	1.30 6.2%	1.44 7.0	3.82 11.4%	2.94 9.0	6.37*
2. Reading: workbooks	2.67 13.6%	4.54 21.8	2.21 10.4%	3.08 14.8	1.62 4.9%	2.17 6.6	1.55
3. Reading: out-loud and silent	4.49 25.7%	3.68 25.7	2.17 10.7%	1.53 7.9	2.50 7.5%	2.04 5.6	7.51
4. Reading: spelling, phonics, grammar	3.32 18.4%	3.03 19.0	1.05 4.3%	2.67 9.9	0.32 1.0%	0.94 2.8	11.00**
5. Reading: other	0.90 3.9%	2.48 10.6	0.92 4.5%	1.20 6.0	0.72 2.2%	1.33 3.8	0.55
6. Reading: total	12.20 65.9%	6.39 32.9	7.64 36.1%	4.66 20.3	9.02 27.0%	4.91 13.5	
7. Unspecified workbooks, worksheets	2.56 14.5%	5.98 30.4	0.92 4.6%	1.47 7.2	0.40 1.2%	1.01 2.9	14.82**
8. Math: manipulative and games	1.55 6.8%	4.50 18.5	1.88 8.3%	2.56 9.9	5.38 15.7%	8.31 23.1	2.90
9. Math: activity cards	0.00 0.0%	0.00 0.0	0.03 0.2%	0.15 0.9	0.58 1.7%	1.09 3.3	1.41
10. Math: workbooks blackboard lessons	1.06 5.8%	1.88 10.6	0.82 4.0%	1.03 5.1	1.22 3.6%	2.47 7.1	4.63
11. Math: total	2.62 12.6%	4.72 20.6	2.73 12.5%	2.62 10.5	7.18 21.0%	8.18 22.8	0.42

													F
12. Science: lesson	0.08	0.37	0.00	0.00	0.00	0.00							1.00
	0.4%	1.6	0.0%	0.0	0.0%	0.0							
13. Science: manipulative and games, etc.	0.00	0.00	0.71	1.15	0.90	1.36							4.12
	0.0%	0.0	3.2%	5.1	2.6%	3.8							
14. Science: total	0.08	0.37	0.71	1.15	0.90	1.36							2.98
	0.4%	1.6	3.2%	5.1	2.6%	3.8							
15. Arts and crafts	0.90	2.14	2.98	2.21	5.92	4.42							1.85
	8.0%	24.0	13.7%	10.4	18.2%	13.0							
16. Play	0.90	1.98	3.19	2.14	4.18	4.79							4.73
	4.5%	10.2	14.8%	9.6	11.7%	12.6							
17. Other	0.92	2.22	3.28	3.85	5.58	5.88							4.16
	4.1%	9.4	15.2%	17.3	18.3%	20.3							
18. Total of all activities	19.43	4.53	21.46	3.60	33.18	4.79							

All F-ratios are based upon 2, 57 degrees of freedom.

*p < .01
**p < .001

Mean = Sum of   Total number of observed events in each classroom
during 15-minute spot observation   Number of visits to
that classroom

Total number of classrooms (= 20)

% =   Mean
Total number of students present

vational data, are reported in Table 1. Analyses of variance for each of the seventeen student activities showed that significant differences occurred only among variables designated as reading categories. Of six reading categories, four showed statistically significant differences: language experience ($F = 6.37$, $df = 2.57$, $p = .01$); out-loud and silent reading ($F = 7.57$, $df = 2.57$, $p = .01$); spelling, phonics, and grammar ($F = 11.00$, $df = 2.57$, $p = .001$); and total of all reading activities ($F = 14.82$, $df = 2.57$, $p = .001$).

Multiple mean comparison tests were done to detect differences among classroom groups. The significant t-test comparisons reported are at or below the .01 level. British open classrooms had 11.4 percent of the students engaged in the language-experience reading method, which was a significantly greater percentage than U.S. traditional classrooms, where 2.6 percent of the students were involved in this type of reading activity. U.S. open classrooms had 6.2 percent of the students engaged in language-experience work, which was not a significantly different percentage from that found in either British open or U.S. traditional classrooms.

The 25.7 percent of U.S. traditional students engaged in out-loud and silent reading was significantly higher than the 10.7 percent of students in U.S. open or 7.5 percent of students in British open classrooms observed in this activity. There was no statistically significant difference between U.S. open and British open classrooms in this respect.

The 18.4 percent of U.S. traditional students engaged in spelling, phonics, and grammar activities was significantly higher than the 1.0 percent of students in British open classrooms engaged in spelling, phonics, and grammar work. There was no difference for U.S. open classrooms, where 4.3 percent of the students were shown doing spelling, phonics, and grammar work.

The greatest amount of combined reading work occurred in U.S. traditional classrooms, where 65.9 percent of the students were counted in some form of reading activity. This was significantly higher than the 36.1 percent of U.S. open students or the 27.0 percent of British open classroom students observed in some form of reading work. There was no difference between U.S. open and British open classrooms for the percentage of students in total of reading activities.

No significant differences were found among the classroom groups for the following student activity variables: reading workbooks; other reading; unspecified workbooks and worksheets, manipulative math and math games, math activity cards, math workbooks and blackboard lessons, combined total of math activities, science lessons, manipulative science and games, combined total of science activities, arts and crafts, play, and other. For all three classroom groups, there was a wide range within each group on many of the student activity variables as exemplified by large standard deviations.

While significant differences were found only for reading activities, some estimate of the top priorities of student activities can be seen by reporting the five most commonly found student activities for each classroom group. For U.S. traditional classrooms, the top five student activities were:

1. Total of reading activities   65.9%
2. Out-loud and silent reading   25.7%
3. Spelling, phonics, and grammar   18.4%
4. Unspecified workbooks and worksheets   14.5%
5. Reading workbooks   13.6%

For U.S. open classrooms, the top five student activities were:

1. Total of reading activities   36.1%
2. Other activities   15.2%
3. Play   14.8%
4. Arts and crafts   13.7%
5. Total of math activities   12.5%

For the British open classrooms, the top five student activities were:

1. Total of reading activities   27.0%
2. Total of math activities   27.0%
3. Other activities   18.3%
4. Play   18.2%
5. Manipulative math and games   15.7%

U.S. traditional classrooms showed a different order of priorities from the U.S. open and British open classrooms. The latter share in common four of the five top activities, whereas the U.S. traditional classrooms shared only one of the top five student activities with the two open classroom groups, namely, total of reading activities. U.S. and British open classrooms placed less reliance on reading work, which was the major emphasis of the U.S. traditional classrooms; instead, both placed greater emphasis on more diverse activities such as those under the "other" category (e.g., social studies, show-and-tell, music, cooking, physical education, health and safety), arts and crafts, and play.

Both the statistical tests on all student activities and the order of priorities of the top five student activities show that there are noticeable differences in student activities between U.S. traditional classrooms and U.S. open or British open classrooms. No statistical differences were found between British open and U.S. open classrooms on any of the seventeen student activity variables. Furthermore, the order of priorities for the British open and U.S. open classrooms was remarkably similar.

Student Stability

Do students wander needlessly around open classrooms, whereas more stable behavior is found in traditional classrooms; or is more aimless student behavior found in traditional classrooms, whereas more involvement occurs in open classrooms? To examine these questions, four categories of student stability were developed and rated by the coders: (1) high stability, (2) moderate stability, (3) low stability, and (4) unknown stability. To rate each student's behavior, coders would locate a student engaged in an activity during the spot observations and see whether the student was still engaged in the same activity during the 45-minute observation. If, for example, six students were originally at an art table doing claywork and six were still there during the in-depth scenario, the rating would be high stability for six students. If only three were there later, the rating would be moderate stability for six students. If only one student remained, the rating would be low stability for six students, and a total absence of students would result in an unknown-stability rating for six students.

"Unknown" was used often by the coders because many teachers would change activities between the time the observers started the spot observations and when the 45-minute observations were recorded. To make a subjective rating would be inappropriate, since often the activity no longer continued not because of the students' motivation but because the teachers had initiated new activities.

Analyses of variance reported in Table 2 revealed that the classroom groups were significantly different on only one of the four categories, namely, low stability. U.S. open classrooms had a higher percentage of students given low-stability ratings compared with British open or U.S. traditional students; i.e., 13.7 percent of the U.S. open, 3.8 percent of British open, and 3.3 percent of U.S. traditional students were given low-stability ratings for their activities.

In general, all classroom groups had highly stable student activities: e.g., U.S. traditional had 57.6 percent; U.S. open had 41.1 percent, and British open had 57.9 percent of student activities given high-stability ratings. Also, all the classroom groups had approximately one-fourth to one-third of their students given "unknown" ratings. This was for three reasons. First, the teachers frequently changed classroom activities for the class while the observers were observing students. Second, many students were unable to be located between the first observation and the second, probably because the children were still in the class but had not been described accurately enough by the observers. Third, some of the students may have wandered out of the classrooms during one of the two observations and thus were recorded once but missed at another observation and marked "unknown."

The data on stability of student activities suggests that teachers in all groups insist upon students' concentrating on school activities and

Table 2. Means, Standard Deviations, Percentages, and F-ratios Based upon Percentages for Stability of Student Activities by Groups

Stability of Student Activity	U.S. Traditional (N = 20) Mean, %	S.D.	U.S. Open (N = 20) Mean, %	S.D.	British Open (N = 20) Mean, %	S.D.	F-ratio
1. High	11.94 57.6%	7.28 29.4	8.81 41.1%	4.81 20.3	17.92 54.9%	7.56 22.9	2.59
2. Moderate	1.35 7.3%	2.82 16.4	2.25 10.1%	3.29 14.2	4.98 14.8%	8.30 24.1	0.84
3. Low	0.68 3.3%	1.70 8.1	2.95 13.7%	3.00 12.2	1.28 3.8%	1.91 5.6	8.31**
4. Unknown	6.20 31.9%	6.10 30.8	7.46 35.1%	4.48 20.6	9.00 26.5%	6.89 19.1	0.66

All F-ratios are based upon 2, 57 degrees of freedom.
** $p < .001$

$$\text{Mean} = \frac{\text{Sum of}\begin{array}{l}\text{Total number of observed events in each classroom}\\ \text{based upon comparison of 15-minute spot observations}\\ \text{with 45-minute in-depth observations}\end{array} \times \begin{array}{l}\text{Number of visits}\\ \text{to that}\\ \text{classroom}\end{array}}{\text{Total number of classrooms} = 20}$$

$$\% = \frac{\text{Mean}}{\text{Total number of students present}}$$

following teacher directions, no matter what activities or style of student behavior the teachers encouraged. However, it should be noted that more students were given low-stability ratings in U.S. open classrooms. The high number of "unknown" ratings reflects the difficulties encountered in survey research where observers unfamiliar to the classrooms have to make two consecutive observations upon which an inferential rating was later made by coders.

Summary and Conclusions

This study upheld the first expectation that open classrooms would have significantly different student learning activities from traditional classrooms, and also supported the second expectation by revealing no differences between British open and U.S. open classrooms for student learning activities. The third expectation, that traditional student learning activities would be more stable than open classroom learning activities, was not supported.

Of seventeen student activity variables, there were significant differences for four reading variables: language experience, out-loud and silent reading; phonics, spelling, and grammar; and total of all reading activities. British students had more language experience work than U.S. traditional students. U.S. traditional students had more out-loud and silent reading than U.S. open or British open students, and more spelling, phonics, and grammar than the British open students. Finally, U.S. traditional students were involved in more reading activities than either U.S. open or British open students.

In rating the stability of student activities, the general pattern was that students in all classrooms were given high- and moderate-stability ratings. More students in U.S. open classrooms were given low-stability ratings, which seems to indicate a potential area for improvement. A high percentage of students in all classroom groups were given "unknown" stability ratings. This higher number of "unknown" stability ratings illustrates the difficulties encountered in survey research when coders, one step removed from the classroom, make inferential ratings based upon a comparison of two observations.

Extrapolations to other student populations must be done with care because this study dealt only with children between the ages of five and eight. Furthermore, practices change with time, and the classrooms visited might be different if observed at another time. It should also be noted that other ways of investigating stability of student activities might have been used. For example, observing a random sample of students over time, or having observers rate student stability directly rather than leaving this to coders.

Important questions still remain after one has conducted a descriptive study such as this. For example, how do the independent variables of open or traditional relate to dependent variables such as achievement scores, student characteristics, student vocational choices, teacher and student satisfaction, attendance, outside interests, economic benefits, and so on? Analyses of individual differences might reveal important comparisons, such as what types of students do best in open or traditional classrooms. Or, one might ask, how do subcomponents of the major independent variables, such as the language-experience method, relate to achievement test scores; or are there different profiles of student activities or stability of activities related to socioeconomic status?

In general, major analytic questions remain about the effects of open education. It should also be stressed that many differences between British open and U.S. open classroom teaching practices can and did occur in other analyses reported elsewhere (Evans, 1972), which makes it imperative to remember the complicated, multivariate nature of open classrooms in America and England. Hopefully, this descriptive study will lay groundwork for other studies which will explore the many facets of open education as they affect children's motivation and learning experiences.

References

Barth, Roland S., *Open Education and the American School.* New York: Agathon Press, 1972.

Barth, Roland S., and Charles H. Rathbone, *A Bibliography of Open Education.* Jointly published by Cambridge, Mass.: Advisory for Open Education; and Newton, Mass.: Education Development Center, Inc., 1971.

Blackie, J., *Inside the Primary School.* London: Her Majesty's Stationery Office, 1967.

Brown, Mary, and Norman Precious, *The Integrated Day in the Primary School.* New York: Agathon Press, 1969.

Cazden, Courtney B., *Transplanting English Infant School Ideas to American Classrooms–and Some Effects on Language Use.* Minneapolis, Minn.: AERA, 1970. Revised mimeographed version of paper presented at American Educational Research Association meeting.

Clegg, Alec B., "The Revolution in the English Elementary Schools," *The National Elementary Principal,* September 1969, *49:1.*

Cook, Ann, and Herbert Mack, "The British Primary School," *Educational Leadership.* November 1969, *27:2.*

Cox, C. B., and A. E. Dyson, "Primary Schools: Moving Progressively Backwards," *Critical Quarterly Society,* London, 1969.

Etzioni, Amitai, "On Crisis in the Classroom," *Harvard Educational Review*, February 1970, *41*, 87–98.

Evans, Judith T., *An Empirical Investigation of the Open Classroom.* Unpublished doctoral dissertation, Harvard University, 1972.

Featherstone, Joseph, *Schools Where Children Learn.* New York: Liveright, 1971.

Gardner, D. E. M., and J. E. Cass, *The Role of the Teacher in the Infant and Nursery School.* Oxford: Pergamon, 1965.

Gump, Paul V., "Intra-setting Analysis: The Third Grade Classroom as a Special But Instructive Case," from E. Willems and H. Raush, *Naturalistic Viewpoints in Psychological Research.* New York: Holt, Rinehart, and Winston, 1969.

Hertzberg, Alvin, and Edward F. Stone, *Schools Are for Children: An American Approach to the Open Classroom.* New York: Schocken, 1971.

Jackson, Philip W., *Life in Classrooms.* New York: Holt, Rinehart and Winston, 1968.

Minuchin, Patricia, et al., *The Psychological Impact of School Experience.* New York: Basic Books, 1969.

Murrow, C., and L. Murrow, *Children Come First.* New York: American Heritage Press, 1971.

Pagen, John, "Backtalk," *Phi Delta Kappa*, March, 1971, *52:7.*

Rathbone, Charles H., *Open Education and the Teacher.* Unpublished doctoral dissertation, Harvard University, 1970.

Rathbone, Charles H. (ed.), *Open Education: The Informal Classroom.* New York: Citation, 1971.

Rogers, Vincent R., *The English Primary School.* New York: Macmillan, 1970.

Rosenshine, B., "Evaluation of Classroom Instruction." *Review of Educational Research*, 1970, *40:279–300.*

Rosenshine, Barak, *Teaching Behaviours and Student Achievement.* Fernhill, 1972.

Sargent, Betsye, *The Integrated Day in an American School.* Boston, Mass.: National Association of Independent Schools, 1970.

Silberman, C. E., *Crisis in the Classroom.* New York: Random House, 1970.

Silberman, C.E. (ed.), *The Open Classroom Reader.* New York: Random House, 1973.

Simon, A., and Boyer, E. G. (eds.), *Mirrors for Behavior: An Anthology of Classroom Observation Instruments*, Vols. 1–6. New York: Teachers College Press, 1966.

Walberg, Herbert J., and Susan Thomas, *Characteristics of Open Education: Toward an Operational Definition.* Newton, Mass.: Education Development Center, Inc., U. S. Office of Education No. OEC-1-7-062805-3963, 1971.

Weber, Lillian, *The British Infant School and Informal Education.* Englewood Cliffs, N.J.: Prentice-Hall, 1971.

CHAPTER 10

Using Systems Analysis to Study Open Classrooms

Nancy L. Dill, *Queens College, The City University of New York*

Open Classrooms as Open Systems

Living systems—whether individuals or populations—are best analyzed as "open systems," i.e., as systems open to exchanges with an environment. Human organizations are living systems (Emery, 1969, p. 8); thus, it would appear to be appropriate to look at "open education" (or more specifically, the "open classroom") in terms of open-systems theory. Such an analysis should be particularly helpful in coming to terms with the notion put forth by many educators that an "open" approach is not an "unstructured" approach.

Chittenden and Bussis (1971), along with others, have tried to deal with the problem posed by the term "open education." While it is probably true that "open education" refers as much to "opening up" the schools as to any fixed method or program, there are a number of ideas that permeate open education as it is currently being practiced.

Open classroom education grows out of the philosophy that for each child learning takes an uneven, episodic path (Kohl, 1969, p. 54) and that children can take responsibility for their own learning if allowed to do so (Muir, 1970). The role of the teacher is to provide an environment in which this process can take place.

The concepts of (1) the integrated day, (2) family grouping, (3) open-space environments, and (4) multiple learning materials have been dealt with in great detail in various literature on open education (Brown and Precious, 1969; Ridgway and Lawton, 1969; Anglo-American Primary School Project, 1971). While these four notions tell us something about the properties of the open classroom experience, the main structural components of any classroom—the curriculum and interaction among participants (teacher and learner/verbal and nonverbal)—remain to be charted.

There is a pressing reason for pursuing this inquiry. Many state Departments of Education are now urging field-based, competency-based teacher education programs (Elam, 1971). If the nature of the curriculum is different in an open classroom, then teacher educators need to know it. And if teachers are to be trained in such a way as to operate optimally in open education settings, then settings displaying that kind of curriculum need to be sought as training sites. If the nature of interaction is different in open education classrooms, then teacher trainers need to know it. Open education teachers who may be certified in the future on the basis of classroom performance need to be evaluated using categories that are appropriate to the kind of teacher-learner interaction found in open classrooms.

A Systems Approach to Curriculum and Teaching

Macdonald (1965) has proposed that teaching and curriculum be regarded as two separate but congruent subsystems—curriculum being the major source of stimuli found in instructional settings. Banathy (1968), Pfeiffer (1968), Umans (1971), and others have advocated a systems approach to instruction. Much of the work in applying systems thinking to educational situations, however, seems to have failed to make use of one crucial systems principle—the notion of *equifinality*. This term refers to the use of different patterns or routes to produce the same final result.

In contrast to equilibrium states in closed systems, which are determined by initial conditions, the state of an open system is determined only by system parameters (Von Bertalanffy, 1962). Feyereisen, Fiorino, and Nowak (1970), however, in their book *Supervision and Curriculum Renewal: A Systems Approach,* do not even incorporate the notion of equifinality.

Processes occurring in machinelike structures follow a fixed pathway. Therefore, the final state will be changed if the initial conditions or the course of processes is altered. In contrast, says Von Bertalanffy (1968), the same final state, the same "goal," may be reached from different initial conditions and along different pathways in organismic processes. This seems to have been what Schwab (1970) had in mind when he called attention to the existential nature of the curriculum and recommended curricular practices which are modifiable by the flow of the individual's experience.

The educational literature of the last ten years is also rich in studies aimed at developing categories that describe interaction in the classroom. According to Simon and Boyer (1970), over seventy-five such category systems now exist. While these systems represent different ways of viewing classroom discourse, they stand together to indicate that when one looks at teaching "the way it is," interaction between teacher and student is of primary importance. In spite of the diversity of existing category systems, however, it is doubtful that one can enter an open classroom with any existing category schema and obtain an adequate picture of the verbal and/or nonverbal interaction of that classroom.

Curriculum theory and classroom interaction analyses have, for the most part, been based on classrooms where teachers stand at the front and confront all youngsters at the same time. Are the theoretical constructs which have been developed over the years in this kind of environment adequate when the framework of instruction becomes an open classroom?

The urgency of research on curriculum and teaching in open classrooms lies in the fact that descriptive classroom studies are at this time the main source of performance criteria (Rosenshine and Furst, 1971). Almost all the current model teacher education programs are dominated by performance criteria stated in behavioral terms (Burdin and Lanzillotti, 1969). Lacking adequate studies on open classrooms, what sources of performance criteria does the field of education have for evaluating the participants in open education?

Properties of Open Systems

Systems thinking plays a dominant role today in a wide variety of fields, and terms such as *systems design, systems analysis,* and *systems engineering* have become commonplace. It is now widely felt that the only meaningful way to study phenomena in the behavioral and social sciences, as well as in the biological sciences, is through the framework of general systems theory (Von Bertalanffy, 1968). It is the purpose of this study to explore the applicability of open systems theory in an attempt to come to some understanding of the curricular and instructional dynamics of an open classroom.

A *system,* put simply, is "all of a thing" (Miller, 1955, p. 515). It can also refers to the degrees to which the system is receptive to all types 1968, p. 55). A system is open if it has *input* and *output.* That is to say, *open systems* involve the flow of energy from the *environment* through the system itself and back into the environment. As Cadwallader (1959, p. 154) has pointed out, an open system, whether social or biological, in a changing environment either changes or perishes. System openness also refers to the degrees to whch the system is receptive to all types of input (Katz and Kahn, 1966, p. 59).

It is possible for an open system to attain a state where the system remains constant as a whole, although there is a continuous flow of component material. This is referred to as a *steady state*. Flanders (1970) has used this notion in his FIAC system. The steady-state ratio (SSR) can be determined by calculating the percentage of all tallies that lie within the ten steady-state cells (1-1, 2-2, 3-3, etc.) (Flanders, 1970, p. 105).

This constancy is maintained because of a continuous exchange between the system and its environment. Systems maintain steady states with regard to many variables by negative *feedback* mechanisms which distribute information to *subsystems*. Miller (1955, p. 514) notes that systems are also usually in balance with their environments, thereby preventing variations in the environments from destroying the systems.

Any system can be further subdivided into *subsystems*. Objects belonging to one subsystem may well be part of the environment of another subsystem. For a given system, the environment is the "set of all objects a change in whose attributes affect the system" (Hall and Fagan, 1968, p. 83) and also those objects whose attributes are changed by the behavior of the system. Open systems theory, with its entropy assumption, emphasizes the close relationship between a structure and its supporting environment. *Negative entropy* implies that systems survive and maintain their characteristic internal order only so long as they import from the environment more energy than they expend in the process of transformation and exportation (Katz and Kahn, 1966, p. 28).

Boundary, in systems thinking, refers to that which separates the system from its environment (Maccia, n.d., p. 141). Input is "the sending of entities from the environment into the system," while output is "the sending of entities from the system into the environment" (Maccia, n.d., p. 141). Input may take the form of information, materials, or personnel, whereas output may take the form of any observable act of a system involving energy exchange across the system's boundary. Outputs vary with different inputs and different configurations of systems elements. Some systems have the property that a portion of their output is fed back to the input to affect system action and succeeding output. Additionally, open systems have the property of equifinality, described above, which is the ability to use different patterns or routes to produce the same final result.

A complex system is composed of subsystems, which in turn have their own subsystems. Most systems exhibit a clearly visible hierarchical structure. The hierarchy of a particular system may be determined by observing who interacts with whom.

Network Analysis as a Tool for Systems Analysis

Network analysis is one of quite a number of analytical procedures which have been developed and put into use in the study of the structure of wholes. More specifically, human organizations are behavioral systems which display activity (Ackoff, 1969, p. 332), and network analysis is a technique used in systems design, planning, and control to show the sequential relationship among activities and events of a system (Johnson, Kast, and Rosenzweig, 1967, p. 316). The analysis is presented in the form of a network which is a visual representation of the system (Evarts, 1964, p. 17). This study explores the extent to which network analysis can handle data on the curricular and instructional components of open classrooms.

A *network* is essentially a flow chart of events that are joined by activity lines to depict their interdependencies and interrelationships (Baker and Eris, 1964, p. 2). *Events* are instantaneous occurrences; they do not consume time or resources (PERT Coordinating Group, 1963, p. 18). An event is usually shown on the network as a circle. Events are used at the beginning and end of all activities, and they are usually identified by a number as well as explanatory nomenclature. Activities, on the other hand, are of two types—real and dummy. *Real activities* are time-consuming tasks, shown on the network as a solid line with an arrow to indicate the direction of sequential activity (Evarts, 1964, p. 94). *Dummy activities* do not consume time or other resources; however, they are constraints which represent the dependency of one event upon another (Baker and Eris, 1964, p. 5). Dummy activities are usually shown on the network as dashed arrows.

Events are numbered sequentially in the network, usually from left to right and top to bottom. A skip-numbering system is usually utilized in order to permit the addition of events without getting numbers out of sequence. Activities are known by the numbers of the beginning and ending events to which they are attached (e.g., activity 10–70 is one which extends from event 10 to event 70).

The above discussion is illustrated by the figures which follow.

A network's *critical path* is the sequence or chain of events and activities, extending from the beginning to the end of the network, requiring the longest time to complete (PERT Coordinating Group, 1963, p. D.1). In this study the critical path is utilized to follow the movements of one youngster over a period of time.

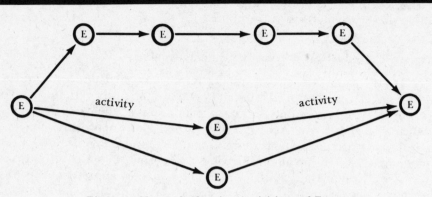

Figure 1. **Network Showing Activities and Events**

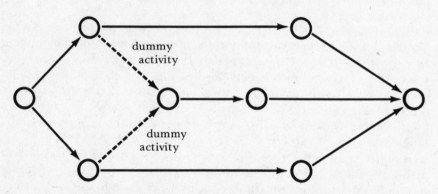

Figure 2. **Network Showing Activities, Events, and Dummy Activities**

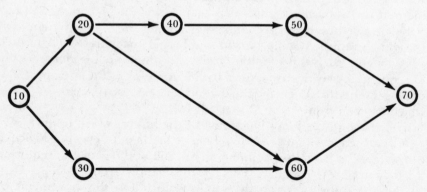

Figure 3. **Network Showing Event Numbering System**

A number of other network procedures should be noted here in order for the reader to get an understanding of how network analysis works. (1) One event often serves as both the ending event for one group of activities and the beginning event for another series. (2) Event bubbles are sometimes drawn in different shapes to make possible rapid identification of activity and event responsibilities. (3) Network *condensation* is a procedure which allows a large network to be reduced to a skeleton network. (4) Network *expansion* is the reverse process, in which more detailed networks are prepared.

A Study of Open Primary Classrooms

Observations.   The open classrooms observed by the investigator were ones in which (1) the researcher had student teachers and was there as a supervisor; (2) the researcher had undergraduate students from an elective course on "Analyzing Teaching Behavior" (who were also student teaching, but the researcher was not the supervisor); or (3) the researcher had graduate students from a research course who were the regular, full-time classroom teachers.

The open classrooms observed were located in public schools both in Queens and elsewhere on Long Island and ranged from K to 6 in grade level. Included among the classrooms observed were a 5-6 and a 4-5-6 combination open classroom. Some observations were videotaped for later analysis.

Curriculum networks.   In some cases a skeleton network was constructed during the observation. The network was later expanded following the observation, using as much detail as the observation had produced. When the observation was videotaped, all network construction was delayed until later viewing of the tape.

Seven kinds of coding were used in addition to the regular numbering of activities and events throughout the network. (1) Youngsters whose activities were being followed or who appeared on the scene frequently were given a number (e.g., 5, 22, etc.). (2) Teachers were coded: T_1, T_2, T_3, etc. (3) Student teachers were coded: ST_1, ST_2, ST_3, etc. (4) Other adults who were often present in the classroom were given letter designations (e.g., P – parent, A – administrator). (5) Time designations were denoted t_1, t_2, t_3, etc. The length of an activity could thus be calculated in the following manner:

$$t_{act} = t_1 - t_2$$

Whenever possible actual clock time was marked down so that these calculations could be subsequently made. (6) Curricular areas were desig-

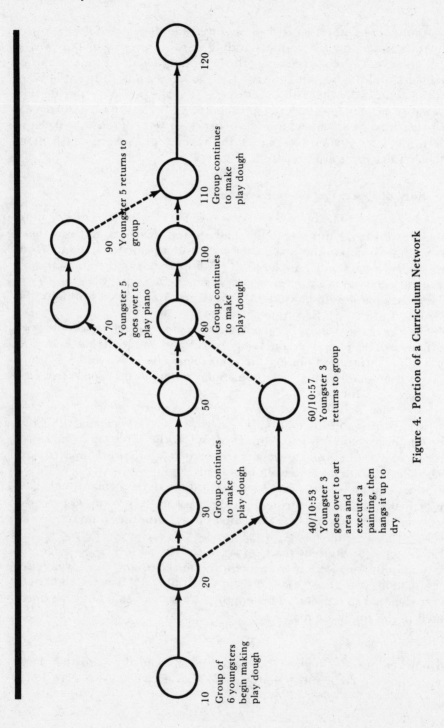

Figure 4. Portion of a Curriculum Network

nated by various letter combinations (e.g., R – reading, SC – science, etc). (7) If a particular curricular program was identifiable as an entity, it was frequently given a number which was used along with the general area designation (e.g., SRA Reading Program might be coded R–2). A portion of a curriculum network is shown in Figure 4.

Interaction networks. Four kinds of designations were used in the interaction networks. Using diamond-shaped symbols to represent events, the four positions

represented, respectively: (1) initiator/responder (the message sender); (2) other person(s) (message receiver); (3) nature of the dialogue; and (4) content area. For example,

Initiator/Responder: S (student)
                   S–5 (student No. 5)
                   ST (student teacher)
                   P (parent)
                   A (administrator)
Other Person: (same as above)
Nature of the dialogue: Questioning
                        Telling
Content Area: R (reading)
              R–2 (SRA Reading)
              SC (science)

The networks were thus series of IODC/RODC's. Figures 5, 6, and 7 illustrate the interaction network components. The brief interactions which these figures represent went something like this:

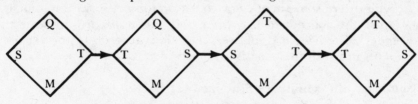

Figure 5. Interaction Network: Student-Teacher

Figure 5:

    S: What did I do wrong here?

    T: Can't you figure it out?

    S: It seems that it's just a mistake in adding it up, but I wasn't sure.

    T: Take a closer look; I believe there is more to it than that.

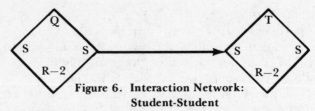

Figure 6. Interaction Network:
Student-Student

Figure 6:

  S: Did you start on level 3?

  S: No, I began with level 4. I'll give you your pretest if you want
  me to.

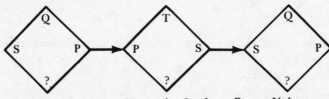

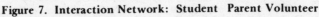

Figure 7. Interaction Network: Student Parent Volunteer

Figure 7:

  S: Do you have a calendar?

  P: Yes

  S: May I borrow it?

Network comparisons.   A variety of comparisons among networks was
possible: (1) one grade level compared with another grade level; (2)
beginning of year compared with later in year for same classroom; (3)
classroom of all one age group compared with classroom with family
grouping; (4) individual youngsters compared with other youngsters in
the same classroom; (5) single-room open classroom compared with an
open classroom operation utilizing multiple classrooms; (6) activities of
boys compared with those of girls.

Activities were sometimes color-coded on the networks for comparisons. Also, the concept of the *critical path* was utilized to indicate the
movement of individual youngsters over time in terms of the activities
and events in which they had been involved.

A Summary of Preliminary Findings

The findings reported here should be viewed as very tentative and
preliminary. There are two reasons for this. First, of course, is the limited number of classrooms observed in the study. The second and more
important reason, however, is the limited theoretical and research base
with respect to open education.

The findings also deal more with curricular aspects than with verbal interaction, simply because of the difficulty of maneuvering videotape-recording equipment around an open classroom. The zoom lens on the Sony VTR camera allows for a visual recording of what is happening at great distances, whereas the accompanying dialogue may or may not be captured. Thus, the visual material collected is more abundant and more clearly rendered on tape than is the auditory material.

Grade-level comparisons.   The flow of events across grade levels turned out to be quite similar. Networks of a third grade did not appear visually to be greatly different from ones of a kindergarten. Similarly, networks of the third grade bore a likeness to upper-grade networks as well.

In networks at all grade levels observed, there seemed to be something of a reversal of roles in terms of verbal interaction. In open classrooms youngsters ask the questions. In the tapes collected in this study, an analysis shows approximately 75 percent of the questions were asked by students.

Time-of-year comparisons.   Networks at all levels grew in complexity with the passing of time throughout the school year. This appears to be a function of the increasing degree to which individual students work completely alone or with only one other person and also a function of the rapidity with which regrouping of combinations of students occurs in an open classroom environment.

In an open classroom during the course of the school year the child increasingly has the freedom to choose those activities in which he wants to become involved. Later in the school year, as children arrive in the morning, they simply start to do things, continuing whatever activities they were engaged in the day before. While at the outset of the school year the teacher might be observed directing groups of children toward certain learning centers or to specific activities, this would rarely be observable later on.

Age-grouping comparisons.   A visual inspection of networks of open classrooms consisting of only one grade in comparison with networks depicting classrooms with groupings that cut across different grades revealed no particular differences except for the increased complexity which accrues to such combination-grade operations because of the larger number of students and staff involved and the resultant increase in available combinations.

Individual-student comparisons.   Sequence in an open classroom is a highly individualistic thing. Some youngsters getting pleasure out of the familiarity of the task, choose to repeat items. Other students, testing their capacities, prefer to plunge ahead, retreating to another level if frustrated or confronted by the reality of low scores on criterion tests. In an open classroom every student appears to take "a different path through the network."

In addition, different students seem to approach their tasks with varying intensities. An art activity, for example, which can frequently fill up 30 minutes in a traditional classroom can be executed in an open classroom in less than 3 minutes or can extend up to 10 or 15 minutes. There appears to be a different rhythm or intensity for each child.

Individuals who look on the surface as if they are doing nothing are often actually engaged in meaningful activity. Activities such as "cleaning the art brushes" or "doing the weather report" perhaps have a deeper structure. They seem to provide the framework within which youngsters can have extended talk among themselves, for example, or begin and/or extend an inquiry they have also been engaged in elsewhere.

Students frequently exercise their options in an open classroom and stay away from certain tasks, projects, or curricular activities. This is to say that many students have favorite curriculum areas; for some, it is mathematics, and for others, it is reading and the language arts. This appears to imply that varying curriculum areas must be made both conceptually and visually attractive to students if they are to have a well-rounded program. It also hints at the necessity for developing with students a management system designed to achieve such a goal that can be self-directed and self-monitored.

Finally, there seems to be a core of verbal subroutines which account for a sizable portion of the interaction in open classrooms. These kernel patterns need to be identified in detail in further research.

Type-of-space comparisons. The activities of an open classroom frequently spill out of the main classroom space into adjoining halls, with a set of stairs providing a mini-stage for impromptu dramatizations, for example. Open-space buildings in and of themselves do not appear to add a noticeable dimension to the patterns of activity.

Boy-girl comparisons. Verbal interaction more often than not involves only two people in an open classroom. This could be a student and a teacher, two students, or a student and a parent volunteer. More than 50 percent of the verbal interchange collected in this study involved only two persons.

In addition, at all grade levels, more often than not a boy would be working with another boy, and a girl would be teamed up with another girl. These are the children's own choosings. Two boys and two girls might be working on similar activities and in shared space, but the close interactions generally involved youngsters of the same sex.

Summary. Open systems theory appears to be a useful framework for viewing the workings of an open classroom. Curriculum areas in an open classroom are subsystems in interrelation with each other—

changes in one curriculum area will of necessity produce changes with respect to all other areas of the curriculum. Interaction may also be viewed within a systems framework. A new student in a classroom complex changes all the interaction patterns, as we are all aware. What is happening in this case is the forming of new subsystems and the dissolving of others.

This study has also found the use of network analysis to be a productive tool in handling information about the involvement of youngsters in various curriculum areas over time and in looking at interaction in open classrooms.

The findings of this study suggest simply the beginning dimensions of a framework that could reflect the changing, dynamic quality of a system such as an open classroom. Additional research is greatly needed in order to map fully the curricular and instructional dynamics involved.

References

Ackoff, R. L., "Systems, Organizations, and Interdisciplinary Research," in F. E. Emery (ed.), *Systems Thinking*. Harmondsworth, England: Penguin Books, 1969.

Anglo-American Primary School Project, *Informal Schools in Britain Today*. New York: Citation Press, 1971.

Baker, B. N., and R. L. Eris, *An Introduction to PERT-CPM*. Homewood, Ill.: Richard D. Irwin, 1964.

Banathy, B. H., *Instructional Systems*. Palo Alto: Fearon House, 1968.

Brown, M., and N. Precious, *The Integrated Day in the Primary School*. New York: Agathon Press, 1969.

Burdin, J. L., and K. Lanzillotti (eds.), *A Reader's Guide to the Comprehensive Models for Preparing Elementary Teachers*. Washington, D. C.: ERIC Clearinghouse on Teacher Education, 1969.

Cadwallader, M. L., "The Cybernetic Analysis of Change in Complex Social Organizations," *American Journal of Sociology*, 1959, *65*, 154–57.

Chittenden, E. A., and A. M. Bussis, "Open Education: Research and Assessment Strategies," paper presented at the annual meeting of the National Association for the Education of Young Children, Minneapolis, November 1971.

Elam, S., *Performance-Based Teacher Education: What Is the State of the Art?* Washington, D. C.: AACTE, 1971.

Emery, F. E. (ed.), *Systems Thinking*. Harmondsworth, England: Penguin Books, 1969.

Evarts, H. F., *Introduction to PERT*. Boston: Allyn and Bacon, 1964.

Feyereisen, K. V., A. J. Fiorino, and A. T. Nowak, *Supervision and Curriculum Renewal: A Systems Approach*. New York: Appleton-Century-Crofts, 1970.

Flanders, N., *Analyzing Teaching Behavior*. Reading, Mass.: Addison-Wesley, 1970.

Hall, A. D., and R. E. Fagan, "Definition of System," in W. Buckley (ed.), *Modern Systems Research for the Behavioral Scientist*. Chicago: Aldine Publishing, 1968.

Johnson, R. A., F. E. Kast, and J. E. Rosenzweig, *The Theory and Management of System.* New York: McGraw-Hill, 1967.

Katz, D., and R. L. Kahn, *The Social Psychology of Organizations.* New York: John Wiley, 1966.

Kohl, H. R., *The Open Classroom.* New York: Random House, 1969.

Maccia, G. S., "An Educational Theory Model: General Systems Theory," in E. E. Maccia, G. S. Maccia, and R. E. Jewell (eds.), *Construction of Educational Theory Models.* Columbus, Ohio: The Ohio State University (n.d.).

Macdonald, J. B., "Educational Models for Instruction—Introduction," in J. B. Macdonald (ed.), *Theories of Instruction.* Washington, D. C.: ASCD, 1965.

Miller, J. G., "Toward a Theory for the Behavioral Sciences," *The American Psychologist,* 1955, p. 515 ff.

Muir, M., "How Children Take Responsibility for Their Learning," in V. R. Rogers (ed.), *Teaching in the British Primary School.* New York: Macmillan, 1970.

PERT Coordinating Group, *PERT Guide to Management Use.* Washington, D. C.: Office of the Secretary of Defense, 1963.

Pfeiffer, J., *New Look at Education: Systems Analysis in Our Schools and Colleges.* New York: Odyssey Press, 1968.

Ridgway, L., and I. Lawton, *Family Grouping in the Primary School.* New York: Agathon Press, 1969.

Rosenshine, B., and N. Furst, "Research on Teacher Performance Criteria," in B. O. Smith (ed.), *Research on Teacher Education: A Symposium.* Englewood Cliffs, N.J.: Prentice-Hall, 1971.

Schwab, J. J., *The Practical: A Language for Curriculum.* Washington, D. C.: Center for the Study of Instruction, NEA, 1970.

Simon, A., and E. G. Boyer (eds.), *Mirrors for Behavior II: An Anthology of Observation Instruments.* Philadelphia: Research for Better Schools, Inc., 1970.

Umans, Shelley, *The Management of Education: A Systematic Design for Educational Revolution.* Garden City, N.Y.: Doubleday, 1971.

Von Bertalanffy, L., "General Systems Theory—A Critical Review," in L. Von Bertalanffy and A. Rapoport (eds.), *General Systems,* 1962 Yearbook of the Society for General Systems Research.

Von Bertalanffy, L., *General System Theory.* New York: George Braziller, 1968.

PART FOUR

Implementation Procedures

CHAPTER 11

Grass-Roots Change and Informal Methods

J. Myron Atkin, *University of Illinois*

INFORMAL primary education in Great Britain after World War II was inspired, nurtured, and promulgated directly at the school level. Right up to the late 1960's it developed without benefit of attention from education officials in London; in its first two decades it was almost totally ignored as well by newspapers and television.

School-based innovation is rare in any country; yet in retrospect it seems essential that open education had to be both localized and inconspicuous to have survived and flourished. How else could extensive variation from traditional practices have occurred? How else could so much flexibility have been maintained? Informal methods also need ample time to enable establishment of suitably high standards for teachers and children; openness that reflects inattention to the quality of children's work is an option that does not reflect a real choice. The early stages of any fundamental change in education, if the teacher is expected to play an active role, are hampered by either uniform expectations or high visibility.

What is grass-roots reform? Who play the key roles? What is there about schools in Great Britain that permitted informal methods to take root? And what forces in the United States militate against educational approaches that rely strongly on the initiative of the individual teacher?

Informal education in Great Britain was devised by teachers—not by professional administrators, not by government bureaucrats, not by education professors or theorists, not by the media, not by the public, and not by the inspectorate. In Great Britain the individual schools are accorded the greatest latitude in developing programs. True, there are traditional practices that shape schooling and that are probably inviolable: the central role of adults, for example; independence from parents, for another. These well-established features of the school system were preserved as informal methods evolved. Nevertheless, within broad limits such as these, change in British education was profound.

A salient difference between Great Britain and the United States when comparing educational systems is the role of the head teacher in the United Kingdom compared with the role of the elementary school principal in the United States. The British head teacher sees himself as an educational leader. He is an individual with ideas about children and how they learn; he spends much of his time working with youngsters; he has a point of view about the good life and about schools. Usually he works in a small school, often only with six or eight teachers. It is reasonably accurate to view a British primary school as a unit consisting of a teacher (the head teacher) with seven or eight assistants. The head teacher is involved centrally in the education of almost every youngster. At best he orchestrates the actions of the other teachers in the school, the articulation of major purpose, the ebb and flow of varying moods. The emotional and intellectual climate is very much a direct extension of the head teacher's own personality.

In the most attractive schools, a sense of standards permeates the building. The head teachers are people with taste and self-confidence. Although they often talk about human capabilities in quaint, romantic terms like "stretching the child," there is usually a firm expectation that the children's math be rigorous, their art craftsmanlike, and their writing clear and creative.

The American principal, on the other hand, usually sees himself as an organizational scientist. He seems to derive basic satisfaction from "improving communication" or "increasing job satisfaction" or "analyzing role behavior." The American school administrator seems most at home in a large and complex organization in which his major satisfactions stem from operating cleverly upon and within bureaucratic complexity.

In the United States the appropriate unit for educational change seems to be the classroom, rather than the school as it is in Britain. In the United States the individual teacher has considerable latitude. In fact, the principal often doesn't seem to care much what the classroom teacher does from an educational point of view. Of course, the parents cannot be complaining too loudly, and the children must not be disruptive, and reports must be filed on time. Furthermore, the children should be performing at expected levels in reading and in mathematics. But otherwise the classroom teacher has considerable freedom; it is upon him rather than the principal that American strategies for change are focused.

Another difference between Great Britain and the United States with respect to development of new educational approaches is that the British schools rely to a minimum degree on educational innovation generated from university campuses. Most of the exciting work stems from imaginative individuals within the local education authorities—aided and abetted by supportive figures in the Department of Education and Science. University personnel are often seen by local school people as stodgy and unimaginative, excessively positivistic and cautious. Most important, the head teachers do not seem to feel that they need to achieve high status among university professors. This last point is in sharp contrast to conditions that often prevail in the United States. American principals and superintendents of schools, except in very large cities, are strongly responsive to the standards and visions of college professors. Professorial concerns often become their concerns, regardless of merit or relevance.

There are other differences between the educational systems of the two countries. In the United States, we tend to think of educational problems the way we think of engineering problems. We favor strategies that require detailed specifications of intent and outcome right from the start. Performance objectives are elaborately identified in detailed form—the way they are in the design of a spacecraft or an automobile. Then the selected objectives are narrowly pursued whether they be in reading, math, or art or in classroom interactions. There is a demand for elaborate rationalization of educational programs with an accompanying justification, usually giving most value to productivity, efficiency, or effectiveness.

For many American education officials, it would seem undesirably fuzzy, even chaotic, to recognize that the most important things that happen to human beings sometimes occur indirectly. While the opportunistic quality that is an essential ingredient of informal methods does not lead either to chaos or mysticism in the best British schools, there is the apparent fear that in the United States we risk such results if we depart from our tightly structured models for educational change.

A central ingredient of the engineering model is the assumption that we achieve our objectives best if we derive practices from research and development. And so we look for demonstrable research results to install new practices in the schools. If we find that children learn long division quickly when given pennies after each correct response, then we seem to assume that such a finding can be translated efficiently and extensively into general practice.

The research and development approach in education received major impetus during the 1960's, when a characteristic feature of social policy formulation was the identification of acute problems and the development of ameliorative programs to attack these problems. To combat poverty, to improve housing, to make our prison system more effective, to fight crime, or to improve the national health, guidelines were mandated from Washington that reflected current explanations for our social ills. For example, it was assumed that programs to attack poverty had failed because the poor were insufficiently involved in making decisions about their own lives. A hallmark of the Federal poverty effort was to require community participation.

In education, the problem was often seen as insufficient identification of the objectives for which we strive in the schools. Major efforts were funded by the federal government to refine goals in sometimes dizzying detail. Collections of "behavioral objectives" were formulated for virtually every aspect of school life.

Informal educational methods require skill in an independent professional who is emboldened to make hundreds of decisions that are tailored to unexpected and unplanned events in the classroom and the community. Confidence and self-esteem are essential if these decisions are to be made well and if the quality of children's work is to be high. Open education is an educational movement poorly tailored to the sharp delineation of a few goals and the single-minded pursuit of these goals regardless of fresh opportunities that arise as well as the varying styles of classroom activity that may be best able to meet these goals in differing situations.

Educational decisions, like most decisions in any complex enterprise, are best made at the level of greatest knowledgeability. No development team removed from the classroom can fully understand the highly personalized needs of a child who has attended four schools in three years and is growing up in the shadow of an older sister, or the youngster who has an abiding and sharply defined interest in birds but computes poorly and doesn't seem to read well, or the teacher who works most effectively by sensing the shifting emotional needs of a group of active and contentious children but who is new in the school and surrounded by other teachers who denigrate this approach. Thus, no school superintendent—much less a remote curriculum development team—can expect fundamental change by continually introducing new goals and methods that the teacher is expected to employ regardless of the unique characteristics of his particular classroom.

For open education to succeed, there must be recognition of the primacy of the teacher in decisionmaking, and professional independence is a prerequisite for this primacy to be established. Furthermore, initiatives must be encouraged and supported. While American teachers are accorded latitude in curriculum matters, it is a freedom born of neglect. Venturesomeness by the individual is not generally valued within the profession; grass-roots initiatives are not the norm. It is an unresolved question whether we have in the United States the combination of individuality and assertiveness that nurtures a movement so dependent on personal and professional responsibility as is open education.

In the United States, the concept of locally initiated reform has been highlighted only in the 1970's, and then partly in reaction to the perceived failure of attempts to change the schools in response to the initiatives of foundations and the Federal government during the 1960's. Millions of dollars were invested in school reform in the dozen years after the launching of Sputnik I in 1957, and the positive results seem to have been meager.* Innovations disappeared after the initiators left. Dissatisfaction with the schools by the media and the general public did not seem to abate as curriculum project after curriculum project was funded and disseminated.

Perhaps there is a serious flaw in strategies for "implementation" and "dissemination" that assume the teacher is a passive client awaiting the good ideas and tested practices designed elsewhere. Such strategies for educational change assume that goals are widely shared among teachers—a questionable assumption in a profession employing well over two million teachers who work for 18,000 separate governing units. As might be expected in so large an enterprise, there is marked variation in abilities, tastes, and fundamental convictions. One teacher considers it essential to capitalize on proximate events that are considered important and spontaneous in the life of a child. Another teacher most values high-quality interaction among children in the class. Another teacher considers her primary role to be the inculcation of basic skills. Educational change strategies that do not recognize such variations can be seen all too easily as special pleading by various interest groups: college-level academics, blacks, labor, women's liberation groups, etc.

Compounding the problem of educational change in the United States is the fact that different goals for our educational system are highlighted at different times, and the targets shift with startling rapidity. At one juncture, teachers are exhorted to attend to the problems of educating talented youngsters, and massive programs are developed for such children. But the spotlight soon shifts to another concern—more effective education of blacks, for example. Programs are instituted to equalize educational opportunities for different racial or ethnic groups. But then

---

* *A Foundation Goes to School: The Ford Foundation Comprehensive School Improvement Program, 1960–1970.* New York: Office of Reports, Ford Foundation, 1972.

the spotlight shifts again, perhaps to environmental problems or sexism in the schoolroom. And so it goes. The media and the funding agencies (including those in the government) shift priorities with such frequency that the classroom teacher is confused. Confused because of the faddish quality of our attention to various educational problems. Worse, perhaps, the teacher is demoralized. Demoralized because of constant exhortation to do something other than what the teacher is often working hard to accomplish now.

Implicit in an engineered approach to educational change is the fact that the teacher is presumed to be ineffective. A new and better program must be established.

Teachers and administrators, nevertheless, have tried to be responsive to new aims highlighted in the media and in the professional journals. When the gifted were emphasized as a neglected group and the education of the gifted was declared a national disgrace, out of a sense of responsibility (as well as a sense of guilt) teachers turned vigorously to the problem. A few years later we highlighted race relations as a prime national disgrace, and schools were seen as an important vehicle for change. School people tended to accept the new declarations of urgency. But then, in search of a new issue, the media and the public turned to joylessness, then the environment, then to the plight of "native Americans." Tired by now, and uncertain, the teacher keeps trying to satisfy the new demands. The result all too often is an enervated and defensive group of professionals. Loss of self-confidence by the teacher is perhaps the saddest effect of all of a strategy for educational change designed to inject new practices into a large and complex system regardless of existing strengths and accomplishments.

Perhaps we need to modify our expectations for change in the educational system. The dicta to modify schools dramatically are based on the expectation that schools can change in significant ways and quickly. Perhaps one reason for the faddism in American education is that we institute new programs to produce changes, then become disenchanted because changes on the scale envisioned do not occur. (We are disenchanted, incidentally, not only with attempts to change the schools but with attempts to modify social programs in virtually all spheres: housing, transportation, environmental quality, crime, and poverty.) Crash program follows crash program. We are victims, partly, of our own lofty goals, plus our sense of impatience. Goals aren't reached because they are unrealistic, even if they are desirable. In the process of continual disappointment, we lose confidence in ourselves.

Strategies for social change that build rather than attack the confidence of professionals may in the long run be the most effective method for progress. But the time scale for these is probably longer, and Americans are an impatient people. It remains to be seen whether or not we can tolerate strategies for reform that assess progress over a decade rather than a year.

The British have a long tradition of independence for local authorities, and this independence extends to the level of school head. It is questionable whether any educational scheme based on a high degree of flexibility for the individual teacher could have taken root unless such a tradition existed. School heads in the United Kingdom have a well-developed sense of individual purpose and priorities. As with most people, their values can be expected to change only slowly. Pressures from the national government or even from the local school district administration that are not consonant with the views of the individual head cannot be expected to have much effect, and that fact is recognized. Indeed, it seems often to be cherished. As a result, local leaders in British education who were attracted to relatively informal approaches were able to establish educational programs that were highly personalized and tailored to the local situation.*

In Britain, broad-scale strategies for educational change capitalized on local variation and innovation. The role of the national group of school inspectors gradually changed from one in which national standards were enforced to one in which local reform efforts were enhanced. Her Majesty's Inspectors—more than 500 individuals drawn from the schools and accorded regal titles—assumed a consultative role, a role in which they assisted the local heads with reform efforts by strengthening the networks of like-minded practitioners around the country and providing material and intellectual support. The fact that the HMI's were drawn from the schools aided their credibility, but most of all it emphasized that practitioners rather than researchers or government bureaucrats were the key figures in modifying the educational system. British teachers are no more talented than those in the United States; yet it was decided to use scarce funds to support their efforts as well as to create new ones.

There are cycles in the ebb and flow of ideas and energy in the work of any teacher. Usually this energy reflects a general impetus toward some change, improvement, and modification in existing practice. Strategies for change that are most effective, particularly if informal methods are to be introduced, are strategies that build on this flow of energy

---

* For a full discussion of the legal and informal structure of British education, see Maurice Kogan, *Informal Schools in Britain Today: The Government of Education.* New York: Citation Press, 1971.

and strengthen it. Such a view of educational change tends to be undramatic, particularly over short periods of time. Undramatic visions of change in educational practice may not be politically appealing in the United States; in fact, to the extent such an observation is correct, it may not be realistic to expect a major move toward open education in America.

An evolutionary view of educational change requires us to become sensitive to natural variations that occur within the system and that seem adaptive and appealing. The problem becomes one of sustaining and possibly extending these variations. A metaphor drawn from evolution suggests different approaches than those suggested by a metaphor drawn from engineering. Scholars would focus more on the context in which change seems to be effectively nurtured than on methods for installing new practices. But these changes demand marked departures from recent practices. Drastic revisions are improbable in our approaches to educational change. Informal education, at least as the British knew it in the late 1960's, is unlikely to be seen on a significant scale in the United States.

CHAPTER 12

In-Class Teacher Training in Open Education

Bernard Spodek *and* **Theodore Manolakes,** *University of Illinois*

AT THIS writing, the University of Illinois Fellowship Program for Teacher Trainers in Early Childhood Education, supported by the U.S. Office of Education under the Education Professions Development Act, is in its fourth year of operation. Its activities consist of (1) preparing teacher educators in early childhood education within the framework of open education and (2) supporting teachers in a number of Illinois school systems through a variety of activities: in-class teacher training, workshops, short courses, conferences, extension courses, seminars, etc. The work within the schools becomes the basis for practicum experiences for our teacher education fellows.

We have also helped to set up two teacher training centers in Wilmette and Arlington Heights, Illinois, as an extension of the teacher training program; these are staffed primarily by public school personnel. Our support of these centers is one way of communicating that change cannot be imposed from the outside but, rather, needs to come from within. Although outsiders can be used to support change, control of the change process must be in the hands of those persons who wish to be changed. This statement grows out of one of the basic ideological assumptions of open education.

In our project we tried not to be viewed as a group of university experts who have the answers to questions relating to implementation of open education; rather, we wished to be seen as colleagues from another institution, with different but complemetary skills, who wanted to work with teachers interested in moving toward an open classroom. Change, we felt, needs to come from within rather than be imposed from without. Outside resources could be invaluable, however, in helping the teachers change, and we could provide some of these resources through our activities. As such, we had no model, but a point of view, some strategies to effect change that could be tested, and a willingness to work alongside the teacher, learning ourselves as we helped.

It may help to make a distinction here between "informal teaching," "integrated curriculum," and "open education." Such a distinction was attempted by Marshall (1972), but her criteria of open education seem inadequate since they did not take into account conceptions of learning, knowledge, power, or school culture which we think are important elements to be included in the criteria of open education. Developing an open classroom is no more a matter of trying to emulate as best we can the practices of English infant schools than it is trying to do what is done in traditional classes but in an "informal" manner. Neither the informality nor the application of specific techniques is an essential part of open education.

We also found, in talking to persons involved in education in England and in reading their literature, that modern British infant school practice is indebted to American educational thought and practice in no small way—a point that was made in the NAEYC small conference on open education in 1970 and in the publication derived from that conference (Engstrom, 1970). The American progressive education tradition as well as the child development and nursery school traditions all contributed to the movement of English primary schools "toward informality."

Nor is open education, by the way, simply a revival of the old progressive education movement. It differs in significant ways, both in its use of curriculum innovations and in its concern with the individual, not necessarily in the context of the group. Open education is an approach to education that we consider more humane and more sensible for children than what is found in traditional schools. But there is no one humanistic model.

The assumptions upon which we operate have been stated elsewhere. Those who are interested in studying the nature of open education might wish to look at the literature of open education, a body of material that is growing at a fast pace. Useful references include reports by Bussis and Chittenden (1969) and Walberg and Thomas (1971), as well as compendia edited by Rathbone (1971) and Nyquist and Hawes (1972).

From our point of view, an open classroom can be characterized in the following ways:

1. School activities are goal-oriented rather than ritual-oriented. Goals include developing intellectual, language, and social skills; developing values; developing ways of dealing with affect; and developing personal autonomy.

2. School activities presented are developmentally appropriate for the children in the group.

3. Children in the classroom are involved in the decisionmaking process of the group. Respect for children underlies the decisionmaking process as well as all teacher-child interactions.

4. Learning is viewed as taking place as a result of the child's acting on the environment, abstracting information, and operating on this information in some intellectual manner.

5. Learning is viewed as taking place as a result of dialogue.

Probably the best short definition of open education can be derived by paraphrasing Paulo Freire (1970). Freire's view of education sees it as taking place when the teacher engages his students in dialogue in which they redefine their universe.

Given the above characteristics, classrooms may have many different physical attributes and varied organizational frameworks and still be open. (One definition of openness is "nondogmatic.")

In assessing our program, we can describe activities and discuss what we have learned as a result of interviewing persons involved and reflecting on these activities. We cannot discuss the consequences of the program either in terms of teacher outcomes or children's outcomes. Since the program itself has been continually in process of re-creation during the last few years, there has been no consistency of treatment. In addition, no change in schools has taken place solely as a result of the things we have done; rather, we have helped teachers and schools create changes they were already disposed toward. These changes might have taken place without us, though probably not with the same ease, the same intensity, or the same depth. Change in any school situation can only be understood and evaluated in the context of the particular situation, and the school situations varied significantly from one to another.

Activities

The activities of the program included in-class teacher training, workshops, consultations, conferences, courses, and seminars. These activities were each designed for different client populations. Our basic premise was that many college-based teacher education courses are too remote from teachers to be effective. They are remote in a spatial sense, in that the teacher must travel away from home to be served by the course. They are also remote in a conceptual sense, for often the content of the course seems to have little relationship to the task in which the teacher is involved on a daily basis. It seemed to us that it might be more sensible to bring the learning experience to the teacher, placing it directly in the school situation and making the content of the learning experience the teacher's own classroom activity, with observation and reflection leading to modification in program or teaching methods and then to an assessment of the change.

During the 1971–72 school year we sent teams of fellows and staff members to our cooperating schools. These teams would spend one to two days a week in a school. At first the concern of our staff was for establishing good working relationships with teachers, based upon a sense of trust and credibility. Staff members and fellows would visit classrooms, observing and helping teachers and meeting informally with individual or groups of teachers whenever possible. When requested, our staff would bring educational material not available to teachers into school or would help the classroom teachers make materials. They would suggest readings for teachers and would demonstrate activities that could be used with children. They would help teachers create learning situations or develop new classroom organizations. In each encounter the staff would try to respond to the needs and requests of the teachers in concrete ways, thus contributing their knowledge and usefulness.

This aspect of our program—directly related to classroom practice— seemed to have great impact. In fact, most teachers in our network identified our program with the individual who came into their school rather than with the program directors or the university. When asked to define our project, teachers characterized it as a group of people from the university interested in open education and wanting to help teachers . . . to give them ideas . . . to become more open in their rooms. This most successful part of our program also created our greatest problems.

Demands on individual staff members were great, and vast amounts of energy were expended on travel. Sometimes we erred in our approach to a specific teacher or in our assessment of local needs. Sometimes the different styles or points of view among fellows and staff members working in the same school led to conflict. Sometimes we were too ignorant ourselves, for *we* were learning from the process just as the teachers and children in the schools were.

As a local need arose, we ran workshops in various schools. These usually included a half day or full day of practice-oriented activity and discourse. We involved the teachers in activities which were adult parallels of those we suggested could be offered to children. The teachers would learn not only from the content of the workshop but from the method employed as well. Art, science, language arts, and music activities were available. Teachers had options in each program and chose from a range of activities at each workshop. Usually they were also asked to report in some way about their involvement in activities.

Discussions would take place relating to the application of what each teacher had learned and to ways of extending classroom practice from the workshop activities. Background and foundation material not directly related to classroom practice would be provided as required, such as demonstrations and discussions to elucidate Piaget's developmental theories. The workshops were requested by the schoolteachers but were planned and implemented by our fellows and staff. We continued to offer these workshops during the 1972–73 year. We also tried to get teachers to develop their own workshops.

During the year we felt the need to move teachers out of their schools for some activities. The pressures on teachers and the teachers' need to respond to their immediate environment suggested that it would be fruitful to hold a number of retreats. These retreats would take place in a comfortable, nonschool environment, such as a university conference center or a state park recreation area.

The formal program of the retreats included discussions and activities similar to those of our workshops. The focus of the program, for example, might be on art, music, language arts, or environmental education and its extensions. The informal program included sharing ideas and concerns among teachers from various school settings and systems, developing group esprit within the total program, and interacting informally with staff members of the project. These retreats also communicated to teachers our view of their importance as persons and as focal figures in the educative process.

We also planned an educational conference in the spring. Such a conference permitted dissemination of our ideas to large groups of people, but did not allow for involvement in depth. Planning of the conference was done by our fellows and provided them with many valuable learning possibilities.

Similarly, a number of school systems have asked for consultation from us. Whenever possible, we try to involve staff and fellows in providing such consultative service, since they have become highly competent. These experiences, too, provide many learning opportunities. Teacher training involves many modes of activities.

Our other formal activities include the provision of coursework and seminars. Our fellows are in doctoral programs at the university and take a variety of courses both in education and in related fields. These are usually relevant either to requirements of the doctoral program or to their work in early childhood education and teacher education.

We also offer courses to teachers in the field. The students of our last year's course were primarily the teachers from a single school building. The course was designed to increase their understanding of open education and to clarify a number of ideas related to this teaching approach. During the academic year we also offered extension courses for teachers in our project. The purpose of this course was twofold: to deal with concepts and implementation of open education in the classroom and to help develop a sense of awareness in teachers of aspects of the process of change. Every other week, teachers are provided with "awareness questions" that require them to collect data in their schools. These data become the basis for course discussions. The experiences of the teachers, we feel, are worthy of study. By operating upon their environment, teachers as well as children can develop significant concepts and understanding—and perhaps redefine their world. In addition, teachers are involved as school groups in developing and implementing workshop activities for the other participants in the course. This reflects our belief that teachers can and should assume greater responsibility for their own professional development.

We are also helping to establish teacher centers, staffed primarily by teachers. We have provided support to these centers by hiring interns who work in children's classes and thus allow teachers to be released from some classroom responsibilities.

Our seminars generally include staff and fellows and take place on campus. Formal seminars for course credit have dealt with the antecedents of open education. Informal seminars, in which invited faculty and students are asked to present aspects of their work somehow related to open education and/or early childhood education, are also held. At times our staff meetings seem to turn into seminars as well, since we try to understand what has happened in the program and possibly why it has happened.

Let us turn to what we have learned as a result of our program. Our evaluation included collecting data through questionnaires and interviews with all those concerned in the program (except the children in the classes affected). Data were collected from a sampling of parents, from all the teachers in all the school settings, from staff members and fellows, and from the directors of the project. Our interviews provided us with a great deal of useful material, much of it consistent with our views of the program's process.

The Relationship Between Adviser and Teacher

The role of the in-class teacher trainer is often viewed as central to the extension of open education, with advisers or consultants serving in this capacity. The difficulty we found in drawing any conclusions from our observations about the role of the adviser and his relationship with the classroom teacher was that this role seemed a constantly shifting and changing one. The one thing that seemed regularly to characterize it was its characteristic *irregularity*. A number of variables in this role seemed to emerge however, partly from these irregularities. These included:

1. *Locus of control.*   The adviser is always using his role and the way in which he works with teachers as a way of communicating the characteristics of open education and the ways that teachers might work with children. Since noncoerciveness is one characteristic of open education, the adviser must act in a collaborative noncoercive manner. This places the control over the relationship between adviser and teacher in the hands of the teacher. The adviser finds that what he does is in response to the needs or demands of the teacher. Often the adviser feels he is not really in control of the situation—not having the option, for example, of responding or not responding to the demands of teachers. Only as a relationship continues does the adviser function in a more autonomous role, with a greater degree of parity between him and the teacher.

Most teachers were satisfied with the support provided by our staff members, who were viewed as nonintrusive and willing to work with, listen to, and round up materials for the teachers. Our staff members were also respected for admitting to not knowing the answers to all questions.

2. *The function of time.*   As the relationship between adviser and advisee continued, change occurred in that relationship and in the function of the adviser. Role attributes that were most important in the beginning of an adviser-advisee relationship seemed less important later, and acts which had earlier been considered inappropriate seemed crucial later.

The function of the adviser needs to be viewed along a time dimension. In our project, for example, the time spent by the advisers in the teacher's classroom seemed crucial at the beginning. As the year progressed, not only did it seem appropriate to spend less time in the teacher's class, but often activities that took place outside the classroom seemed to become more important and more appropriate.

The amount of time that elapsed between classroom visits also seemed an important factor. These intervals allowed the teacher to reflect, to react to the content of her sessions with the adviser, and to act on suggestions and ideas. What the optimum time between classroom visits is, we could not determine. Our visits occurred weekly. This was a greater time span between visits than had occurred in our Washington School project during the previous year, where an adviser was almost constantly available in the school and there was thus a lesser time span than in other situations in which we have been involved, where visits also occurred monthly. This span of time—i.e., one week between visits—*seemed* appropriate for what we were doing.

The amount of time that each of the staff members devoted to each teacher was directly dependent upon the relationship of the teacher and the staff member. All the teachers interviewed, except one, wished that each staff member could spend more time in the classroom or visit for longer periods during the week. We have no way of knowing whether giving more time would have improved the relationships between teacher and adviser or would have accelerated change in classroom procedures.

One disadvantage in the structure of our project, with the schools involved being as much as 150 miles away from the university, was that some teachers had immediate needs that could not be met. Time between visits was fixed, and there was less flexibility in schedules than there might have been. Face-to-face contact seemed to be important. None of the teachers interviewed mentioned using the telephone to contact advisers, although such contact was certainly possible. They either didn't think of it or couldn't call long distance from their school, or else the teachers felt the need for a face-to-face relationship.

3. *Development of trust or credibility.*   The basis for any helping relationship is the degree of trust felt between client and helper. For the adviser, the trust aspect of the relationship seemed less a function of a feeling of safety on the part of the teacher and more a function of the degree of credibility the adviser had. The adviser had to establish himself as one who could be helpful and who had something of practical worth to offer the teacher. Whether this need to test the adviser was a function of the fact that the adviser was connected with a university rather than an official school agency is beyond our ability to know. (Universities are not the most credible educational agencies when it comes to performance of service in the context of public schools.) However, the establishment of credibility did seem to be an individual matter. Teachers with varied experiences asked for consultative service even when they had been operating "open" for some time, and not all advisers were used to the same degree. If anything, the more-experienced teachers felt neglected as a result of their "longevity" in open education, since less-experienced teachers were often asking for help that advisers felt more compelled to give.

4. *Intrusion of local constraints.*   In each setting we found that the role of the adviser was determined not only by the individual teachers and advisers involved but also by various constraints within the local situation. A teachers' strike and the residue of conflict that resulted from the response of the local board of education severely limited what could be done by an adviser in one setting, as well as how much effort the none-too-willing teachers would put out for any education function. In

another situation the difficult relationship between the teachers and the principal seriously influenced the role the adviser played there, even though there were no formal ties between the adviser and the school administration. Other constraints we identified included:

a. Absence or presence of leadership within a school: Though leadership might come from either an administrator or a teacher, some form of leadership needed to be established in a school for change to take place.

b. Perceived support of the project by the administration: Administrators who originally voiced support of our project and our approach to education sometimes seemed less than enthusiastic over the long haul. The way that teachers viewed the administrators' support and the constancy of their point of view was influential.

c. Architecture of the building: The organization of space seemed to be an influence on teacher flexibility. One building in which we worked was designed with open spaces. Other buildings had walls removed to encourage team teaching and flexible grouping. But open spaces did not always support open education. Often the possibility of additional auditory and visual distractions served to inhibit informality.

d. Staffing patterns: The organization of human resources also influenced flexibility. Team teaching, like open spaces, often proved inhibiting. Inflexible scheduling of groups working with individual teachers sometimes resulted. In addition, the need to keep peace within teams served as a rein on innovation, with teams often agreeing to a "least common denominator" approach to planning.

5. *The function of expectations.*   Another set of variables that seem to control the relationship between teacher and adviser are the expectations held by both parties. The teacher, in entering the relationship, has already anticipated what will be considered appropriate or inappropriate. The need to extend the expectations of both parties thus becomes evident. The sooner the staff member and the teacher discuss their mutual purposes, the more productive their relationship tends to be.

The fact that our project had as one of its goals the training of future teacher trainers may have been a strong point in limiting original expectations, for the teacher viewed the staff members as generally knowledgeable but also as another developing person. The partnership in learning formed between individual staff members and individual teachers seems a necessary part of the process of change. It also seems necessary that the feeling of "partnership" be an expression of a sharing relationship, not simply a pretense.

6. *Skills and resources needed for the function of the adviser.*   Advisers,

as suggested above, need to be viewed as competent in order to build credibility; they also need competence in order to function. But what are the dimensions of competency that are essential? Is there a body of knowledge or a set of skills that each person must have in order to be effective in this capacity? Do certain attitudes or beliefs need to be held?

In the literature of education, a dichotomy has often been constructed between a core of process skills that supervisors or teachers might have and a body of substantive knowledge that is deemed necessary for each situation. This process/content dichotomy is also related to the generalist/specialist distinction that is often made. Since a professional cannot be highly competent in education in all subject areas or on all age levels, should advisers limit themselves to particular areas or age levels, or can they be equally effective in helping teachers at many grade levels and in many curriculum areas?

While none of our advisers was competent in every area of the curriculum in which they had to deal or in teaching at every grade level, each did have to some degree an area of specialization in which his substantive knowledge was greater than in others. Some were better at science activities or in the arts; some had teaching experience with older or with younger children. Beyond that, however, they had to use what might be called process skills to move people along. Perhaps their performance in one area of the program allowed their credibility to be carried over to other areas? Perhaps the conventional dichotomy is not that strict after all?

A general knowledge of children and schools and of principles of child growth and development as well as substantial familiarity with oneself as a professional, including one's knowledge and skills in educational practice, seems to be part of the important "repertoire" needed by each staff member—as does a belief that the teachers were willing and able to change and that the adviser is capable of helping others to effect such change.

7. *Professional/personal needs.*   A number of different causes seem to motivate persons to join the education profession, and different personal needs seem to be met by those who move up the competency ladder within the profession. To speculate whether a teacher decides to work with children because of an internal drive to provide help for others, or whether the teacher must feel a degree of control over other people's lives, is beyond the scope of this presentation, but the effective adviser seems to be successful because he places himself in an extending relationship with another human being. The adviser needs to influence, but without exerting control over the teacher's actions in the classroom.

These personal dimensions of the adviser's role are in need of study. How an adviser operates seems to be a function of the kinds of satisfaction received from the role as well as a function of personal style. Where satisfactions were less direct, conflict or frustration was often created.

Our advisers all had a background of successful teaching. Often the need to work at influencing another person to provide a particular educational service for children, which appeared obvious to them and could be provided directly without much difficulty, caused frustration for the adviser. The acceptance of "teacher error" was something that advisers had to develop.

8. *Building autonomy.*   While teachers controlled the relationship with the advisers, the advisers were able to influence this relationship over time. One of the needs of our project, we felt, was to help teachers function with a higher degree of autonomy. As time passes, the adviser should be needed less and less. To some extent the adviser's personal satisfactions, however, were a function of being needed by the teacher. The more an adviser felt needed by teachers, the more the adviser felt he was performing a legitimate service.

The weaning of advisers from teachers, and vice versa, is a complicated process. If the relationship develops successfully, the adviser should be viewed as one more of the many resources available to a teacher in providing the best educational opportunities for the children in her class, and so the adviser's importance should diminish. Whether or not this lesser status will also diminish personal satisfactions for the adviser is probably as much a function of the adviser's personal maturity as anything else. Perhaps in an open system with new teachers continually entering, this will not present a problem.

Two very apparent strengths of our project lay in the fact that it required voluntary entry on the teacher's part and that, in the first year of action, growth was evidenced at least in some teachers. Growth of the teacher can be viewed as a move toward autonomy. To what extent autonomy will persist or continue to develop when external supports are withdrawn is something we must wait to find out.

9. *"Layering" of teachers.*   As we have worked with teachers during the past few years in the process of teacher change, we have found that just as the change process is a complex phenomenon, so the teacher is a complex phenomenon. Teachers who have volunteered to work with us are committed to change; yet the process of change moves along for them in fits and starts. At certain times the process of change moves smoothly as teachers are willing to modify their classroom structures and practices. At other times it seems as if a great deal of resistance to change is building up in the teacher, even when the change has been

accepted verbally. Nor could each teacher involved in the project change in the same way or at the same rate.

Our original explanation of the movement of teachers toward open education was postulated on a "plateau" effect. We viewed the process of change as a linear effect, moving in a positive direction at different rates at different times. It seemed as if teachers would make significant moves toward an open classroom, then stop or slow down, resting or consolidating gains. We are now rejecting this notion and attempting to explain the process through what might be called the "onion construct." Teachers may be viewed as being made up of principles and practices that can be arranged at various levels. The external levels might include such things as accepted room arrangements, specific selected texts, or classroom materials. Closer to the core of this set come specific instructional strategies. Still further in may be found goals for children and teachers. Within the very core of the teacher are a set of professional beliefs and values, beliefs about the nature of childhood, the nature of education or schooling, the role of the teacher, and so on. And innermost are a set of personal beliefs and values which we feel are outside our domain to deal with and modify.

It seems to us that the ease or difficulty associated with changing a particular characteristic of a teacher's method is a function of the distance that characteristic lies from the internal professional core of the teacher. Characteristics in the external layers of the teacher are more responsive to external stimuli or pressures, and hence are easier to change. Teachers, for example, seldom resist reorganizing the physical arrangement of the classroom or creating activity centers. The way in which furniture is arranged in the classroom may not be viewed as critical by many teachers. As we move on to deeper layers, greater resistance to change is felt. It is harder to affect the reading program in a primary classroom than the science program, since the reading program is viewed as a more essential part of primary education than is science. Characteristics closest to the innermost layers of beliefs are even more resistant to change. It is difficult for many teachers to share real decisionmaking power with children or with parents, for the teacher may view the decisionmaking role as one of the most crucial in education. Understanding the depth of layering of a particular practice might help the adviser to develop more effective strategies for change, as well as help him accept resistance and difficulties related to certain kinds of change.

Similarly, teachers tend to distrust what appears to be ambiguous learning; i.e., if the teacher can't legitimatize in her own mind a certain experience to be provided the children, it isn't viewed as a learning experience. A trip to a newspaper office may be seen as a very important part of school experience by one teacher and as simply a break from classroom routine by another. The concern for building appropriate skills in mathematics and reading is overwhelming in the primary grades. The expressive arts and social studies were never mentioned in our evaluation interviews as prime areas of concern, and science was mentioned only once. In spite of the lack of mention, these areas were included among learning activities in our cooperating school buildings. For example, art displays and dramatic plays were going on as well as scientific investigation and writing. Yet, though teachers engaged in these activities, they still did not view the "arts" to be as vital as the "skills." Teachers seem quite satisfied to leave to chance the richness of learning associated with the activities of art or science, but they are extremely hesitant to loosen up in the fundamental skill areas, which were still being formally taught. At the end of our first year, there continued to be some confusion among teachers that open education forsakes the skills necessary for mathematics and reading, and so these areas of the program were least changed.

10. *Continuity/discontinuity and the process of change.*   All the teachers involved have commented that they have grown somewhat as a result of our project and that they are doing something differently in their classroom at the end of their first year of involvement. Throughout our interviews the teachers seemed to be torn between what they read about open education and what they were actually doing in their classrooms. They felt inadequate in terms of implementing what they read, and all commented that moving toward open classrooms takes time and careful thought. Most of the teachers commented that they felt comfortable with the old structure of teaching. Also, none of our teachers presented themselves as being consistent in their teaching that year. They remarked that some days they would be "open" and some days "traditional." Most of what they did in their classroom was based on how they felt at the time in relation to what they thought the children needed.

This often led to a situation in which contradictions were introduced into the classroom. Children were told they could be free to select activities and extend personal interests in the classroom. At the same time teachers were concerned about covering the required course of study. Children were often given contradictory messages about what constituted success in the class or about what power and degree of freedom they actually had. Such contradictions might have made it more difficult for children to cope in these transition classes, for the rules governing behavior and relationships were less explicit and less constant than those in more traditional classrooms.

The bulk of the teachers interviewed did not seem confident in their ability to extend an activity or an interest of the child into related areas. The comments were: "What do you do after a child completes the geoboard?" "They are interested in crows. What next?" "Do you carry on this activity for the whole year?" "What do you do when a child has finished an activity?" Many of the teachers have been trying to supply the children with various activities to "keep them busy" or to "motivate" them. They needed assistance in identifying the many alternatives that materials have to offer and what may evolve as a result of their possible uses by the child. Most of the teachers say they have really individualized their teaching (regardless of whether or not they say they are "open"), because they feel they know the child better. At the same time they seemed baffled about how to provide experiences for children. This leads us to believe that these teachers are trying to individualize activities in their classrooms while maintaining a group orientation—possibly the basis for another set of contradictions.

The constant encouragement and support that each staff member provided for teachers at each of the sites served as reassurance for the classroom teachers and helped them through a difficult period of change. "It was nice to be able to talk to someone about this." "Whenever we met as teachers, we talked about our faults." "It was gratifying to be able to talk to someone who understands our problems."

These, then, are some of the dimensions of the advisory role and its relationship to teachers that we have identified as worthy of study. We have learned some during the past few years; we are continually becoming aware of how much more we need to learn. The strategies for studying the open classroom need to extend beyond psychometrics. Such studies should probably rely heavily on ethnographic techniques. The interrelatedness of the dimensions we identified requires that, to understand the process adequately, they must be observed in a natural setting with a minimum of intrusion from the researcher. We are trying to expand our documentation of the process of change toward openness through a number of studies: ethnographic studies of classrooms, documentation of the development of teacher centers, observations of schools and classes, informal and formal interactions with teachers, and study of teacher belief systems. We find the combination of action and study or reflection an appropriate strategy to use in serving and studying education.

References

Bussis, A. M., and E. A. Chittenden, *Analysis of an Approach to Open Education: Interim Report*. Princeton, N.J.: Educational Testing Service, 1969.

Engstrom, G. (ed.), *Open Education*. Washington, D. C.: National Association for the Education of Young Children, 1970.

Freire, P., *Pedagogy of the Oppressed*. New York: Herder and Herder, 1970.

Marshall, H. H., "Criteria for an Open Classroom," *Young Children,* 1972, *28:1,* 13–19.

Nyquist, E. B., and G. R. Hawes, *Open Education: A Source Book for Parents and Teachers*. New York: Bantam Books, 1972.

Rathbone, C. A., *Open Education: The Informal Classroom*. New York: Citation Press, 1971.

Walberg, H. J. and S. C. Thomas, *Characteristics of Open Education: Toward an Operational Definition*. Cambridge, Mass.: Educational Development Center, 1971.

CHAPTER 13

A Descriptive Analysis of Experiences of Five First-Year Teachers Attempting Open Education

Jerome De Bruin, *University of Toledo*

THE MAJOR purpose of this study was to examine and analyze the experiences of five first-year teachers who were committed to an "open education" approach for children. These beginning teachers had been part of a one-semester program in England which coupled a study in a teacher training college with practice in a primary school in Bristol. They also had additional work at the University of Illinois related to open education.

For the study, four sources of information were chosen as appropriate for generating descriptive data: (1) anecdotal descriptions related by the subjects themselves in interviews held by the investigator, (2) diaries written by the subjects, (3) photographs of the classrooms and learning environments taken at different intervals during the study, and (4) direct observation by the investigator.

The investigator served as participant observer and spent an average of six days per month at Adams School. The subjects were interviewed every two months on any changes in their perception of open education teaching plans, problems encountered, and avenues they had used to alleviate these problems. In the interviews, the subjects also gave detailed descriptions of their experiences in teaching. Diaries allowed the investigator to keep pace with events in the classrooms between visits. Photographs were used to illustrate naturalistic settings and written descriptions from photographs aided the investigator in writing the study. The study covered the 1971-72 school year.

A Framework for Analysis

The data gathered included 2,200 pages of written material from transcriptions of 55 ninety-minute cassette tapes, written pages of diaries, written personal notes, and written descriptions of 700 photographs. An analytic framework was culled from this material to pinpoint specific problem areas in the subjects' attempts to implement open education and to identify emerging patterns of concern. The framework increased in complexity and was composed of conceptual themes and threads, patterns of concern identified in specific observations of events, anecdotes, and written descriptions.

In general, themes were identified by the frequency with which that theme was noted by the teachers. As a result of general groupings, the investigator was able to identify five major themes after the first week of study. Minor themes were also evident but were not noted as often by the teachers and therefore not included. A number of minor themes that later gained in importance were then considered major themes and included after the first, third, sixth, and ninth months of the study.

The themes seemed to orchestrate in importance at various intervals during the study. An attempt was made to separate the problems encountered by the five teachers into specific problems dealing with open education and problems that did not appear to be related to open education, but this was abandoned because the problems seemed so intertwined that this operation seemed inappropriate.

Five themes were identified after the first week of school: (1) teachers' strike and influence of the teachers' organization, (2) lack of an open school philosophy, (3) physical design of an open-spaced building, (4) race, and (5) typical first-year teacher problems such as classroom organization, discipline, and organization for teaching.

After the first month, the number of themes increased from five to eight. The new themes included the influence of "semitraditional" teachers, concern for evaluation methodologies, and specific interest center problems.

Four additional themes were identified three months after the study began: a growing concern for mastery of basic academic skills, growing parental concern and pressure, the children's apparent inability to handle responsibility in an open education environment, and the lack of personal growth (social, emotional, and cultural growth outside of teaching) on the part of each of the five subjects.

Seven more themes became significant after six months. These themes included concern over the continuity of open education after the children entered junior high school, the quality of work, the appropriate use of space, the development of schemes of open education, the issue of play, the element of choice in learning, and increased concern over dialogue among staff members and the principal.

A total of 19 basic themes and 63 examples of supporting threads made up the analytic framework. These represented unsolved problems that hindered the five teachers' attempts at implementing open education. For purposes of further analysis, the themes and threads will be considered under the following broad headings: school philosophy, influence of other teachers, physical design and structure of an open-spaced school, influence of parents, technical aspects of teaching, and attitudes of children.

School Philosophy

Because Adams School was a new facility, the principal did not express an overall philosophy of education. In reference to open education, the principal stated, "We are going to move slowly toward open education and hopefully take the parents along with us. . . ." However, he didn't express these views to the staff. Rather, he adhered to a philosophy of non-intervention and played a rather passive role as a facilitator of open education. He hoped that teachers would get together, talk and select a method of teaching that would eventually evolve into a working educational philosophy for Adams School.

The lack of an expressed school philosophy, coupled with the principal's position of non-intervention, led the five teachers to formulate their own philosophy of teaching. Generally, they chose to start out in a fairly traditional manner, planning to "get their feet on the ground" before attempting to "open up." Ironically, they chose a traditional method of teaching even though the bulk of their teacher training had been in open education. This choice of a cautious approach to teaching resulted from their lack of professional experience and their desire to avoid any hostility generated by other teachers.

The lack of an expressed open education philosophy was apparent throughout the year. However, an attempt to involve open education in the philosophy of Adams School was initiated by the principal in late October when he asked his staff to respond to Barth's "Assumptions about Learning and Knowledge" (Barth, 1971). The five teachers responded favorably to these assumptions, a response that reaffirmed their commitment to open education. The difficult task for these teachers, however, was the actual implementation of this commitment.

In January, a change in the staff's attitude occurred when teachers began to communicate extensively with each other about attempts to "open up." The principal also took a more active role in running the school as he set down procedural rules and time schedules for special areas. However, he continued to play a non-interventionist role concerning open education. This appeared to be one of the obstacles that may have hindered the implementation of open education throughout the year. The teachers needed his support and active classroom participation in the "opening up" process, but the principal did not involve himself in this way.

Influence of Other Teachers

Most of the members of the staff other than the five teachers knew very little about the basic ideas and practices of open education. This ignorance inhibited the implementation of open education because conflicting views existed in the school on proper noise levels, room arrangements, curriculum, pod structure, grouping patterns, teaching methods, record keeping, and the utilization of time and space. The five teachers often were forced to compromise their ideas and methods in order to maintain harmony among all teachers in the pod. This resulted in the employment of traditional methods of teaching by the five teachers.

The problem of influencing successful traditional teachers to change to open education was perplexing to the five teachers. Generally, they decided that they would first have to prove themselves as teachers and then attempt to show the experienced traditional teachers the merits of open education. It seemed virtually impossible for them to succeed, however, because of the concern shown by traditional teachers for the loud noises emanating from the five teachers' "open" classrooms. Teachers often questioned the five about the method of education that would tolerate such noise levels. Once again, in defense, the five teachers reverted to more traditional methods of teaching and the implementation of open education was impeded.

The need for the five to work with experienced teachers and support personnel trained in open education was apparent. The task of implementing open education would certainly have been less difficult for the five teachers if the need for support of well-seasoned veteran teachers in open education could have been met.

An integral component of open education is that teachers should experience personal growth (social, emotional, and cultural growth) along with professional growth. Teaching and activities related to teaching consumed most of the five teachers' waking hours throughout most of the school year. All five expressed concern for their personal lives outside of teaching but allowed little time for this personal development. The five teachers experienced difficulty in maintaining this delicate balance between meeting personal and professional needs which, if maintained, might have aided the development of the continual learning process necessary in open education.

In the midst of many frustrations throughout the year, the five teachers maintained the deep professional commitment necessary for open education. Although shaken at times, it remained their greatest asset as they continued to believe that open education was the way to go.

A teachers' strike at the beginning of the school year and the influence of the teachers' organization hindered the implementation of open education because it placed the five teachers in a difficult and complex situation. They were forced to make a decision on whether to strike and side with the teachers' organization or teach and side with the administration. They were considerate of other people's feelings but soon realized that they were forced to hurt the feelings of some people (contrary to a basic tenet of open education) in favor of not hurting the feelings of the children and themselves. After serious consideration was given to numerous aspects of the problem, they decided to teach during the strike. The most difficult part was not making the decision but rather accepting the consequences of the decision. The harassment from fellow teachers was one such consequence; the injury to professional relationships another.

The most important consequence was that the strike virtually blocked all lines of communication between the non-striking teachers and their striking colleagues. It didn't allow sufficient time for communication between teachers who may have promoted an understanding of and agreement on a method of teaching for each pod. Instead, the five teachers retreated to their own individual classrooms without ever having an opportunity to discuss educational approaches with their fellow teachers.

Pressure applied by the teachers' organization impeded the implementation of open education when it forced a veto of the principal's plan to replace two teachers (who had left due to pregnancy and marriage) with eight qualified teacher aides. (The aide proposal was designed to make the task of implementing open education easier for the classroom teachers. Aides would have taken over clerical duties, thus giving more time to classroom teachers to implement open education.) The plan seemed feasible but the teachers' organization, being suspicious of any attempt to replace classroom teachers with aides, vetoed the proposal. Several of the open education teachers called the decision a travesty. They felt that it greatly reduced their chances of implementing open education because they would not have the necessary support personnel.

Physical Design and Structure
of an Open-Spaced School

Adams School was an "open-plan" school. Since the five teachers had not learned to use the school as it was designed to be used, the physical design and structure of the school actually interfered with the implementation of open education. It allowed noise to travel and permitted a flow of children from room to room, to the consternation of the other teachers. The five teachers themselves were not aware of the increased noise level while they were busily engaged in activities with children. By the end of the first month of school, the teachers wanted separate classrooms with four solid walls and one entrance with a door.

It was apparent that the five teachers had difficulty adjusting to small pie-shaped open teaching areas. They feared that children would leave the classroom whenever they wanted since no doors prevented this. After their fears were confirmed, the five teachers began to restrict children's movements. Both the control of noise and flow of children fostered more meaningful relationships with other teachers in the pod but hindered the five teachers' attempts at implementing open education, forcing them to use more formal methods of instruction.

Influence of Parents

Significant concerns voiced by parents also blocked attempts by the five teachers to implement open education. Parents showed great concern for their children's school achievement. They demanded that traditional textbooks be used to cover the "basics" and that tests be used to assess mastery. The five teachers tried to convince the parents that American education is too pressure-packed, with its emphasis on competition and the memorization of facts. They talked with parents about the British infant school system of education, which to them was less pressured and which placed an emphasis on warmth, individual creativity, self-development, and group social interaction. They also attempted to convey the idea that they were attempting not to transplant British infant school education to Adams School but rather to develop a model suitable to American society. The parents seemed unimpressed. As a result of confrontation, the five teachers often gave in and geared their instruction to comply with the parents' wishes. The parents also voiced their concern about discipline in the classroom. They viewed open education as being too free and thus a threat to their own methods of discipline.

There appear to be several other reasons why the parents resisted the idea of open education. Adams School was not "their" school. Except for an informal teacher helper program, the parents were not involved in the school, nor had the parents been given a choice as to whether they wanted their children to participate in open classes or remain in formal classes. The parents also viewed the principal's role of non-intervention as a specific weakness in his approach to discipline in the school. His vacillation regarding open education only seemed to reinforce the parents' doubts about the appropriateness of this approach. In addition, open education was different from the type of education they had experienced. They didn't understand the basic assumptions, ideas, and principles underlying the approach and were suspicious of it. They masked their lack of understanding by saying that the method allowed the kids too much freedom and lacked discipline and structure.

Technical Aspects of Teaching

As a result of parental pressure to cover the basics in sequential format, the five teachers increasingly utilized traditional textbooks rather than interest centers. This was particularly true in the reading program, since Adams School was a member of a pilot project for reading that would be evaluated in the future. The adoption of the traditional sequential format was epitomized on a warm Indian summer day in October when a teacher had her class make a snowman because that was the next lesson in the book.

The concern for covering the basics by using traditional assignments became a problem because it didn't meet individual differences. The children used traditional assignments as a wedge to do less work, and could be heard saying, "Wow, you have to do that much! I only have to do this much," or "Well, if you only have to do a little bit, I'm going to do only that too."

There were attempts to meet individual differences by devising "schemes" to move toward open education. Teaming, departmentalization, and ability grouping were three such schemes. Movable walls were set up and taken down on numerous occasions. A master schedule of departmentalization for fifth and sixth grades was utilized and later dropped when cross-age grouping patterns were eliminated. Fourth-grade teachers developed a "clubhouse" scheme of teaching which featured an independent area for kids who displayed acceptable behavior. Third-grade teachers structured their day traditionally and grouped their students by ability in several subject matter areas. Second-grade teachers departmentalized science and social studies and exchanged kids who had previously been behavior problems. Other attempted schemes included self-scheduling and "open education" on a limited-time-only basis.

All five teachers experienced little success in implementing open education by the employment of these schemes. The schemes were developed primarily to curtail chronic behavior problems and were so tightly structured that they lacked provisions for a valid choice. They also lacked provisions for teachers to help children learn how to make proper choices, and little freedom was allowed children in negotiating a choice of activity with their teachers.

In the fifth-grade individualization scheme, children noted, "We have a choice but not a 'real' choice." Their choice was often limited to the *order* in which assignments could be done but not the activity itself. They were·often engaged in different activities on an individual basis but the activities continued to be prescribed by the teacher on assignment sheets.

In fourth grade, the children who were in the independent area had a choice of activities but generally the activities were limited because of a lack of manipulative materials in the interest centers.

In a departmentalized scheme, the teachers learned that some subjects were easier to "open up" than others; with science, for instance, it was easier than with reading. It seemed easier to open up with older children than with younger ones. It also seemed that the five learned that some teachers and children would never be able to adjust to, and work in, a more open environment.

With increased communication, walls were removed permanently from between a number of rooms. This led to a marked improvement in the utilization of space. The flow of children between rooms increased and children from different pods communicated more with each other. The movable walls placed in a U-shaped design made excellent carrels for quiet study and also provided increased surface area for the display of children's work. In some instances, removing the walls also led to a decrease in noise level. Despite these improvements, several of the five teachers continued to be disappointed and frustrated in their efforts to implement open education: they seemed to expect too much in too little time.

Increased planning and communication by teachers led to the use of interest centers in some pods. However, the traditional teachers viewed interest centers as an extension of learning rather than a primary mode of instruction. This lack of a well-defined purpose in the use of interest centers hindered the implementation of open education. Interest centers were used as a reward for "good work." Often the purpose of interest centers was to give the "top kids" something to do so the "slow kids" could catch up with their regular textbook assignments. Some children, therefore, never had a chance to use these centers.

There was also a misconception in the use of manipulative materials, which were often used as crutches for "slow kids" who were unable to grasp a concept. Rarely were they used by "top kids." Thus, the "top kids" could often verbalize a concept but frequently did not have a concrete understanding of the concept. Also, the "slow kids" would be ridiculed by the "top kids" for being dependent upon and using manipulative materials.

A lack of time and paucity of materials were additional reasons why open education was not implemented on a large scale with the use of interest centers. The five teachers had little time to procure materials and set up interest centers, so they limited the number of interest centers in their rooms. When they did succeed in setting up a center, they had difficulty introducing children to the center and replenishing the center once interest had waned. They also experienced difficulty in developing self-propelling activities that did not require teacher intervention. Not knowing how to rejuvenate interest centers, the teachers often closed down the centers, thus denying an opportunity for children to return to a center at a later time. Another problem in developing interest centers was the possessiveness of the children who refused to give up their desks to be used for interest center activity. The desks and their contents were the children's anchor. Their lack of adjustment to a new school led to an unwillingness to forgo traditional practices and possessions.

There were spurts of activity in several interest centers during the year. The amount of time devoted to "open" activity was related to the number and understanding of the potential value of manipulative materials on hand. An increase in the use of these manipulative materials also led to a decrease in traditional textbook activity and an increase in the display and quality of children's work. The quality of questions asked by both teachers and children also seemed to improve at these times.

The five teachers sometimes lacked the necessary content background that would take the children beyond a superficial understanding of the activities in the centers. For example, it was difficult for the children to become familiar with the differences between series and parallel circuits in *Batteries and Bulbs* (Elementary Science Study, 1966), when the teacher was not familiar with the two types of circuitry.

The children's desire to learn by a traditional method of teaching caught the five teachers off guard. They thought the children would enjoy working in interest centers. After a third-grade teacher set up seven centers in math, a child asked, "Why can't we have math out of our books like we used to have it? It's much better that way!" The teacher looked surprised and shocked. She had no answer to the difficult question, "What do I do if the kids choose to learn the traditional way?"

With the use of interest centers, record keeping became a problem and hindered further development of open education. It was difficult to evaluate the children's growth; to know where the children were academically and to keep records of what activities they were engaged in previously. It was also difficult to report student progress to the parents.

The need for further development of an accurate record keeping system was apparent. To some extent, several teachers employed a procedure of keeping records similar to one described by Cazden (1969), jotting notes during the day, writing them up at the end of the week.

The concern for the lack of continuity of open education into the junior high school affected the five teachers. They feared that the children would become emotionally upset when they entered junior high school and were forced to sit in their seats and be quiet. Their concern for continuity was legitimate. They often wondered whether children would be adaptable to the rigors of junior high school after experiencing attempted open education at Adams School. This was one reason given for a reluctance to attempt open education on a large scale.

Attempting to solve a myriad of first year teacher problems took valuable time away from the actual implementation of open education. Discipline was a constant worry for the five first-year teachers. Many ways of solving behavior problems were tried as teachers searched for the best method to suit their needs, often using methods antagonistic to open education. The "plus-minus" system became popular for extreme cases of deviant behavior: for every good deed, the child received a plus mark; for every bad deed, a minus mark. The teacher met with the child twice a day, totaled the marks and sent the card home to the parents.

Other methods of discipline included peer approval, isolation, taking away minutes from recess, giving points to groups who exhibited good behavior, high-low seating arrangements, and various rearrangements of desks. Unfortunately, the teachers found little success in attempts to develop the children's self-discipline, so necessary for open education to flourish.

Attitudes of Children

The problem of racial conflicts influenced attempts at open education because the friction and tension generated by the conflicts ran contrary to basic tenets of open education. The children attending school represented four groups; black, low income white, middle income white and middle to upper class white. Blacks made up only five per cent of the school population and felt outnumbered and dominated by the white children and the all-white staff. A number of low income and middle class whites were bused fifteen miles and came to school reflecting their parents' animosity at their being bused long distances. The absence of playground equipment perpetuated opportunities for racial strife because there was nothing to occupy children's time. The playground was the scene of a number of small racial skirmishes throughout the year.

The racial problems at Adams School subsided somewhat during the year but there were still some extortion threats against white children by black children. The principal called in a black principal to talk to the staff. The black principal had no answers and indicated there wouldn't be an answer to racial strife until society found an answer. Adams School was a little society all in itself, and its members looked to the principal for leadership.

Here as in Barth's study (1972), black children may have been venting their parents' adverse feelings toward open education when taking part in racial incidents. Black parents sometimes viewed open education as a threat to the advancement of their children in life—a life that reflects a test-oriented American society that requires mastery of the basics through traditional methods. They spoke of the lack of discipline in open education and demanded that teachers incorporate strong discipline in addition to teaching the basics as an avenue that would allow their children to "get ahead" in life.

The five teachers showed sympathy for minority group children. They realized the effects of an impoverished home life. They believed that the future of these children looked bleak, but they didn't know how to reach them or how to help them learn. Early in the year, one of their ways of working with the black children was to give them special privileges at the expense of others. That only seemed to intensify the problem. However, in time, the teachers stopped granting special privileges and there was a decrease in the number of racial incidents. Another apparent reason for the lessening racial tension was greater communication between the parents and the teachers as many teachers incorporated special social studies units on minority groups into the program.

The five teachers cited the children as a stumbling block to the implementation of open education. The children were faced with a major adjustment when coming from traditional backgrounds to a "new, open" building, a "new" staff and a "new method" of learning. A continuing large number of transfers, both in and out of Adams School during the year, also complicated their adjustment. The children often did not follow directions. This may have been due to unclear directions given by teachers or the use of activity cards that were too difficult for some children to read.

The five first-year teachers often indicated that "American kids aren't like English kids." This feeling may have been the result of the five teachers' slow adjustment to teaching different age levels. In England they gained experience with five-, six- and seven-year-olds; now they were faced with the task of working with eight- through fourteen-year-olds. It is difficult to assess whether the age difference or the cultural difference was of greater importance.

The allegations by the five that the children were unable to accept responsibility may have been a defense mechanism used by the teachers to express their frustrations inherent in a stressful Adams School situation. Their occasional accusations that the kids lacked responsibility may have resulted from the egocentricity of teachers themselves, who were blind to many of their own shortcomings and took solace in blaming difficulties and failures on the children. Perhaps the major reason the children had not accepted responsibility was that of time, too little time devoted to responsibilities in class each day and too little time to learn these responsibilities during the year.

The establishment of trust was an integral part of the teaching philosophy employed by the five teachers. A "thrust for trust" was in process when the teachers gave the children a "little freedom" (usually the privilege of working at an interest center) and then took it away if they thought the children had abused the freedom by misbehaving. This extending and denying trust was a constant struggle and often led to stricter controls, more resistance, and added misunderstanding of trust. Occasionally, sending children to the office or to the learning center became an escape for the teachers when the struggle for trust became too much to cope with. The children's lack of respect for property was also a problem in establishing trust. One teacher had placed some carefully fabricated structures in the corridor which were soon smashed and/or dismantled. Stealing also was widespread. The principal remarked,

"It's pretty darn hard to develop trust when they are stealing you blind out the back door."

A small amount of progress had been made in the "thrust for trust" with the establishment of classroom meetings run by students. This procedure increased dialogue among teachers and kids while kids assumed greater responsibility in handling classroom routine. It appeared that greater responsibility given to children enhanced the establishment of trust and facilitated the implementation of open education.

The issue of play seemed to hinder the implementation of open education because the teachers devoted much time to the task of attempting to make a distinction between "work and play." The five teachers struggled to develop the skill to decide if what the child was doing was pointless or meaningful learning. Perhaps only the center of the educational process, the child, truly knows this distinction.

Reflections

What was accomplished by this study? It has identified salient problems in the attempt to implement open education at Adams School. Some of these problems included the action of professional teachers' organizations, an absence of an expressed open school philosophy, insufficient administrative participatory support, the influence of semi-traditional teachers, the physical design and structure of the open school, and a lack of appropriate materials and activities for open education. Other problems that were identified included a lack of extensive preparation for this method of teaching, opposition of parents, the children's adjustment to open education, time and energy expended on first-year teacher problems, and the inability to move from a commitment to open education to its implementation. While these particular problems will not arise in every implementation of open education, some similar ones are certain to exist.

For open education to be successfully implemented, it is felt that a workable system must be developed which would pose possible solutions to the problems such as those identified in this study.

Need for Individuals with a Firm Commitment to Open Education

Because of the vast amount of time and energy needed to implement open education, it is important that teachers and administrators carefully examine their own personal commitment to open education in terms of their willingness to change. They must ask themselves: (1) Am I truly willing to change? (2) Am I willing to make a firm commitment to open education, accept its assumptions and its concomitant forms of school life? (3) Am I willing to sacrifice the time and energy to support that commitment? If affirmative answers cannot be given to these three basic questions, open education should not be attempted. If they can be given, teachers and administrators may consider change as being slow, occurring over an extended period of time and deepening in levels over time.

Progress in the implementation of open education may be related to the deepening of layers in the "onion construct" presented by Spodek and Manolakes in this volume (Chapter 12), as it is easier and takes less time to change the external layers than value-laden layers closer to the core. The successful implementation of open education may well be dependent upon viewing open education as a way of life that features a coalescence of *both* professional and personal values and beliefs in the core. It is a balance in this coalesence that teachers must develop and maintain if open education is to be successfully implemented. A firm personal commitment to open education is one way to preserve this balance.

While a firm personal commitment towards open education is important, the above observations demonstrate that commitment alone is not enough. The actions of other teachers as well as the principal can influence the success of any implementation. The concern about academic achievement and the provision of time to try out new methods, to test ideas, and even to fail are important. The support or opposition of parents is also a vital consideration. Even the physical facilities can help or hinder a move towards open education.

Not to be forgotten is the ability of teachers to implement their commitment through professional acts. The first-year teachers studied here lacked the background and competencies to turn their commitment into a reality. Nor was there adequate support in the field to help these teachers gain the professional strengths they needed.

Any attempt to move toward open education needs to begin with an assessment of resources in support of open education, outer resources as well as inner ones. Devaney (1973) in a study of implementation of open education in the United States identified those resources as being a supportive principal, a flexible view of curriculum, the availability of an advisory service, the support of parents, and a view of the teacher as a learner. The need for these resources is supported by this study. Devaney's report presents a checklist that one could use to determine the level of support and to provide information to make adequate plans in a campaign of implementation.

Need for Ongoing Research

The potential avenues for further research in open education are many and need to be pursued. There is a need for a longitudinal study of the experiences of the five teachers in this study to follow up their efforts to implement open education over a longer period of time. The five subjects' performance at Adams School could be compared with the performances of others who had gained experience in England but who taught in traditionally built schools during their first year of teaching. A study by McCall (1973) provides some insight into the performance of other first-year teachers who had gained experience in England. There is also a need to compare the performance of teachers with British experience in open education with those who had no British experience.

Future research needs to focus on the following questions to nurture the growth of open education: (1) Is it possible to train teachers for open education? (2) What kinds of teachers (age, experience, qualities) can best implement open education? (3) Is it possible for teachers to implement open education if they do not view it as a way of life? (4) What method is most effective for the implementation of open education? (5) Is it possible to separate normal first-year teacher problems from those specifically applicable to first attempts at open education? (6) Are there available methods developed to write both singly and collectively about a group of teachers attempting open education? and (7) How does one evaluate both teacher and pupil performance in open education? Future research needs to focus on these important questions.

The value of this study for the investigator lies in further reflection upon personal and professional values and beliefs and how this study has altered them, if at all. The position of Chittenden and Bussis (1971) that the study of knowledge and belief systems is a fruitful step toward unraveling the dynamics of both the open teaching process and the teacher changing process applies to the investigator and is also a matter for future reflection.

In a final analysis, it seems necessary to re-emphasize the fact that open education must be viewed as a profound change in goals as well as method of education. Teacher educators who profess the ideas of love, warmth, and joy inherent in open education in their dealings with pre-service and in-service education must develop methods that reflect these ideas in practice. Teachers and administrators in turn must do the same. The real test for credibility of a proponent of open education is the extent to which he utilizes these ideas in his total professional life.

References

Barth, R. S., "So You Want to Change to an Open Classroom." *Phi Delta Kappan,* Vol. LIII, no. 2, October 1971. (Elaborated in Barth, 1972.)

Barth, R. S., *Open Education and the American School.* New York: Agathon Press, 1972.

Bussis, A. M., and E. A. Chittenden, *Analysis of an Approach to Open Education.* Princeton, N.J.: Educational Testing Service, 1970.

Cazden, C. B., *Infant School.* Newton, Mass.: Education Development Center, 1969.

De Bruin, J. E., "A Descriptive Analysis of Experiences of Five First Year Teachers Attempting Open Education." Unpublished doctoral dissertation, University of Illinois, 1972.

Devaney, K., *Developing Open Education in America: A Review of Theory and Practice in Public Schools.* San Francisco, Calif.: Farwest Laboratory for Research and Development, August 1973.

Elementary Science Study, *Batteries and Bulbs.* Newton, Mass.: Education Development Center, 1966.

McCall, D., *The Bristol, England, Program at the University of Illinois: Its Impact on First Participants at the End of Their First Year of Teaching.* Unpublished doctoral dissertation, University of Illinois, 1973.

CHAPTER 14

Using the British Experience

Vincent R. Rogers, *University of Connecticut*

AS I WRITE THIS, in early June, thousands of American teachers are preparing for a journey which can be compared to a Muslim's pilgrimage to Mecca. There *is* a religious fervor associated with this mass summertime exodus; one will shortly see the light and be saved. Surely years of effortless teaching will follow in an educational Shangri-la, during which all children will read at or above grade level, while loving school and shamelessly adoring their teacher.

Strangely enough, a visit to a British primary school *can* have an impact on American teachers that is comparable to a religious conversion. Our teachers are usually inspired and enthused and often return to their jobs with a new vision of what education might be. Difficulties generally arise, however, as teachers try to implement some of the ideas they saw working so well in British schools, and there is often a period (sometimes temporary, sometimes permanent) of disillusionment which can end in recanting.

How, then, can we make use of the British experience in ways that may have some permanent bearing on our work? What is it that can be exported and what cannot? What *should* be exported and what *should* not? How can an American put the British experience in some meaningful perspective?

Perhaps we should begin by examining some of the broad cultural differences that exist between our two countries—differences that are important *not* because they tell us that "It can't be done" in America but, rather, differences that put into clearer focus the reasons for the remarkable success the British have enjoyed, the problems we may encounter in our attempts to move in similar directions, and the ways to resolve such problems.

Anyone who has spent some time in Great Britain *and* on the European continent recognizes immediately the schizophrenic view we often hold of the United Kingdom. If one arrives first in England, we are delighted at the differences between American and British ways. We are conveniently abroad, if you will, in a country full of "foreign" surprises and quite manageable contrasts. As one moves on to France, Italy, Spain, Scandinavia, or perhaps Eastern Europe, he often finds himself losing some of the "comfortableness" of touring in Britain; he is now more certainly in alien lands, and travel becomes more challenging. If one is fortunate enough to return to Great Britain for a few days before a final flight back to the States, he is struck with the sense of already being "home" as he goes through British customs and boards the airport bus to London.

All of which is a long-winded way of saying that there *are* noticeable, perhaps measurable differences between the lifeways of Britons and Americans, as well as some very basic similarities. In my opinion, the differences, while worth noting, do not in any way suggest an insurmountable barrier to the development of more open or informal schools for American children. Nevertheless, an understanding of such differences is probably helpful to anyone interested in moving toward openness in an American community, and it is in this sense that we examine such differences in the paragraphs that follow.

To begin with, the British are *not* engaged in an academic race with the Soviet Union or any other nation. That is, having given up pretensions to (and responsibilities for) "world leadership," the British can get on with the problem of improving the quality of life in their country with minimal concern for outside pressures. They can afford the luxury of "looking inward," of self-examination, and of the commitment of significant proportions of their budget and energies to bringing about domestic change. All of which means, of course, that education may exist more for its own sake than as a way of glorifying one's country in some sort of academic Olympics.

Other general differences might also be noted: for example, the way the British theater flourishes, not only in London but in provincial towns as well; the very strong interest in art, dance, and music, which suggests that the importance of the arts in schools is at least partially a reflection of broader interest in these areas among the British people as a whole.

Certainly, British society is more stratified than America is—class still rears its ugly head—and people are more likely to "know their place" and not interfere with "professionals."

British child-rearing habits, at least among the middle class, seem to emphasize more than we do the importance of independence and responsibility for a child, even at ages as young as six or seven; thus children coming to school are able, perhaps, to fit more easily into open classrooms which function best when children do, in fact, possess these qualities.

One might also comment on the role of T˅ (far greater emphasis on quality rather than quantity in children's programming), the church (everyone belongs, but nobody goes), the ubiquitous "public" (private) schools that do in fact offer educational alternatives to those who can afford to pay, the relative openness of British society toward a great variety of political, social, and economic views. The list seems endless.

The point is that cultural differences *do* exist between us, and those differences should be understood. Whether or not those differences are of an order that would make the growth of open or informal education impossible in the United States is an entirely different question, however—and that question I am prepared to answer in the negative.

There are other differences, however, that relate more closely to the educational enterprise in Great Britain that have a greater bearing on the direction primary education has taken in that country. It would be difficult indeed to assess the growth of British open schools without some understanding of these conditions. The views which follow are certainly not intended to be a conclusive listing. They should, however, touch on the major differences related to the growth, financing, organizing, and managing of primary schools in Great Britain.

To begin with, there is much that is centrally or nationally controlled in British education. The allocation of funds for school buildings, for example, is handled at national rather than local levels, as is the establishment of salary scales for teachers, the minimum age at which children may leave high school and enter the job market (now sixteen), the number of years required for primary school teachers' training (three), etc. Glaringly absent from this list of national powers is any reference (with the exception of mandated religious instruction) to either *curriculum* or *methodology*.

The British "Schools Council for Curriculum and Examinations," now generally referred to as "the Schools Council," was organized in 1964—about the same time that various American curriculum-reform projects were being funded by the Federal government in what we refer to as the "curriculum revolution" of the 1960's. Nowhere can the contrast between British and American approaches to curricular and methodological change be contrasted more sharply. The Schools Council began with the basic assumption that each *school* should and would take full responsibility for the development of its own curriculum and its pedagogy—based essentially on the needs of the children in a given local community. The Council would give every possible assistance in the task, but change *begins* in the local school. The contrast with American approaches during the same period needs no elaboration here; the story is all too familiar to most of us.

If curricular and methodological change are largely a *local* responsibility in Britain, so also are they almost exclusively the province of the *professional* educational community. The general public, the universities, the educational publishing industry—all these played a relatively minor role in the evolvement of British primary education as we know it today. This is not to say that parents, publishers, and university scholars had *no* influence on the shape of primary education in Britain; rather, their influence was (and is) minimal by American standards. It is still safe to say that *local professionals*—for better or for worse—bear the burden of developing and improving British primary education.

Change occurred in Great Britain, therefore, gradually—almost gently—coming largely from within, occurring here and there, in pockets where conditions for change were ripe, not monolithically or on a grand scale. John Coe, the perceptive, articulate head of primary education in the county of Oxfordshire, is fond of telling the story of Edith Moorhouse, one of the great early leaders of the movement toward informal education in that lovely region, as she sat in the evenings at her home with a small group of primary headmistresses and teachers, knitting and talking about children. There were no elaborate lists of goals and objectives to be achieved, deadlines to be met, nor tests to be given. Rather, there was good talk about children, how they learn and grow, and what this might mean to teachers.

Similarly, Stewart Mason, the chief education officer for many years in the county of Leicestershire, was fond of personally inviting a group of heads and/or teachers to come with him for a day to look in on "a marvelous teacher" working somewhere in the county. He took a personal interest in change and in the people who could most likely bring it about. He needed and took *time*. He coaxed and argued—but he did not dictate.

Curricular and methodological change came (and continues to come), then, in Great Britain on a local level, fostered and inspired by professionals. We must also keep very clearly in mind that when we say "professionals," we include in the most significant possible way the classroom teacher. The materials developed in the most famous of the Schools Council projects, the Nuffield Maths and Science Programs are "cases in point." (It should be pointed out at once that teachers played a major role in the development of these programs as members of development teams.) These materials are designed to stimulate teachers—to help them grow, become more flexible, more spontaneous, and more responsible for making day-to-day curricular and methodological decisions. The British have faith in the classroom teacher as the ultimate change agent; she is the "sine qua non" of meaningful, lasting change. This, too, contrasts considerably with generally accepted strategies for change in American schools.

Hand-in-hand with the development of a truly professional role for classroom teachers is the evolvement of a similar role for the British "head teacher," or principal. Clearly, a good deal of the autonomy and flexibility of many classroom teachers stems from parallel freedoms (and responsibilities) for "heads." As most American educators know, there are few city-wide or county-wide curricular or methodological decisions made that bind all of a district's primary schools to a given procedure or set of materials. The head is expected to take the lead in these areas in his school; and most of the heads who have provided the magnificent leadership we have seen so often in Great Britain's finest informal primary schools have utilized their freedom to bolster the role of the teacher as a responsible, flexible, decisionmaking professional.

It is equally important to note that British schools are financed in ways that differ radically from what we are used to in the United States. Funds come to local schools through general, state, or central government grants. The local property tax accounts for about 5 percent of educational revenue. In addition, there are few strings attached to these grants, so that each Local Education Authority is free to spend its money as it sees fit. The L.E.A. then is not faced with the problem of having budgets approved at town elections each year. This obviously removes a great deal of political and other pressure from local educators and allows for long-range planning and a degree of continuity in education that many of us find sadly lacking in our own school districts.

Perhaps a more subtle, yet no less significant, difference between educational tradition in Great Britain and America involves what the British would call the "pastoral function." To quote Tim McMullen (1967),

> Parents may cavil at masters' interference and excess of authority; masters may object to being involved in burdensome trivia about clothes and manners and hair and behavior on buses . . . whatever the objections, whatever the shortcomings, the fact remains that the intention of English schooling is more whole, complete, and inclusive than that of any other country.

This concern quite possibly accounts for the willingness of so many British primary school teachers to willingly take a broad view of education, valuing the total growth of the child, and placing much emphasis on the role of art, music, dance, poetry, and drama—as well as the "3 R's." Similarly, this may explain the British preference for small schools where teachers may get to know children (and each other) well, where there is much human response to children's problems and needs, and where the possibility for assessing and aiding the total growth of the child exists more fully than it does in what the British sometimes call "the American factory schools."

In any case, the Establishment view of education in Great Britain is, on the whole, child-centered and open. The *Plowden Report* gives a semiofficial blessing to the sorts of changes that have been growing gradually in British schools for thirty years. An open teacher may be encountering difficulty with a conservative head, but her battle is somewhat less lonely than it would be in most American schools, because it is widely acknowledged that British primary schools should be more child-centered, more informal. Clearly, this gives a kind of support and direction to primary teachers in Great Britain that is sadly lacking in our own schools.

One might list other differences—for example, the differing approaches to the in-service education of teachers in both countries, including the role of the adviser and teachers' center, and the lack of salary increment incentives tied to such training in Great Britain. However, it seems to me that we have hit upon some of the most significant differences between our two systems. Let me conclude again with the admonition that, while these pages may help to explain some important differences between us, they *do not*, in my opinion, add up to a manifesto for the status quo for American educators.

The British Achievement

Lilian Katz (1973, p. 7) once wrote that the basic question facing American educators was not "How can we teach children the specific academic skills they need?" but, rather, "How can we teach children the skills they need while at the same time strengthening and enhancing their feelings of self-respect, self-responsibility, and sense of dignity— their capacity for curiosity, exploration, investigation, for tenderness, compassion, understanding and insight?"

To suggest that the British succeed in this Herculean task in every respect and with all their children would, of course, be nonsense. On the other hand, they *have* achieved a balance among the cognitive and affective domains that we have not, as well as a balance between the skills areas of the curriculum and the expressive arts.

Anyone who has visited a good informal primary school in Great Britain recognizes this immediately. British teachers do more than pay lip service to such areas as art, music, dance, and drama; they *do* care about the total development of the child, and they try (often with very large classes and tiny budgets) to bring about a more total, holistic, and complete growth in their children.

We know, of course, that there are no "either-or's" in education. Many American teachers try to achieve this balance, and some British teachers don't. But when one looks at the general thrust, the basic direction of primary education in both countries, it becomes clear that there is a general acceptance of this position in Great Britain that actively influences the day-to-day life of children in classrooms. It would be difficult to suggest that this was equally true in the United States. This then, is a major achievement for any educational system in any time or place.

A second achievement of British primary education is the *scale* on which this more humane, child-centered education is practiced there. After all, there have always been experimental schools of one kind or another in most countries—educational mavericks pitted against the conventional wisdom of the time. Such schools still exist, many of them in the United States. The point is that never before in the history of Western education has there been anything like the situation that currently exists in Great Britain. A large percentage of the state-supported schools of a highly industrialized nation are, in fact, significantly different from conventional or traditional primary schools as they exist in other Western countries. One may quarrel with the percentage. Is it 30? 25? or 40 percent? No one knows for sure. But it is clear that the number is very large by any standard, and even more impressive when one visits those bastions of open education such as Oxfordshire, where out of perhaps 160 primary schools, it may be said that 100 or so are clearly "open," while almost all the others are moving in that direction.

I think it is this factor that impresses so many American visitors. After all, one *expects* to see schools that are different in the private sector, or in university "laboratory" schools. One *does not* expect to find them in the slums of London, Birmingham, Nottingham, and Bristol as well as in posh suburban areas and many parts of rural England. This latter point may well be a third major achievement of British education worth noting; i.e., informal schools have grown and prospered in every imaginable setting, and with children representing a dozen or more different cultural and racial groups.

A fourth achievement—and perhaps this should have come first if we were listing these in order of importance or significance—is that this massive change came about through the efforts of quite "ordinary" teachers. These were not bright young things fresh out of Cambridge or Oxford, ready to change the world. They were (and are) both old and young—mostly with three-year training college diplomas rather than university degrees, often with families to raise, dilapidated facilities to work in, and niggardly salaries. They are not genetically different from American teachers, and we dare not assume that intelligence, wit, creativity, and sensitivity have been bred into British teachers much as we breed speed and stamina in thoroughbred race horses. The point is that these "ordinary" people became quite extraordinary teachers largely because British "heads," H.M.I's, local advisers, officials in the Department of Education in London, chief education officers, and others in positions of authority have always assumed that the key to good education is the classroom teacher. He or she cannot be bypassed, and schools fail or succeed mostly because of the quality of the classroom teacher.

As early as 1918 we find this idea stated in the Department of Education and Sciences (then called the "Board of Education") *Handbook of Suggestions for the Consideration of Teachers* (Kogan, 1971, p. 13):

> The only uniformative practice that the Board of Education desires to see in the teaching of the public elementary schools is that each teacher shall think for himself, and work out for himself such methods of teaching as may use his powers to the best advantage and best suited to the particular needs and conditions of the school. Uniformity in detail of practice is not desirable . . . even if it were obtainable."

In Great Britain, then, the classroom teacher has been the nucleus about which educational change has occurred. The classroom teacher is a decisionmaker, curriculum worker, and student of children. She is, in the best sense of the word, a *professional.* Again we must caution that this is far from a universal condition. There are British teachers who do *not* fit this mold, and American teachers who *do.* Nevertheless, the overall direction in Great Britain has been to place great value on the role of the classroom teacher, and this seems to me an achievement of tremendous importance.

A fifth achievement has to do with the remarkable balance British primary education has achieved among what David Hawkins (1969, 1974) refers to as "I, Thou, and It." In Hawkins's phrase, "I" is the teacher, "Thou" the child, and "It" the materials with which one learns. In the best of the British open schools, teachers *and* children constantly make significant contributions to daily classroom life. The British have so far avoided the excesses of the "progressive movement" in the United States, where the schools moved perhaps to an extremely child-centered approach. Teachers intervened as little as possible, and an almost Rousseau-like attitude seemed to dominate.

Similarly, the British have avoided the excesses of modern American elementary schools vis-à-vis their use of mountains of commercially published materials of all sorts. Such materials exist in British schools, as do an almost unbelievable variety of "found" or "junk" materials of all kinds, along with the great "natural" materials of the world—sand, water, clay, earth, stones, etc.

The British primary school at its best, then, seems neither teacher- nor child-dominated; nor are such schools heavily influenced by what we in America have come to call the "Ed Biz." There is indeed an intelligent balance—and this seems to me to be a major educational achievement.

Finally, I am deeply impressed with the British teachers' search for *quality* in the work children produce; indeed, I am impressed with the importance they place on the *work* children produce as opposed, say, to test results. The poetry, art, and literature we have seen displayed; the plays and "dance" or movement we have been privileged to watch— all suggest a quest for quality or standards that goes far beyond mere test performance.

I once recall a visit to an American school by a British headmaster, who was shown a group of drawings recently completed by a class of 8-year-olds. Each picture was done on paper of similar size and shape, the same materials had been used in each drawing, and all dealt more or less with the same topic or theme. They were displayed neatly, fifteen or twenty of them in a row above the blackboard. When asked to comment on the drawings, he said (with appropriate apologies) that what he saw in each drawing was perhaps 20 to 30 minutes of work. And, of course, he was right. They had all been begun and completed in a 40-minute "art class," and their quality was uniformly uninspired.

This is not to suggest that American children do not produce beautiful drawings—they often do. Nor should we assume that every piece of work produced by a British child is a masterpiece. The British teacher does seem to recognize, however, that quality is important. She wants the best she can get from every child, and she also recognizes that one does not, for the most part, get "quality" in 30- or 40-minute segments.

The good open teacher, then, in her quest for quality, has managed to look at the daily schedule (what the British would call the "timetable") in a completely flexible way, allowing *time* for in-depth work by individual children and largely working *with* the natural rhythm of a child's learning rather than against it.

These two attributes—the search by many teachers for quality and the concurrent recognition of the need for time and flexibility in the day-to-day activities of children—represent to me a major educational achievement. Other writers would no doubt single out additional aspects of the British experience that should have been listed here. I am reasonably certain, however, that the achievements I chose to emphasize would be included at some point in their analyses by virtually all students of British education.

Weaknesses in British Education

In the last chapter of my book *Teaching in the British Primary School* (Rogers, 1970, p. 301), which included a section devoted to criticisms of informal education, I concluded:

> There is so much that is magnificently "right" in the British primary schools I know that I hesitate to conclude this chapter on a critical note. At their best, these schools are nothing short of superb. They do, in fact, offer "another way" to those of us who are willing to listen and examine our own practices—however agonizing such a reappraisal might be.

I would begin this section with the same admonition. Criticism of British primary schools is both possible and necessary if they are to continue to grow and evolve into better and better places in which children may live and learn. Criticism is important, too, if we are to delineate which aspects of British primary education should not and need not be exported to the United States.

On the other hand, exposing such weaknesses (if indeed they *are* weaknesses—surely there will not be universal agreement with my analysis) should not imply anything less than an enthusiastic endorsement of the British primary school on my part.

Let me begin my critical analysis of the British primary school, then, with a criticism I raised in *Teaching in the British Primary School* (pp. 297–299). At this writing, I see no reason to retract it; on the contrary, I think it important enough to restate in full:

> A more direct criticism is exemplified by a description of an afternoon spent in what was in many ways a fascinating primary school in rural Leicestershire. During the entire afternoon the children were free to carry out projects that were of interest to them. There was a great deal of arts and crafts activity—carpentry, weaving, block printing, and so on. The children were obviously well behaved, busy, and interested in their work. Yet I could not help but feel that this happy, involved group of children were somehow existing in the middle of what we all know to be a terribly complex, rapidly changing world—divorced from its reality, protected from its problems, and uninvolved in its conflicts and dilemmas.
>
> Somehow, the "real" world that children explore in such schools is often a rather limited version of reality. It is a real world of fields, streams, trees, rocks, stones, flowers, birds and insects, if it is a country school. If it is a city school, it is a real world of traffic patterns, nearby shops, local museums and libraries, parks and gardens. The "real world" is often conceived of

as that part of the world which is nearby; more precisely, that which can be seen, felt, smelled, touched, or listened to.

One might suggest then, that after all there are limits to how far one can go with personal concrete experience as *the* essential teaching technique. Children can study only a small part of the world by direct observation and experience, and one must question the hours spent in making, building, and *physically* "doing"; hours that could, conceivably, be used in other ways as well. One wonders, for example, if in studying the woolen industry the process of making wool does not get treated all out of proportion to some of the related economic, social, and, in fact, even political problems that might be implied in such a study—granting, of course, that much of this "activity" would be intellectual rather than physical, vicarious more than direct.

One might argue, of course, that this is the job of the *secondary* school; that primary children are concerned with the properties, origins, uses and manufacture of wool, and not with related economic, social or political problems. Surely the gathering of in-depth experiences is crucial to the learning of primary children; whether such experience gathering precludes consideration of the types of questions mentioned above is, however, an unresolved pedagogical issue at this time.

In any event, if one largely limits the objects of one's study to those found only in the local environment, it is difficult to see how the school can play a significant role in helping children understand the broader world in which they live. Conflict exists about Rhodesia and about the immigrant-settled sections of British cities such as Wolverhampton and Bradford. These problems are important to all British children—not only to those living in areas directly affected by such conflict. The fact that they do not always lend themselves to direct or "concrete" experience does not render them any the less important.

The real world of social conflict exists, and no school, no teacher, no syllabus will ever completely isolate children from it. Yet the schools' responsibility would seem to include some attempts at increasing children's awareness of the inadequacies and inequalities that exist in both their local and their wider environments. Failing this, children will muddle through, picking up ideas and attitudes wherever they find them and becoming more and more aware (perhaps through harsh personal experience) about the conflict that exists between the school world and the world of social reality.

A second, somewhat related point concerns the tendency in English primary schools largely to ignore the results of a growing body of research dealing with the development of attitudes, values, prejudices and stereotypes in young children. One American researcher, for example, has summarized some of the more striking conclusions that seem to have emerged from a host of studies dealing with the development of and causes of prejudice in children. Among her findings are (Arter, 1959, pp. 185–189):

1. Inter-group prejudice in children makes its appearance at an early age—sometimes in children as young as four. [*These findings are in direct conflict with the view commonly held among many teachers I talked with here, i.e.,*

*that negative feelings toward particular groups do not arise until or shortly before
adolescence.*]

2. Apparently, these studies tend to support the conclusion that segrega-
tion, prejudice, discrimination and their social concomitants potentially damage the personalities of *all* children—those in the majority as well as those
in the minority.

3. Experimental programs such as the Philadelphia Early Childhood Project and others indicate that specific activities in schools can help to diminish,
or even reverse, racial and other prejudices.

Similarly, the research of Merriam (1931), Turner (1967), Easton and
Hess (1962), and others dealing with the political socialization of the
young indicates that political attitudes and values develop (whether
teachers like it or not) during the primary school years. Apparently a
vast array of factors (from television to the casual comments of a school
bus driver) influence and contribute to the development of such values.

Now, none of this suggests that racial problems in England approach
the severity of those in the United States (although they are growing)
or that, if these studies were replicated here, similar results would occur.
Nevertheless, they *do* suggest that the primary school years are a truly
crucial educational period in a child's life—a period during which formal
education *could* consciously begin to counterattack many of the negative
influences that affect children's lives. Attitudes and values *are* being
formed, some of them based on fair and honest answers to children's
questions given by perceptive and sensitive parents, others based on the
worst kind of rumor and gossip. The schools and, in particular, the
social studies exist as a possible vehicle for reasoned and objective exploration of the child's wider world. Whether or not they will be utilized
more effectively for this purpose remains to be seen.

These questions seem to me to be particularly important for American
educators to consider. The problems of Blacks, Chicanos, Puerto Ricans,
and other minority groups will not simply go away. Any version of open
education that hopes to survive in the United States must provide a
positive response to the problems so clearly visible in our society.

A third criticism is best summed up by Ian Lister's comment (Plumb,
1964, p. 166):

We in England must acknowledge that the very liberty, flexibility and variety
of the educational structure have ensured that experiment should be limited
and isolated, and have often encouraged tribalism in educational organization and staunch conservatism in educational practice.

There are, then, evils as well as strengths in diversity. One of these
evils is surely the relative haphazardness of curricular development in
general, the lack of mutual attacks on mutual problems, the tendency
to "go it alone," blithely unaware of what others are doing. This sometimes results in meaningless repetition of studies, topics, or themes, and

also, to a degree, curricular unrelatedness that seems neither wise nor necessary.

A fourth criticism involves the tendency to play down the possible value of educational media and technology as if somehow these devices, in and of themselves, were inherently "bad." Obviously they are neither good nor bad, but can be used wisely *or* foolishly by the human beings operating them. One way or another the hardware is here—and much of it has tremendously exciting potential. If open education becomes identified in the United States with an antitechnology view, or as an approach that is looking backward rather than forward, out-of-date and out-of-tune with the time, it will be difficult to foster its growth in America.

I referred earlier to the relatively passive role played by nonprofessionals in the evolvement of the open school in Great Britain. This becomes particularly striking when one considers the role British parents play in affecting change in their schools. Basically, their role is relatively slight, although this *is* rapidly changing, particularly in counties such as Oxfordshire.

There are times when all of us who have ever taught school would be envious of any society in which parents could be ignored—or even told to "Go to the devil" if the occasion warranted. All in all, however, I think the British lose more than they gain when parents, for whatever reasons, are shut off from the day-to-day activities of the school. Most of the heads and teachers I have talked with recognize this, and there is a strong movement among open educators to involve parents more fully in their children's education. Nevertheless, by American standards, parent involvement is still relatively slight. The fact that many of our parents *are* deeply involved in elementary education, either through the PTA or in other ways, must in the long run be considered a good thing. To push for disengagement simply because British parents by tradition have not been greatly involved in their children's schooling would be to import the wrong product.

Finally, one might refer to the rather obvious differences that exist in Great Britain between primary and secondary education. So far, the exciting movement to create more child-centered, flexible, and open schools for primary-age children has barely touched the secondary schools. While we have not begun to *solve* that problem in the United States, I find the contrast less glaring here. In addition, almost everyone seems to recognize the *need* for greater communication among those working in elementary and secondary education in the United States. In many communities serious attempts have been made to bring about a degree of continuity in a child's education, and this strikes me as a significant strength of American education.

Relevance of the British Experience for Americans

I began this chapter with a reference to the very large number of American teachers who are crossing the Atlantic each summer to see firsthand the exciting changes that have taken place in primary education in Great Britain. There is no question that this experience has an impact upon the great majority of our teachers. They generally *are* impressed by what they see, and they do return to their own classrooms inspired and eager to begin to move toward more open ways.

Whether or not such teachers will meet with any degree of success at all depends upon a great many factors—some related to the competence and personality of the individual teacher, some related to the particular set of local conditions in which the teacher must work, and some related to far broader problems, problems having to do with a number of beliefs and attitudes that have, over time, become part of the American educational culture. For example:

1. We seem to place great value on what is new. "Innovation," "new directions," and "revolution" are words and phrases that appear over and over again in our professional literature and at our professional meetings. We must be publicly involved in "innovations," and any idea that has been with us for three years or more is in danger of becoming "old hat." This penchant for fads and fashion initially helped bring open education to the attention of American educators. It may also prove to be at least partly responsible for its death.

2. We have a tremendous, rather naïve, and often irresponsible and immature faith in the "expert" to solve our problems. "Experts" usually come from universities or the billion-dollar-a-year publishing and manufacturing industry we refer to as the "Ed Biz." This means that we look for global solutions where local initiative and understanding are called for. It means we dodge our own responsibility to create and adjust and assume that, after all, the "experts" know best.

3. We believe very strongly that success comes in being "better than" someone else. Our rhetoric about the importance of the individual growth of each child in terms of his own abilities, interests, and needs is drowned out in a chorus of nationally standardized tests. Parents (and far too many teachers!) are not so much interested in what a child has produced—in how he relates to other human beings—his individual strengths and weaknesses. Many would gladly forgo this kind of information if only they could be told that their child scored at the 90th percentile or that he or she is in the "top" half or third or tenth of his class.

4. American teachers have been taught, sometimes subtly and sometimes directly, that they are not really very good, or able, or competent. They cannot *do,* therefore they teach; yet, *doing* in a hundred different

ways is the essence of good teaching. Strangely enough, most teachers do live interesting and varied lives outside the classroom. I am constantly amazed at the interests and experiences of the teachers who show up in my classes. Getting them to feel that they *do* have something to offer and share with children—their art and poetry, their wit and humor, their successes and failures, their emotions and feelings—is a central problem in moving our schools toward "openness."

There are, of course, other ideas that belong in this list. I invite the reader to add his own observations. It is important to note, however, that attitudes, values, and beliefs *are* subject to change. Nothing is forever, and most of the most cherished notions middle-aged Americans hold concerning the way life ought to be lived in this country are being challenged as they have never been before. Indeed, there may be hope for significant change in American education precisely because it is difficult to imagine today's high school and college-age students being contented *for their children* with education as *they* experienced it.

I recently attended my daughter's high school graduation ceremonies. The program began with the high school stage band playing "Sentimental Journey" at a fairly quick tempo while the Class of 1973 almost danced (but certainly did not *march*) down the aisles to the stage. Each wore a graduation gown of his own choosing, different in color and design. The theme of the ceremony was "individuality," and this idea dominated every phase of the proceedings. The program ended with the graduates leaving the hall to the strains of "Sunrise, Sunset" from *Fiddler on the Roof*. No pomp and circumstance here! Rather, a joyous affirmation of our right to be ourselves.

What will these young adults demand of education when they become parents? No one knows for sure, but I see little reason to assume that the "American educational culture" I referred to earlier must stay always the same.

In any case, and despite these very real problems—these "educational hang-ups" that so many of us suffer from—there *are importable ideas* that we can and should consider which do have a chance to succeed in the United States. What is it, then, that we can learn and utilize from the British experience?

First of all, and in a general sense, the British have demonstrated beyond question that, in a highly industrialized Western nation with a value system and culture much more similar than dissimilar to ours, a form of elementary education that is neither dull, boring, oppressive, nor meaningless can survive and prosper. This surely should give us stimulation, hope, and inspiration for the future.

More specifically, we can and should think deeply about the implications of the notion, so often stated by John Coe of Oxfordshire in his many visits to us, that the best preparation for living richly and fully as an adult is to live richly and fully as a child. This does not mean adopting in a robotlike fashion all the procedures and techniques utilized by Oxfordshire teachers. There is little point for children in the North End of Hartford, Connecticut, to get deeply involved in the gathering, carding, and weaving of wool, for example. The woolen industry is a traditional and important aspect of Oxfordshire life; American teachers must find American parallels in their communities. Nevertheless, engaging children in practical and concrete studies of the traditions, industries, art, architecture, hopes, aspirations, and problems of their own people and locales is surely part of what it means to live richly and fully as a child.

It is of great importance that we consider new ways to help American teachers to grow both personally and professionally, to become the best they can become in the same way that we wish this for children. I am suggesting that those in positions of power and authority in American education reconsider, in light of the British experience, the singular importance of the classroom teacher as the principal instrument in the education of a child while he is within the confines of the institution we call the school. It is in this sense that two institutions of great importance in Great Britain—the "Teachers' Centre" and the "Advisory"— might be studied with a view toward adopting or adapting them to American use.

A fourth insight that seems quite adaptable to the American experience concerns aspects of the practice of "family grouping," or—to put it in the simplest terms—organizing schools so that teachers may work with a given group of children for at least a two-year period. If, in fact, so much depends in teaching upon *getting to know well the students* one is working with, it seems foolish indeed to arbitrarily move children from teacher to teacher every September. The children need not cover so wide an age range as they do in many British schools, although there are good arguments in favor of such groupings. Teachers might simply move on with their classes of 8- or 9- or 10-year-olds for another year. In any event, and however organized, it does seem important that we develop ways to get to know and understand children better. Working with them for longer periods of time as classroom teachers is one way to help achieve that goal.

A fifth "lesson" can be stated simply and quickly: it will take *time* to move toward openness, either as individual classroom teachers or as administrators seeking to bring about change on a larger scale. As much as we may want it, we cannot have instant change. The British have been developing open schools for thirty years. Significant, as opposed to superficial, change will only come with time, and American educators should be developing 5- and 10-year plans rather than beginning a new program in September, evaluating in June, and (probably) making a judgment concerning the "success" or "failure" of the new program over the summer.

We might also give special attention to the question of size as we consider the construction of new schools or the renovating of old. If we are in fact interested in creating more humane educational environments for teachers and children—schools where teachers know children well, where children know each other, where *teachers* feel part of a closely knit group that shows significant professional responsibility, and where principals know both teachers and children—then we must consider alternatives to bigness. This may be possible through the subdividing of larger schools, as well as through the building of smaller schools. In any case, the British experience will be of particular value to America in this case.

These ideas seem to me to be eminently importable; they have little to do with cultural differences between our two societies. They are directly related to some of the most pressing problems facing American education today and *are* achievable within the existing American milieu. They do not require expenditure of exorbitant sums of money, elimination of compulsory education, or the de-schooling of our society. More than anything else, we need the *will* to do these things and the patience necessary to allow them a chance of success.

References

Arter, R., "The Effects of Prejudice in Children," *Children,* 1959, *6,* 185–189.

Easton, D., and R. Hess, "The Child's Political World," *The Midwest Journal of Political Science,* 1962, *6,* 229–246.

Handbook of Suggestions for the Consideration of Teachers, 1918. Cited by M. Kogan, *The Government of Education.* New York: Citation Press, 1971.

Hawkins, David, "I, Thou, and It," *Mathematics Teaching,* No. 46, Spring, 1969. Reprinted in Hawkins, *The Informed Vision: Essays on Learning and Human Nature.* New York: Agathon Press, 1974.

Katz, L., in D. Hearn, J. Burdin, and L. Katz (eds.), *Current Research and Perspectives in Open Education.* Washington, D. C.: EKNE, 1973.

Kogan, M., *The Government of Education.* New York: Citation Press, 1971.

McMullen, T., Unpublished report for Schools Council, June 1967.

Merriam, C. E., *The Making of Citizens: A Comparative Study of Methods of Civic Training.* Chicago: University of Chicago Press, 1931.

Plumb, J. H. (ed.), *Crises in the Humanities.* London: Penguin Books, 1964.

Rogers, V. (ed.), *Teaching in the British Primary School.* New York: Macmillan, 1970.

Turner, M. E., *The Child Within the Group: An Experiment in Self-Government.* Stanford, Cal.: Stanford University Press, 1967.

Index